Four Plays by Hjalmar Bergman

Hjalmar Bergman

FOUR
PLAYS

BY

HJALMAR
BERGMAN

With Introductions by Stina Bergman
Edited by Walter Johnson

UNIVERSITY OF WASHINGTON PRESS
Seattle and London

THE AMERICAN-SCANDINAVIAN FOUNDATION
New York

Preface

When Örebro opened its city theater in the late winter of 1965, it had very appropriately been named the Hjalmar Bergman Theater in honor of the more recent of the two famous playwrights born in Örebro. While Olaus Petri or Master Olof (ca. 1493–1552), the Lutheran reformer, had had relatively little time to devote to writing plays and had no rich native theater tradition from which to benefit, Hjalmar Bergman (1883–1931) was fortunate enough to be able to make creative writing his profession at a time when Sweden had not only had several generations of great literary achievement but had had a rich theater tradition since the eighteenth century. The novel had been flourishing since Carl Jonas Love Almqvist's day at the beginning of the nineteenth century, and August Strindberg (1849–1912) not only had surpassed every one of many Swedish predecessors within drama but had written plays which made him the unsurpassed modern dramatist.

As a novelist, Hjalmar Bergman is outranked by none of his countrymen and only by Strindberg as a dramatist. Although he never succeeded in writing all the hundreds of plays he is supposed to have wanted to write, he did write a great many, a substantial number of which have become parts of the standard repertory of the Swedish theater and several of which have also become popular abroad. The plays that are best known, most frequently produced, and most highly appreciated by theater audiences are *The Baron's Will* (a dramatization of the 1910 novel *Hans nåds testamente*); *Mr. Sleeman Is Coming* (1917, published as one of the plays in the volume *Marionettspel*, "Marionette Plays"); *An Experiment* (*Ett experiment*, 1918); *Markurells of Wadköping* (a 1929 dramatization of the novel *Markurells i Wadköping*, 1919); *Swedenhielms* (1925); *The Riffraff* (*Patrasket*, 1928); and *The Legend* (*Sagan*, written in 1919–20 and published in 1942). To these should perhaps be added *Granny and Her God*, which is two Britishers' dramatization of the 1920 novel, *Farmor och Vår Herre*.

Like Strindberg, Hjalmar Bergman was intensely interested in people. Shy, retiring master observer that he was, he watched them, listened to them, and found them anything but simple. Many of them were eccentric, odd, and these he found particularly fascinating but believable. But concerned with himself and his personal problems though he was, his major interest throughout his whole career was not his own being but the whole human tragicomedy of which he was merely an integral and illuminating part.

Hjalmar Bergman's world is a moral world in the sense that he feels that there is a clear distinction between right and wrong, between good and evil. How that affects his thinking about human beings and the world in which they exist can perhaps be most easily clarified by two quotations, one from *Swedenhielms* and one from the novel *Mor i Surtre* (1917). In the play, Dr. Swedenhielm says: "We are born as human beings; we age into trolls." And Mother Boel in the novel says: "It's like this—one goes about arranging and arranging and arranging. Until things get pretty close to as good as they can be. Seems like. And then the devil gives the world a half turn. And one can't find one's way any longer in one's own petticoat."

Bergman is basically pessimistic about the fate of Everyman in this imperfect world: the young like Anne-Marie in *Mr. Sleeman Is Coming* are essentially good and innocent, but they are helpless when confronted by evil in the form of the crippled, the apathetic, the bitter, and the powerful. By the time the young wake to the horror of the adult world, they themselves are well on their way to becoming like their elders. The adult is concealed under layers of camouflage, and, when these are removed, all that remains is a pitifully helpless, defenseless human creature.

Bergman knew about the tremendously great role chance plays in human life; he knew about such human weaknesses as the tendency to tyrannize when one can; he was very much aware of the blind play of human drives; he had a strong feeling that life is ultimately meaningless. Since he felt there is much good in people, in spite of everything, he believed man is to be pitied; but he believed that life—irrational, fascinating, and unpredictable—is a tragicomedy.

Although he read widely and learned from many, he never became a mere disciple or a blind imitator of anyone. His favorite writers—Strindberg, Lagerlöf, Ibsen, Dickens, Dostoevski, and Maeterlinck—as well as such lesser men as Musset undoubtedly taught him much as did *The Arabian Nights* and the Bible, but, as will be seen when one reads his plays or his novels, he is an original genius, not a pale copy of anyone else.

He had the gift for seeing the grotesque humor in much of life and for putting it into words. He had a sure feeling for moods in all their nuances. He had a particularly good eye and ear for detecting mad and fantastic situations. He had a sense for both brutality and gentleness. He had a liking for what is surprising and unpredictable. He had, moreover, a great joy in telling stories. Fortunately, too, he had an almost overwhelmingly impressive sense for word values; in fact, as the host of Bergman devotees would testify, he is one of the great artists in the use of words. Not only did he have much to say, but he said it unforgettably well.

The plays in this volume may serve as an introduction to a few of the many merits of Hjalmar Bergman. *Markurells of Wadköping* is not only a delightful comedy with hilarious situations and fascinating intrigues and a study of one aspect of the Swedish respect for education, but, perhaps most important of all from Bergman's point of view, a serious drama in which a troll who is what his environment has made him succeeds in rising above egotism and its attendant pride. *The Baron's Will* is, I think, more than a delightful folk comedy verging on farce. It is, among other things, a revelation of universal human frailties and human strength. *Swedenhielms,* labeled by many Swedes as *the* national comedy, is a warm, sympathetic, and adequately close scrutiny of various Swedish "types" of individuals on various levels. The fourth play, *Mr. Sleeman Is Coming,* is a gem, as many producers and actors have discovered. A one-act horror play, a shadow play, close to Strindberg's expressionistic dramas and Maeterlinck's symbolic ones, it is a serious drama with tragic implications. It is at once a grisly comedy and a horrifying tragedy, in which Bergman illustrates his view of the human condition.

Preceding each of the translations in this volume is a short causerie by Stina Bergman, Hjalmar Bergman's widow. These delightful little "chats" are typical of Fru Bergman, as anyone who has had the privilege of knowing her and of seeing her appear in public knows.

WALTER JOHNSON

Contents

Illustrations

Four Plays by Hjalmar Bergman

Introduction to
MARKURELLS
OF WADKÖPING

IN CENTRAL SWEDEN there are two cities which had a great deal of influence upon Hjalmar Bergman's creative writing. The first is Örebro, where he was born in 1883 and where he attended primary school; the other is Västerås, where he took his matriculation examination in 1900. Neither of these cities can be identified as the one in Bergman's novels, because the author merged the two and created his own fictional city, which he called Wadköping. Both the people of Örebro and those of Västerås recognize their own city in the imaginary one that has become so famous that warm disputes have arisen from time to time as each tried to claim Wadköping for its own. Actually, the city belongs to nobody but Hjalmar Bergman. Here he placed the many figures who appear in his books; here he settled his fictitious families; and here he omitted neither cathedral nor bishop's mansion, neither city hall nor school.

Hjalmar Bergman's schooldays in Örebro were one long martyrdom for him. He was tormented by both his schoolmates and his teachers. The little boy was so frightened by all this that it is said he stood in a corner outside the school every morning and vomited before he dared to go in. Terror,

3

which later was to play such a large part in Bergman's works, began here and reached its climax forty years later in his last novel, *Jack the Clown*.

This child was afflicted with a sensitivity so great and an imagination so uninhibited that he suffered from what *might* happen long before the events actually took place. He was large and heavy—altogether too fat, and altogether too shy. He was awkward and slow, and he could neither dance nor take part in sports. For this he was teased by his schoolmates and looked down upon by his teachers. He regarded ordinary school-boy pranks as stupid, and consequently went about by himself trying to figure out ways to keep his schoolmates away from him.

He discovered a way—he learned to think. Quietly and methodically he began to study philosophy and psychology, the history of religions, and what we would now call sociology. And after a few years of reading all that he could find on these subjects he found that he no longer needed to remain silent when his schoolmates teased him. He answered them quickly and bitingly until at last they left him alone.

He came from a rich, respected family. His father was manager of the savings bank but also had extensive business connections outside the bank. The household consisted of father and mother, two sisters, Hjalmar, and a faithful retainer, Amanda. The boy loved Amanda most of all, because she had the rare wisdom to leave the boy alone in the imaginary world he had early begun to build for himself. As an adult he wrote the following in a letter to his wife. "I am thinking of the time when I was little and built seven worlds, one on top of the other. What a job for a little boy between three and nine—to build seven worlds! You sometimes chide me about being lazy, but think of what I have accomplished, how well I have earned my rest."

Amanda respected his seven worlds, and as they sat together in the maid's little room, the builder confided to her about how the work was progressing. But if his mother or either of his sisters should turn up in Amanda's room, he fell silent, afraid that they would laugh at him if they ever found out any of his secrets. He was a strange child, whom even his father and his mother sometimes found it difficult to understand; and he remained strange all his life.

When he was only two years away from the matriculation examinations, he failed in German. This made his father so angry that he took the boy out of school, despite the fact that the boy said the grade was justified since he had neglected his German lessons the whole year. Instead of continuing in the local school he accompanied his father to Germany that summer and studied so intensively while there that he felt able to finish his examination as a private student a whole year before his schoolmates at Örebro.

The matriculation examination was a peculiarly Swedish phenomenon. It was a series of tests of preparation designed to demonstrate whether the student was ready for further training at the senior college or university. Early in the spring, when the sun shone nearly around the clock, the matriculation examination was given in all the schools throughout the country. The visible signs of having passed the examinations were the little white velvet caps and the slender canes which distinguished the new "students" as they filled streets and squares with singing and shouting. And the traditional student song was heard everywhere, with both young and old chiming in.

A private student was one who for some reason or another wished to take his matriculation examination in some school other than the one in which he had passed the required courses. He enrolled in a school in another town, studied there a year, and took the examination with that school's own pupils. This is exactly what Hjalmar Bergman did. He was bold enough to enroll in the highest class and was especially happy when he got his student cap a year before his classmates in Örebro. His father was gratified, too. He nodded a bit mockingly when he met the German teacher from the Örebro school, for even a small measure of revenge is still revenge.

Hjalmar returned home to Örebro and was greeted with the traditional festivities, but he did not stay there long. He began the series of long trips through the continent which were to continue all his life. And he also began to occupy himself with the city which was to become his own, Wadköping.

In 1919, he wrote his great novel about the innkeeper Harald Hilding Markurell and his family in Wadköping. It marked a turning point in Bergman's work. The sense of humor which no one had ever denied him but which was often hidden by the serious overtones of the earlier novels was now set free, livelier and more easily grasped. This does not mean that his view of life had changed particularly since he first began writing in 1905, but that he began to bring out the comic side of his fictional people and to give them freer rein to move us to laughter. And he chose as the central figure of this novel a person who for all his faults and virtues was still a living human being, no better and no worse than you or I. But it was a black day in the history of Wadköping when H. H. Markurell moved into town sitting on top of the furniture van with his beautiful wife at his side and his new-born son in his arms. Here began a period in the city's history which was full of both tragedy and comedy.

Markurell is a troll—fox-red—a dangerous troll who moves like a cyclone without sympathy for those shoved aside right and left. He is sly, often cruel, really a very unpleasant person; but he has one virtue that redeems all his inhumane acts— his love for his son. The story of Markurell is the story of a man whose heart is not warmed by anything on earth but this love. He lives for his son, amasses money for his son, makes himself the most powerful man in Wadköping so that Wadköping in turn will treat his son better than it has treated him. His love for the son is sheer adoration. But the author, who is so skillful in reading the human heart and who knows the ten commandments (Thou shalt have no other gods before me) feels that H. H. Markurell has broken the law. He smites him; and he smites him hard. The day the son, Johan, is to take the examinations, Markurell learns (everybody in town except the father and the son already knew it) that Johan is really the son of his bitterest enemy, Judge de Lorche.

The success this novel met with in the beginning grew and grew over the years. The book has been translated into nine languages and published in many editions. The English translation, by Mrs. Classen, appeared in 1924 and has long been out of print. The translations into Serbo-Croatian, Russian, Rumanian, Czech, and Flemish all appeared within recent years; and the dramatization of the novel which Hjalmar Bergman himself made has been produced several thousand times and is still being played in Scandinavia.

Its dramatic history began when the author wrote a radio play at the request of the head of the Swedish Radio Theater, the famous theater figure, Per Lindberg. Then Victor Sjöström came home from his seven years in Hollywood and asked Hjalmar Bergman to write a film story about Markurell. Incidentally, this was one of the first sound movies in Sweden. Then the theaters began asking for a stage version; and they got one. It is this version which is printed here. By this time the author had had enough of H. H. Markurell. He said, "If anyone, no matter who he is, asks me to work over the old man any more, I'll refuse, because I'm fed up with him."

When Bergman was born, Örebro was only a small town, but now it has grown into a large industrial city which honors and admires its son. In 1965, the city built a large beautiful theater and named it after Hjalmar Bergman. It was inaugurated with a Bergman comedy, *His Grace's Mistress* (*Hans Nåds Maitresse*), and the season was ended with *Markurells*. And at least a hundred young people who had just finished their matriculation examinations asked to appear as unpaid extras in the last scene, in which the students come marching in with Johan at their head. The old and yet eternally young Swedish student song, written by Prince Gustaf, poured out over the audience: "Let us sing of the student's happy days. . . ."

STINA BERGMAN

MARKURELLS
OF WADKÖPING

A Comedy in Three Acts

TRANSLATED BY HENRY PERSON

Characters

HILDING MARKURELL, *innkeeper. The ugliest, slipperiest, most dangerous man in the world. Between 50 and 60, with thick, fox-red hair. When not occupied with particularly vexing problems, he is a very well-bred, urbane person—one who always knows what is fitting and proper. Ordinarily grave and dignified, he is at times pathetically naïve; yet he is a man who fawns upon nobody. He has a pince-nez hanging by a loop. Though never on his nose for more than a few seconds at a time, it is often in use. When he finds it necessary to ponder or to avoid giving an answer, he polishes the lenses slowly and deliberately. He has the unpleasant habit of picking at his teeth with his thumbnail when deep in thought. Though not pretty, this does help him concentrate. He is violent in anger, pitiable when suffering, ludicrous when exhilarated, and boundless in his affection for his son.*

MRS. MARKURELL, *his wife. A magnificently good-looking red-haired woman of about 40. Easygoing, even a trifle indolent, but with a sturdy peasant vigor in speech and gesture when aroused by either sorrow or joy.*

JOHAN MARKURELL, *their son. A bright, easygoing lad of 18, full of good nature and animal spirits. Black-haired and handsome, likable and fun-loving, he handles any situation with ease and aplomb.*

CARL-MAGNUS DE LORCHE, *District Judge. About 55, black-haired and handsome. Refined, elegant, but with a certain brittleness about him. A one-time big business tycoon at the end of his tether. Not exactly haughty, but a trifle reserved.*

COUNTESS DE LORCHE, *his wife. 45 years old. A small, slender woman with a keen intelligence and a will of iron. The only human being for whom Markurell shows not only respect, but something close to veneration.*

STROM, *the barber. 40 or 50 years old. Markurell's stooge, who betrays his master out of sheer malevolence. Small, skinny, and sickly, he has a sharp, whining voice. He tosses out his poisonous thoughts and insinuations with an innocent expression on his face, but with a deliberate stress on the crucial words which brings out his unmistakably malicious meaning.*

HEADMASTER BILLBERG. *A gruff, venerable old gentleman.*

ASSISTANT HEADMASTER BARFOTH. *A man of gentle poetic temperament, with a kind heart and a melodious voice.*

DISTRICT GOVERNOR RUTTENSCHOLD. *Old, feeble, and a bit stupid.*

GENERAL LOEWEN. *Old, but robust and respect-inspiring.*

THE PROFESSOR, *an official examiner. A serious, learned gentleman with a deep, rumbling voice.*

CATHEDRAL DEAN, *an official examiner. A good-natured prelate type.*

STROM, *school caretaker. Small and quick.*

ASSORTED STUDENTS, *and a melancholy "lone voice."*

Note: In the original, Strom = Ström, Ruttenschold = Rüttenschöld [ed.]

Settings

ACT I

SCENE I. *Markurell's office. A very large old-fashioned room with a large door at right, and a small tapestry door near the footlights, left. Farther forward left, a window. Between the smaller door and the window stands a safe. Beside one wall, an old sofa-bed with a spread, made up for sleeping. Against another wall, a long table. In a corner, a smaller table with a built-in cabinet above it. An old dresser, etc., if necessary.*

SCENE 2. *Johan's room. A small, pleasant garret room. Sports gear in the corners; a little bookshelf with a dictionary and*

some schoolbooks; on top of it a phonograph. A radio, some stuffed birds, a punching bag. In the middle of the floor, a large table piled helter-skelter with open books.
SCENE 3. *The office.*

ACT II
SCENE 1. *Outside the school gate (Scene 1 may be omitted). Immediately over the footlights hangs a painted scene representing the schoolhouse, with the huge school gate in the middle. The scene representing the inn can stand beside it ready for immediate use.*
SCENE 2. *Main dining room at the inn. A huge room. Entrance far in the left background. Right and left beside the footlights, small doors leading to kitchen and living quarters. A bar with taps, and a cashier's cage in which Mrs. Markurell presides when it pleases her. Behind the bar, shelves of bottles, glasses, small kegs, chinaware, etc. Chairs and tables.*
SCENE 3. *Faculty room at the school. A very ordinary room.*

ACT III
SCENE 1. *Main dining room at the inn.*
SCENE 2. *Markurell's office.*

The action takes place in Wadköping, circa 1920.

ACT I

Scene 1. Markurell's office

Strom, the barber, sits in a chair near the front with his back to the door. He is alone, rehearsing the "role" he is to play at the impending meeting of the charitable foundation, FRIENDS OF THE POOR. *Silently he asks for the floor, bows slightly toward an imaginary chairman, and rises. With a superior air he proposes a motion which is plainly of great significance, then sits down again. With eyes half closed and head turning slowly from right to left, he "listens in" on the murmurings his motion has presumably given rise to. Then he asks for the floor again, and begins with gesture and mimicry to carry on a silent harangue in which he seems to uphold his argument vigorously and shrewdly. Mrs. Markurell enters, carrying a small tray with glasses and a decanter. She stares at Strom in some astonishment; then she bursts into laughter.*

MRS. MARKURELL: Well, I'll be darned—you look like you're practicing your lesson in the art of bowing and scraping.

STROM: Not being slavish by nature, Mrs. Markurell, when I have some bowing to do, I need some practice first. Maybe you never need any, my dear Mrs. Markurell.

MRS. MARKURELL: Are you looking for my husband?

13

STROM: As far as I know, Markurell isn't at home.

MRS. MARKURELL (*petulantly*): And incidentally that's rather strange. Why should they have arranged to have the meeting just for his convenience when he intends to be gone?

STROM: Aw! Maybe it's on Johan's account.

MRS. MARKURELL: What sort of nonsense is that?

STROM: Well, tomorrow is finals day in the matriculation exams, so . . .

MRS. MARKURELL: What's that got to do with the foundation's annual business meeting?

STROM: My, my, my, but the fair sex is obtuse. The fairer the obtuser, you might say . . . (*Bowing*)

MRS. MARKURELL (*annoyed*): Cut out the nonsense. What connection is there between the meeting and Johan's examination?

STROM: It will give me great pleasure to start Mrs. Markurell sort of thinking. Look! The headmaster himself is secretary of the board of directors, the district governor is chairman, the general and assistant Barfoth are auditors. And so on . . . only big wheels . . . headmasters, instructors, members of the examination board, and so forth and so on . . . Well, do you begin to get the idea?

MRS. MARKURELL (*shoving the tray aside, quietly, but sternly*): Out with it now, barber!

STROM (*seriously*): Well, look . . . it's this way. If anything unpleasant should happen at the meeting, nobody can blame Markurell for it as long as he isn't there. And they can't appeal to him, and so forth and so on, and they can't get angry at him, either. So then there's no danger that Johan will run into any prejudice during the exam.

MRS. MARKURELL: Ah . . . nonsense!

STROM (*sanctimoniously*): Just as I said to Markurell. They surely can't be prejudiced against Johan simply because his father is . . . is . . . er . . . is present at the meeting. But you know how it is; the minute anything has to do with Johan he gets so apprehensive and so timid it's downright unnatural.

MRS. MARKURELL (*with restrained curiosity*): Ah . . . when did you last talk with Markurell, Mr. Strom?

STROM: He was in the shop this morning. Had to have his hair cut and get prettied up . . . father of a graduate, you know . . . must look the part . . .

MRS. MARKURELL (*more friendly and confidential*): And . . . ah . . . and that's when he told you to go to the meeting in his place?

STROM: Well, after all, I happen to be a member of the foundation just like the big shots and have a seat and a vote, as they say.

MRS. MARKURELL: Yes, of course. Strom is dependable. Markurell confides in him. Well, so he gave you a job to do . . . eh?

STROM (*innocently*): Not that I recall.

MRS. MARKURELL: It's a secret, maybe?

STROM: In that case, I recall nothing.

MRS. MARKURELL: Until the job is done, eh?

STROM: Then I'll remember even less. And Markurell will remember least of all.

MRS. MARKURELL (*coaxingly*): And has Judge de Lorche also been at your shop today?

STROM: He comes every day.

MRS. MARKURELL: And I suppose you entertained him with gossip as usual?

STROM: Of course! That's part of the trade.

MRS. MARKURELL: Oh, now I understand. And where is Markurell hanging out now?

STROM: How should I know? If he isn't at home, he must be somewhere else; and if he isn't somewhere else, he must be at home. As far as I know, he can't be in two places at the same time.

MRS. MARKURELL (*who has come close to the window, suddenly impatient*): Okay then, if you're not going to tell me anything, don't hang around and babble. Disappear! I want to be alone . . .

STROM (*cowed, slinking toward door*): Yes, but . . . the meeting is set for here in the office . . .

MRS. MARKURELL: Disappear, I said! The meeting won't be for half an hour. Step out into the bar and have a glass of beer, or Scotch, or whatever you feel like . . .

STROM: Thank you, thank you. It might be a good idea to fortify myself before I . . .

MRS. MARKURELL (*as the barber cautiously approaches the window for a peek*): Well, are you going to get going?

STROM: Certainly, certainly . . . I understand that you want to be alone, Mrs. Markurell. Since you're so generous with your drinks . . . (*Exits through small door, left*)

(*Mrs. Markurell remains standing motionless, deep in unpleasant reflections. Suddenly she hurries over to the safe but, as someone knocks at the larger door, returns with equal haste.*)

MRS. MARKURELL (*very curtly*): Come in.

(*Judge de Lorche enters . . . smiling, nonchalant.*)

DE LORCHE: Good morning

MRS. MARKURELL (*grumpily, but less curtly*): The same to you.

DE LORCHE (*extending a hand to her*): Well . . . here I am, as I said.

MRS. MARKURELL (*sullen, takes his hand hesitantly*): Yes . . . so I see.

DE LORCHE: Is it true that Markurell is not coming to the meeting? Yes indeed, he's got good sense, our friend Markurell. (*Smiling*) But why so still and quiet?

MRS. MARKURELL: What do you expect me to say?

DE LORCHE: Have you . . . thought about the matter?

MRS. MARKURELL (*withdrawing her hand, crossly*): Naturally, I've thought about it . . . but look, it just won't do.

DE LORCHE (*concealing his displeasure with a smile*): Really? I thought we were pretty well agreed. Weren't we? When we talked over the phone a little while ago . . .

MRS. MARKURELL: Yes, sure, yes . . . because then I hadn't had a chance to think it over. I'm afraid of Markurell . . .

DE LORCHE: But, my dear, he's not going to know anything about it.

MRS. MARKURELL: Well . . . I just don't know what there is that he's not going to find out about in the end. His stooge, the barber, was in here just now. Spying, maybe . . . you never can tell for sure . . .

DE LORCHE: Spying? On what? The whole thing is the merest formality.

MRS. MARKURELL: Yes, of course. But do you suppose that Markurell will consider it a mere formality? That we take papers out of his safe without his permission . . . ?

DE LORCHE (*suddenly*): By the way . . . did you manage to get hold of the key?

MRS. MARKURELL (*proudly, and with a certain distaste*): *Managed* to get hold of? Markurell doesn't hide any keys from me, ever. There aren't many he trusts, I can tell you that. But when he trusts anyone, he trusts them all the way! Because he's a *man,* you see, a *real* man! And not a phony! And that's why I don't like all this sneaking around behind his back.

DE LORCHE: Come, come, now; be reasonable. I'm not asking for my promissory note . . . only the shares I put up for security. I assure you that Markurell himself would have let me have the papers . . .

MRS. MARKURELL: Oh, would he? Fine! . . . then go to Markurell and . . .

DE LORCHE: No, no, my dear . . . you know how it is. Markurell and I aren't exactly the best of friends. If he had a chance to get anything on me he wouldn't pass it up. He just doesn't seem to be able to forget that unfortunate incident of many years ago . . .

MRS. MARKURELL (*angrily*): When Carl-Magnus was so big and powerful, and poor Markurell was so awfully, awfully small and weak. But you know how it goes, Carl-Magnus, times change . . .

DE LORCHE: And we with them. I am unhappily aware of it, my dear Mrs. Markurell. (*Glancing at the clock*) Well, time flies . . . How are you getting along otherwise? How is it with Johan? Has he got the examination jitters?

MRS. MARKURELL (*crossly, but with ill-concealed maternal pride*): Him! Oh, how I wish he *would* have them! Then he might pay more attention to his books and less to girls and dancing and running around. I'm really worried about tomorrow. And the less said about Markurell the better . . . he's on the verge of a nervous breakdown.

DE LORCHE (*with a slightly forced laugh*): The boy will get along all right . . . he has his mother's intelligence.

MRS. MARKURELL: He's gifted enough, all right, as far as that goes. Learning a lesson is as easy for him as falling off a log. When it happens to please his royal highness!

DE LORCHE (*seriously*): I only wish my Louis had it that easy. But to make up for it, he's a hard worker. You know, it's funny about those two lads . . . so unlike each other, and yet such good friends—almost like foster brothers.

MRS. MARKURELL (*who has been slowly approaching the safe during the last few remarks, absent-mindedly*): Yes, of course . . . that's the sort of friendship that never dies . . . between the boys . . . now, if I was absolutely sure . . .

DE LORCHE (*quickly, emphatically, but with self-control*): On my word of honor! (*After a moment's hesitation, Mrs. Markurell takes a key ring from her pocket and opens the safe. The judge covers his excitement with a broad forced smile.*)

MRS. MARKURELL (*rummaging energetically among papers and envelopes*): Well, now that . . . that Markurell is so busy worrying about Johan and the examination these days . . . maybe he won't be doing much rooting around in the box . . . Would the foundation's name be on the cover?

DE LORCHE: No, no, no . . . it had *my* name . . .

MRS. MARKURELL: Not here; but on this one it says "180 shares of United Metals" . . .

DE LORCHE: That's it . . . that's it . . .

MRS. MARKURELL: All right, then, here they are.

DE LORCHE (*as he takes the envelope, his self-control leaves him for an instant*): My dear friend . . . my very dearest friend . . . I can hardly tell you what a great favor . . .

MRS. MARKURELL (*avoiding his thanks, closes the safe and lays the keys on the desk. A trifle sourly*): Not necessary, it shows in your face . . . dripping sweat from pure ecstasy.

(*Pricking up her ears, suddenly*) Sh! Quiet! (*She tiptoes quickly over to the smaller door; de Lorche moves toward the larger. She whispers*) No, no . . . give the papers here . . . give me the . . . (*De Lorche holds out the envelope, but drops it, and the shares fall out. At the same instant Markurell steps quickly and silently in through the smaller door, which he closes behind him without taking his eyes off the two accomplices.*)

MARKURELL (*after a moment or two, grinning and bowing*): Most humble servant. Welcome to my lowly dwelling, Sir District Judge, Knight Commander, and so forth and so on. The honor almost overwhelms me, I might say. (*Slight pause*) Just in case I should seem a wee bit inquisitive . . .

DE LORCHE: There is a meeting . . . the foundation . . . it is well known . . .

MARKURELL: Sure, the foundation is well known. (*Quickly tiptoes over to his wife*) Listen to me, you! What's going on around here? Who told the barber he could sit in the bar and booze it up all by himself? Huh? You? And on the house, at that!

MRS. MARKURELL (*trying to conceal her agitation by scoffing*): Well, I never knew you were that tight with your small change . . . especially when it concerns one of your own stooges . . .

MARKURELL: Naw! You can be sure I don't operate like that! Anybody serves me faithfully, I pay him. But the one who doesn't had better watch his step. Understand? Because I see everything, hear everything, and know everything! Now march . . . on the double! Get out to the bar and see that he doesn't get himself drunk.

MRS. MARKURELL (*defiantly*): I'll go if I feel like it!

MARKURELL (*suddenly tender*): But of course . . . little turtle dove . . . little sugar plum . . . of course, you want to do just as I . . . (*He appears to stroke her arms lovingly.*)

MRS. MARKURELL (*jerking away*): Ouch! Quit pinching me, you dirty ruffian! (*Exits straightbacked through smaller door.*)

MARKURELL (*grinning*): Tee hee hee! Now you take women . . . they're so responsive to the slightest little caress . . . have you ever noticed that? (*He walks slowly toward de Lorche.*)

DE LORCHE (*with a forced smile*): Mrs. Markurell and I were talking about our sons. I had just asked her if Johan had the examination jitters.

MARKURELL (*changing his expression—or pretending to change it—from sheer surprise*): Just think of that! The district judge took the trouble to come here a half hour early just to inquire about Johan's welfare. My, my . . . yes, indeed, that's the sort of thing that touches a father's heart . . . thanks . . . my profoundest thanks! (*Taking the judge's hand, he pumps it heartily and bows so deeply that his left hand reaches nearly to the floor. Gathering up the shares and rising to his feet, he looks the judge straight in the eye. Then he continues, seriously*) Look here, this stuff is altogether too valuable to toss on the floor. But, then, women don't understand business and matters of form and suchlike. They're not as shrewd as us along those lines. These papers are worth a lot of money. They could also be worth a few years in prison, if the worst comes to the worst.

DE LORCHE (*disconcerted*): I don't understand . . . I don't understand at all . . .

MARKURELL: Naw! It's hard for a person to understand his own disgrace and shame. But I can tell you, judge, that it's even harder when the disgrace is undeserved . . .

DE LORCHE: I still protest that I don't understand . . .

MARKURELL: Of course not! You have never had a taste of undeserved disgrace. But I . . . (*coming closer—forcefully, but quietly*) de Lorche, do you recall when you presided over your first trial? And tried to get Markurell, the stump farmer's son, convicted of theft?

DE LORCHE: What sort of nonsense is this, Markurell? It certainly wasn't *my* fault . . .

MARKURELL (*interrupting*): . . . that I was acquitted. No, that was no fault of yours. You did all you could to get me convicted. And just look . . . I'd almost have to laugh if I wasn't serious by nature. To see de Lorche standing here in the stump farmer's lad's house—and guilty—I mean *nearly,* of course—nearly guilty of stealing—eh?

DE LORCHE (*with an effort to preserve his dignity*): First and foremost let me call your attention to the fact that your own wife gave me the papers . . .

MARKURELL: Yeah—the petticoat road—that's a fine shortcut! And I am supposed to believe that my wife helped rob her husband out of sheer gratitude for having pulled teats in your father's barn years ago . . .

DE LORCHE (*sternly*): Watch your language! If you had been at home I would have come to you. Specifically, I want to trade a promissory note on my relatives District Governor Ruttenschold and General Loewen for the shares you hold as security for my loan . . .

MARKURELL: District Governor and General—that's very elegant, I'm sure. I honor the gentlemen, but not their bank accounts. Look, their bank accounts are nearly as anemic as your own!

DE LORCHE (*nervously*): I could—perhaps—find other endorsers—besides, it's merely a formality.

MARKURELL: Yes, yes, of course that's what it is. Tell me . . . would I maybe get the shares back again . . . later . . . ?

DE LORCHE (*rising quickly to the bait*): Certainly . . . just so . . . why of course, Mr. Markurell . . . you'd get them back again . . .

MARKURELL: Gee, but I've got an awful itch to play guessing games! When would I get them back? Soon?

DE LORCHE: Naturally you'd get them back soon . . . very soon . . . shall we say . . .

MARKURELL: No—let me make one more guess. I would get them back after the meeting of the foundation. Providing that it's peaceful and agreeable . . . a real cosy sort of brotherly get-together . . . eh?

DE LORCHE (*perceiving that he has betrayed himself, an instant later, constrainedly*): Markurell, I ask if you would be willing to accept a promissory note in place of the shares, and thus do me a great favor.

MARKURELL: Ju . . . ssst for old times' sake . . . eh?

DE LORCHE: You certainly carry a grudge an awfully long time, Markurell!

MARKURELL (*quickly*): Oh, no! Not I! Vengeance is *mine,* saith the Lord. And if someone saws himself off a limb, that's not *my* fault.

DE LORCHE (*bitterly*): But you can use it for your own advantage!

MARKURELL: A good father must provide for his household. Specifically, I have a son. Unh, unh! Possibly you are aware of it. His name is Johan. You also have a son, judge. Whose name is Louis. But what really counts is the surname. Johan's father isn't called de Lorche or any other elegant name. His father is only called Markurell; and since that name has no

particular prestige, I'll have to see to it that I leave him some
other . . . and better . . . inheritance.

DE LORCHE (*extremely upset, almost cringing*): I entreat . . .
I implore Markurell's consideration . . .

MARKURELL (*vehemently*): . . . was taken away from him
when he was young and ignorant during the months that he
waited for the verdict.

DE LORCHE (*with an attempt at dignity*): That verdict was *not
guilty*.

MARKURELL: Yes, just think . . . it *was!* Even though the district judge worked like a bird dog to turn up something in-
criminating . . .

DE LORCHE: I did my duty.

MARKURELL (*after a brief silence*): Uh . . . huh . . . yeah . . .
A man has to do his duty, of course. (*Taking the keys from
the desk and returning the envelope to the safe, he locks it
and ostentatiously puts the keys into his pocket. Then he
stands directly before de Lorche.*) Once upon a time there
was a simple farmer lad who didn't know any tricks at all.
Then he ran afoul of a certain district judge who made a
man out of the boy. As long as people merely teased me, I
stayed a meek, well-behaved dummy. But when they also
wanted to disgrace me . . . that's when I started to get wise.
(*With the feline, crafty quickness characteristic of him in
moments of excitement, he suddenly leans forward and grabs
de Lorche's lapels, so unexpectedly that the latter involuntarily recoils.*) So thanks, district judge . . . thanks for the
chance to learn a few turns! Without them, I wouldn't be
standing here. (*Releasing him, and regarding him a moment
with narrowed eyes*) And that judge . . . de Lorche! . . .
wouldn't be standing there (*He spits the words out*) . . .
like a beggar!

(*The office door opens with a loud clatter, and two fussy women hurriedly enter.*)

FIRST WOMAN: We aren't too late, are we?

SECOND WOMAN: Somebody said that Carl-Magnus was already here. (*They greet the judge.*)

MARKURELL: Oh, no, not by any means. You ladies aren't late at all; it was just that the judge came a little too early. (*He makes off through the smaller door, left, just as several ladies and gentlemen enter through the door, right—the district governor first, the others immediately following. While greetings are being exchanged all around, some of the members busy themselves with moving the large table, around which the meeting is to be held, to the center of the room.*)

DISTRICT GOVERNOR: Ahem . . . yes, dear friends, our meeting today is a very important one . . .

FIRST WOMAN: Yes, isn't it true! And isn't it a beautiful ideal that we are dedicated to . . . helping one another . . . to always . . . good afternoon, my dear . . . always help one another.

DISTRICT GOVERNOR: Ahem, yes, this meeting is probably so very important that I dare say that we can scarcely overestimate how important it is. But I hope that . . .

SECOND WOMAN (*interrupting*): Yes, Julius . . . hope! That is what really sustains mankind. I always say when some friend comes to me looking for help, which I am unfortunately not in a position to give, "Hope, my friend . . . hope!"

DISTRICT GOVERNOR (*angry at being interrupted*): But I hope, my dear friends, that we are all agreed with one another that this meeting is a very important one!

(*All seat themselves around the table—de Lorche at the head of the table, right; the district governor midway on one side; the headmaster on the other. He takes a handful of*

*papers from a briefcase he has brought with him. Last of all
barber Strom enters through the door by which Markurell
has left. He slides into a chair at one side of the table, near
the footlights. As he crosses the floor to take his place, he
salutes everyone respectfully. Nobody pays him any attention.*)

HEADMASTER: Ladies and gentlemen! At the forty-ninth annual
meeting of the charitable foundation FRIENDS OF THE POOR
the following members are present: Governor Ruttenschold,
chairman; District Judge de Lorche, treasurer; yours truly,
Headmaster Billberg; also innkeeper Markurell . . .

STROM (*rising*): Mr. Markurell asked me to say that he is
detained by very pressing business affairs.

(*De Lorche, rising and walking over to the headmaster,
whispers into his ear. Billberg looks a little surprised and
uncomprehending. As de Lorche returns to his seat, the headmaster continues.*)

BILLBERG: We have before us for our approval the auditors'
report for the past year, signed by General Loewen and by
Assistant Headmaster Barfoth, both present.

(*The two mentioned incline their heads slightly.*)

STROM (*rising again, somewhat diffidently*): Mr. Chairman . . .

DISTRICT GOVERNOR: Mr. Strom has the floor.

STROM: I request a recheck of the foundation's accounts.

DISTRICT GOVERNOR: Wha—— what's that? A recheck . . . this
is an insult to de Lorche . . .

(*Immediately upon Strom's entry into the arena the judge
gives an involuntary twitch, though the attack from that
quarter was not unexpected. Meanwhile, having quickly regained his composure, he answers the general with a shrug of
his shoulders and a smile; but the old general, getting angry,*)

*rises and, pounding his fist upon the table so violently that
the headmaster drops his pen, he bursts out)*

GENERAL: Actually it is an insult to the foundation's auditors—
Mr. Barfoth and myself!

*(By now, even the fussy old ladies understand that some-
thing really serious is up. They cluck their tongues and gasp.
Barfoth's sensitive soul bursts into flame. Rising, he declaims
with righteous indignation)*

BARFOTH: I swear upon my honor and conscience that the accounts have been examined with scrupulous accuracy and per-
spicuity . . .

STROM *(mildly)*: And you have, of course, checked over the
foundation's securities also? Stocks and bonds . . .

BARFOTH *(utterly dumfounded, stares at the general)*: Should
. . . should . . . we . . . have done that?

GENERAL *(rolling his eyes threateningly and coughing to cover
his confusion)*: Hem! Hem!

HEADMASTER *(interrupting, positively)*: I beg to inform you all
that the foundation's securities are deposited in a safety deposit vault according to the testimony *ex officio* of notary
public . . .

STROM *(turning to de Lorche)*: That's just fine! The notary
public happens to be Judge de Lorche. Perhaps we may request the key to that safety deposit box?

DISTRICT GOVERNOR *(gaveling the table loudly)*: I hereby de-
clare that barber Strom is out of order. *(The commotion in-
creases and becomes general as the chairman pounds his
gavel, but subsides immediately when the judge rises.)*

DE LORCHE *(completely self-controlled and superior)*: Would
Mr. Strom be so good as to ask his master Mr. Markurell to
appear in person?

STROM (*rising hastily*): Gladly! (*Almost runs out the door, left*)

DE LORCHE: Mr. Chairman, I move that we table this business until Mr. Markurell arrives.

(*The District Governor raises his gavel, lets it fall, and sits there expectantly. General silence. The ladies whisper to each other "such brazen behavior toward Carl-Magnus— what's the man thinking of . . ." The headmaster fusses with his papers; the other men simply stare at the table. De Lorche's gaze strays to the smaller door a few times. [Note: This silence must not be too protracted.] Strom slinks in again, alone.*)

STROM (*blandly*): Our host asks me to say that he is still tied up in an important transaction, but that it is nevertheless always a good idea to have an extra audit.

(*Hubbub, with mixed dissatisfaction and agreement. "It's always a good idea! Such impudence! It's a disgrace, that's what it is, etc. Let's hear Carl-Magnus."*)

DE LORCHE (*rises, forcing a smile*): Naturally I have nothing . . . absolutely nothing . . . against an extra audit . . .

GENERAL (*who is sitting beside the judge, rising, and patting de Lorche genially on the shoulder*): A thousand thanks for those words, brother. Otherwise, it might look a bit queer.

HEADMASTER (*rising. He is angry*): Mr. Chairman, it is my opinion that we shall have to call off the meeting since it doesn't seem to suit board member Markurell's pleasure to be present. We shall have to arrange an extra meeting when our landlord has fewer weighty matters to take care of.

(*District Governor gavels the table. All rise and push back their chairs.*)

DISTRICT GOVERNOR: That was the worst . . . that was the most . . . I've ever experienced in my whole long life!

FIRST WOMAN: Yes, but calm down, my dear friend. You can't know for sure whether you know what Markurell means.

DISTRICT GOVERNOR (*angrily*): What's that you're saying? Don't I know what I mean?

SECOND WOMAN (*irritated*): My dear sir, you don't understand what she's talking about.

GENERAL (*who is hard of hearing, hisses*): I don't know what I'm talking about, eh? Well, in spite of that, I'll have you know that I'm still the District Governor!

(*They withdraw. By now de Lorche has managed to gather up all his papers. He leaves the stage, alone. [Note: The stage must be empty around him, to emphasize his utter aloneness.] The general and the headmaster stand together. After de Lorche has left, the general nods his head in the direction of the door and speaks.*)

GENERAL: There goes a man who has just pronounced his own doom. I have expected it for a long time. How the public executioner, Mr. Markurell, intends to give him the business, I don't know. But in all probability the affair will be unpleasant for all of us. (*As they leave, the curtain falls. Off stage a phonograph plays the latest hit.*)

SCENE 2. Johan's room

At a large table cluttered with books, Johan sits with an opened book in his hands cramming for his examination. Rocking back and forth in his chair more or less in time with the phonograph music emanating from somewhere on his bookshelf, he mumbles and prattles as, pencil in hand, he underlines portions of the text. Markurell sits across the table studying a map. Rising angrily, he shuts off the phonograph.

MARKURELL: That'll be about enough music for now!

JOHAN: Apo-ca-ta-sta-sis, apo-ca-ta-sta-sis . . . apocatastasis. Tell me, old boy, have you the slightest idea of what *apocatastasis* is?

MARKURELL (*who has returned to the table*): Has it something to do with apothecary?

JOHAN: You flunked! *Apocatastasis* is the reunion of souls and the restoration of everything to its earlier state. A very comforting doctrine. You and I shall meet again in the sweet bye and bye, old boy, even if I flunk tomorrow's exam and have to leave the country as a consequence . . .

MARKURELL (*alarmed*): What did you say, boy?

JOHAN: Obviously I'll have to run away. It's all arranged. If we flunk the exam, Louis de Lorche and I are going to sea. He has written to a shipowner in Gothenburg who is a good friend of his dad's. But for the time being I'm banking on apocatastasis. One of the examiners is a cathedral dean, so I'm boning up on church history on the side for all I'm worth. I've learned by heart everything from the fact that Origen's mama hid his clothes—ingenious old girl, eh—to where Tertullian was one of the church's most remarkable men . . .

MARKURELL: Do you know for sure you'll get a question on that?

JOHAN: Five'll get you ten that I won't. But a graduate ought to know *something* at least. If they ask me about anything else, I'll be a little hard of hearing and drag in Origen. Two whole

pages, you understand, without pause or stop, all the way up
to apocatastasis. Boy! There's a first-class, sixty-four-dollar
word to choke on!

MARKURELL: But what good will that do?

JOHAN: Well, then I'll have to go out for a drink of water, and
by the time I get back they'll be questioning someone else,
and Markurell's answer has been accepted. Sharp lad—they'll
say to themselves—he's already got beyond eschat—— the
doctrine of last things.

MARKURELL (*sternly*): Come now, Johan, be serious! We'll
take something else now. (*Rummaging among the books,
he comes upon one that looks brand new.*) What sort of book
is this that's in such good shape? No dog ears! Not even any
thumbprints! You've never even opened this one! What is it?
(*Leafing through it*) Chemistry.

JOHAN: Calm yourself, pa, calm yourself! The headmaster
knows that I don't know the first thing about chemistry . . .
and that's a tremendous advantage for me.

MARKURELL: What's that? Advantage?

JOHAN: He can't very well ask a fellow something he knows
he doesn't know. It'd look awfully bad for him to give me
a question in chemistry. It'd be disloyal . . . show a complete
lack of school spirit.

MARKURELL: But . . . but . . . what about the visiting examiners?

JOHAN: The examiners? Ah, yes. Well, like all transients they
inject a certain note of insecurity in an otherwise well-
ordered society. And their well-known lack of any of the
gentler feelings naturally arouses certain misgivings.

MARKURELL (*who has been gazing intently into his son's face,
lays the book before him and pats him coaxingly on the*

shoulder): Look now, learn a chunk of this by heart, too. To beat them over the head with, so to speak, just in case . . .

JOHAN: One of the examiners is related to the judge, you can be sure.

MARKURELL: So . . . o?

JOHAN: They're eating dinner with de Lorche tonight . . . with headmaster, District Governor, and all the blue-blooded relatives.

MARKURELL: So . . . o . . . o?

JOHAN: It'll be swell for Louis, you understand. The old boys will all be Dutch uncles to him, of course. And tomorrow they'll still feel some gratitude toward his charming mother and his unfortunate father.

MARKURELL (*uncertainly*): Unfortunate? Who has been saying that the judge is unfortunate?

JOHAN: The whole town, of course. Everybody in town says that that wicked old Mr. Markurell intends to force the nice district judge into bankruptcy.

MARKURELL: Oh, well . . . people *will* talk!

JOHAN: The headmaster is at the meeting downstairs . . .

MARKURELL: I know, I know. That's why I'm staying away. I don't want to bark anyone's shins—at least not tonight.

JOHAN: Now listen, old boy; listen to what I'm telling you. You ought to go down to the meeting and swear a sacred oath that you have no intention of forcing Judge de Lorche into bankruptcy. Just think how happy the headmaster would be! And afterward, the whole town!

MARKURELL: That's . . . that's something you don't understand about . . . some notion your mother has put into your head. Just because she knew the judge when she was young and worked for his folks at Stortofta, I should lose out on a big

deal? Nix, my lad, nix! And you can tell her so from me as
long as she doesn't dare to mention it herself.

JOHAN (*derisively*): Dare? Come off of it, pa, it's me you're
talkin' to. When have you ever seen mama afraid of you?
Or of anyone else, for that matter?

MARKURELL (*impatiently*): That's something you don't understand about. But another thing . . . Don't you think that
you ought to go over to the judge's tonight and call on your
friend Louis?

JOHAN: Friend! How can he be a friend to a son of *yours?*

MARKURELL: Pooh-pooh. Son here, son there . . . forget it!
Nobody pays any attention to that. And then you could
get acquainted with the examiners, too. Look here—things
like that never hurt a person.

JOHAN: They crossed over the terrace just a little while ago.
Admiring the view!

MARKURELL (*agitated*): The examiners! . . . And you didn't
tell me about it! We could have invited them in and treated
them to champagne . . .

JOHAN: That's what I figured. And that's why I kept still. Don't
like to see my dad make a fool of himself.

MARKURELL: Oh, well . . . it isn't too late yet . . .

JOHAN: . . . to make a fool of yourself. Yes, God be praised,
it is for *today*. But tomorrow morning you can serve them
coffee in bed, and make bosom pals out of them by slipping
them an extra roll.

MARKURELL: Now look here—don't make me mad! Listen,
Johan . . . be a good boy now, and go over to the de Lorches'
after you've crammed down a bit of chemistry . . .

JOHAN: Sure thing! If you'll be a dutiful husband and father
and go down to the meeting on the double and rescue de
Lorche. That would really be something to move my filial

heart—to sit at the de Lorches' dinner table and hear my father being praised!

MARKURELL (*suddenly*): Someone's knocking!

HEADMASTER (*calls from outside the door*): Is Markurell there?

JOHAN: It's the headmaster. Choose now, father of mine, between sordid Mammon and me! Are you going to the meeting, or aren't you?

MARKURELL (*infuriated, but irresolute*): Mammon and you . . . what sort of nonsense is *that?* Mammon and you!

JOHAN (*oratorically*): Let Fate decide the issue then, my poor misguided father, since your conscience refuses to speak. (*Changing his tone*) Won't you step in, Mr. Billberg; papa is here . . .

HEADMASTER (*entering, reproachfully*): Markurell! How shall I ever explain your behavior? You absent yourself from a meeting which was moved over here simply to suit *your* convenience. A meeting at which your word would have had such tremendous importance for hundreds of people.

JOHAN: Papa is so worried about the examination that I've had to calm him down a bit. But he'll go now.

HEADMASTER: Now! This is a *fine* time for it. After I've had to adjourn the meeting with the explanation that Mr. Markurell had more important matters to take care of today!

MARKURELL: Johan? Are you going to the judge's?

JOHAN: I'm afraid not; it's too late now.

MARKURELL: Then go down and tell your mother to do something about dinner. I'm hungry. Perhaps Mr. Billberg will do us the honor of . . .

HEADMASTER: It would have been a pleasure . . . Unfortunately, I already have an engagament . . .

MARKURELL: I know that! At the judge's—with the board of examiners. Now you know, Johan, we'll be alone. Speak to your mother. But don't you try to sneak out, you! If you're not going to the de Lorches', you must promise to stay home and study chemistry!

JOHAN (*solemnly, after a moment's reflection*): I give you my word not to step out the door. (*Exits*)

MARKURELL: It'll probably be one of these here corruption dinners . . . as they say, at the judge's? So that their boy will have it a little easier-like tomorrow . . .

HEADMASTER (*upset*): Markurell! What sort of wild and nasty suspicions have you been dreaming up now?

MARKURELL: This here kind of an exam is the very devil to deal with! A fellow can't figure out just how to handle it. You yourself are incorruptible, I know well enough. And now if the lad passes tomorrow—and it's a cinch that he will, eh? A matter of course, eh?

BILLBERG: Such things are never a matter of course. But we may hope.

MARKURELL: No! Look, I don't intend to merely hope. "Certainty is the only necessity," as the books say. If Johan passes, it will make me happy. And if a person is happy, he can find a way out for everyone concerned—judge, headmaster, the whole shebang. That things are in an awful mess all around, I know well enough; but they're not so bad that they can't be fixed up. It's easy and simple if you just try to be human. (*Changing his tone, tensely*) But look! . . . if the lad, contrary to all justice, should unfairly be failed . . .

HEADMASTER: Stop it, Markurell, before you end up saying something stupid. Even the beginning of it shows a certain likeness to cattle dealing.

MARKURELL (*soothingly, calmly*): Buying livestock is no trick for a person who's got the money. But who is really the ox in this case? . . . who is it that's to be slaughtered?

HEADMASTER (*a trifle disconcerted*): This is no matter for
joking. You know perfectly well that we teachers want very
much for *all* our lads to succeed . . .

MARKURELL (*cutting him short*): Thanks! But look, somehow
I'm most concerned about my *own* lad's success. So there
is more urgency about him. And in this town I am well
known, you might say; so there certainly can't be any doubt
about Johan's ability. Just look! Just look at all those books!
And every one of them open! But what sort of queer fish
have we got for examiners?

HEADMASTER (*loftily*): They are appointed by the government
to supervise the . . .

MARKURELL: The government has nothing to do with raising
my boy—I'll supervise him myself. But tell me, Billberg,
how could a person butter up those old fogies? How should
you go about it? The judge is entertaining them at dinner.
How about if I should treat them to a real first-class smörgåsbord during the morning recess? Hall decorated with flowers and flags—music, singing, and champagne! You're
invited, too, naturally!

HEADMASTER (*with great dignity*): Fortunately—and I mean
fortunately—it cannot be done. The recess period is altogether too short. But *after* the examination it might be . . .

MARKURELL (*hissing*): *After* the exam! When the grades are
all decided! What good would it do to taffy the old geezers
then? Listen, Billberg, couldn't a fellow shake hands with
them, sort of? In case the smörgåsbord idea won't work. I
could slip them each . . .

HEADMASTER (*staring at him paralyzed*): I . . . I . . . I . . .
Have you gone stark mad?

MARKURELL: Don't start carrying on! If the minister can accept
a ten-spot for confirming a lad, then one of those examiners

ought to be able to take a hundred for graduating him. If it's done in good taste, of course. Refined, you know. "A proper greeting and a warm handshake," as they used to say at district court sessions when a person needed dependable witnesses . . .

HEADMASTER: Let me go! Get out of my way! Markurell, I am leaving this bandits' nest at once!

MARKURELL (*holding him back*): Oh come, now! Surely you can take a little joke. At least, people usually can if they have a clear conscience. You know perfectly well that I wouldn't stoop to thieves' tricks and raw stuff where the lad is concerned. No, not then . . . wouldn't think of it. But I've got something in my hind pocket—something really high-class . . .

HEADMASTER (*despairingly*): The saints preserve us! What now?

MARKURELL (*mysteriously*): You'll see tomorrow. It'll be a surprise that will set you all back on your haunches. But it'll be high-class! Refined . . . elegant . . . A-number-one! Everybody in town will be astonished to learn there's such a wonderful man in our city!

HEADMASTER (*wringing his hands hopelessly*): Oh, ye gods, ye heavenly powers above! What on earth have you come up with now?

MARKURELL: Yeah, try to figure that out, you . . . you . . . tormentor of small boys . . . you bully! I may be as gentle and polite as can be right now—but I can change! So now you've got something else to puzzle over—and you've got to have it all figured out by the time your alarm rings in the morning. (*Emphatically*) If I see the judge's boy in a student's cap tomorrow, and not my boy—then this evening's dinner party is going to cost you gentlemen plenty! Try to sell your shares in United Metals *then!* I'll buy them at two cents a bushel!

HEADMASTER (*flaring up*): That's about the worst . . . the rawest . . . Do you expect to gain anything by threats? From *me?* From the headmaster of the school? This is the most shameless . . . My hat! Where is my hat? (*Rushing toward the door*) Mrs. Markurell! Where is Mrs. Markurell?

CURTAIN

MRS. MARKURELL: I'm here, Mr. Billberg—in the office!

Curtain rises upon SCENE 3. The office

Mrs. Markurell and barber Strom are clearing up after the meeting. They continue with this work throughout the scene. Mrs. Markurell feeds jobs to Strom as fast as they occur to her. He can polish glassware and silver, pick up scraps of paper from the floor, rearrange chairs, etc. He does whatever she wordlessly signals for him to do.

MRS. MARKURELL: Now you'll see that Markurell has driven the headmaster into an apoplectic fit. Is that any way to behave just when Johan is about to take the matriculation exam?

STROM: Markurell knows exactly what he's doing. First he treats people so coarse and raw that they're about to choke; then he gets refined—he thinks—and expects people to kiss him from sheer surprise.

BILLBERG (*rushing in from left*): Mrs. Markurell, it pains me to have to say it—but your husband is insane. To put it plainly, he's trying to scare me . . . or bribe me . . .

STROM: If you asked me, I'd say that you'd better let yourself be scared—or bribed—whichever is most convenient.

BILLBERG: Sir!!??

STROM: You'll bear a heavy responsibility if Johan fails. Just think of the widows and orphans . . .

BILLBERG: This place is a madhouse! Do you intend to murder people in case the boy fails? Widows and orphans?

STROM: Of course not! Markurell will only ruin the *judge*. And if de Lorche goes under, then United Metals and the benevolent foundation will go to hell along with him. Just think— our only large charitable organization! That will be a real treat for the poor children in Wadköping.

MRS. MARKURELL: The Milk Fund will go down along with it . . . and the Symphony Society, and the S.P.C.A. . . .

STROM: Not to mention a lot of the school's scholarship funds. The judge manages most of the treasuries, but Markurell manages the judge. And that's really a responsibility, sir. Here—have a clean handkerchief in case your sweating embarrasses you. (*Offers him a handkerchief*)

HEADMASTER (*pacing back and forth in distress and perplexity, thrusts it aside*): Can you imagine it! He asked me in all seriousness if he should slip the examiners a tip!

(*Door at right opens with a bang. Markurell, who has been listening outside, enters.*)

MARKURELL: Wow! Is that proper, refined language from a headmaster! *Tips* you give to people like *him*. (*Pointing at the barber, who immediately sticks out his hand with a sardonic leer*) But look—for headmasters and professors and other learned fogies you grant a stipend for scientific research. That's what *they* need. That isn't bribery; that's something high-class.

HEADMASTER (*furious*): And with that you expect to gloss over the fact that Johan is weak in several subjects and lazy in all of them! (*This charge hurled against Johan immediately secures Markurell an ally in his wife, who drops what she is doing and steps over beside him.*)

MRS. MARKURELL (*rather wrought up*): Weak? Lazy? No! Don't give us any of *that!* Johan is *my* boy, and he's neither weak nor lazy.

MARKURELL (*so happy over his wife's remark that he slips an arm affectionately around her*): Weak! Lazy! You saw yourself how he sat there dripping with sweat in the middle of a dozen textbooks up in his room. And, as I said, if he doesn't get a good grade, then the headmaster and a few others will have a chance to find out how Markurell can act when he's a little unhappy. See?

BILLBERG (*choking*): He's stark raving mad—ready for a straitjacket.

STROM (*extending a friendly invitation*): Try putting him in one, Billberg. Try it! Go ahead!

MRS. MARKURELL (*though usually stingy with her caresses, pats her husband's cheek and says proudly*): There's only one person who has ever been able to put a halter on this particular man. And then it was done in Ekersta Church with bell and book.

MARKURELL (*squeezing her waist and beaming lovingly upon her*): Yeah, yeah, that's right! But there had been some preliminary preparation.

STROM (*smoothly and sanctimoniously*): Figuratively speaking, yes . . .

MARKURELL (*giving him a little shove*): Shame on you for a tattletale—talking like that about a fine church wedding and a figure . . . At the same time!

BILLBERG (*wandering about the room like a lost soul, addresses*

Mrs. Markurell): And he is utterly inconsiderate of other people's feelings as well. And underhanded! He has his stooges spread scandal about de Lorche to drive down the shares in United Metals. What he wants to do, of course, is to buy them himself at a discount.

MRS. MARKURELL: Oh, well, it's always a good idea to buy cheap.

MARKURELL (*grinning*): That ought to shut him up! But that I should spread scandal about de Lorche out of malice . . . (*He seems to be hunting for something in the room. Suddenly he goes over to the wardrobe and, after peeking under it, lies down on his stomach and creeps under it. Then, kicking his legs about, he screams angrily.*) Grab hold of my legs and pull me out, damn it! I'm getting the Bible!

(*All three have been observing his behavior in some astonishment. Presently the wife and Strom each grab a leg and pull and haul away. Markurell reappears with a huge Carolinian Bible in his arms. While Mrs. Markurell dusts off her husband's clothes, he even more carefully dusts off the Bible.*)

MARKURELL: You're supposed to be a Christian—and you throw God's word on the floor! Shame! (*Opening the book with a solemn expression, he draws the headmaster toward him by the lapels. He means no disrespect by this—for Markurell feels almost like a bishop as he stands there with the sacred book in his arms. Pointing*) Read here! On the family page. Born—and so forth—Johan Hilding Carl-Magnus Markurell. Johan—that's the boy; Hilding—that's me. Carl-Magnus is for his godfather. (*Turning a page*) It says right here plain and clear who the godparents were—and first of all comes Carl-Magnus de Lorche, district judge! (*Laying the book carefully upon the desk, he returns to the headmaster.*) Would I destroy my son's godfather out of sheer malice? Oh,

for shame! But look—business is business! It doesn't say so
in the catechism, but lots of Christians believe it anyway.

BILLBERG (*stares at Markurell, dumb with despair, then jerks
himself free*): My hat! Get me my hat! Then I can get out
of here!

STROM (*handing him his hat*): Here you are. Good-bye, Mr.
Billberg, always at your service—shave and a haircut—first-
class service . . . and very reasonable prices—exactly like
Mr. Markurell, who only wants one measly little student cap
in exchange for a major industry. Good-bye, good-bye.

MRS. MARKURELL: Jeez! Strom . . . he's really got the old boy
going!

STROM: I started him sort of thinking-like, Mrs. Markurell. I
have always enjoyed getting people to start thinking . . .

MARKURELL: And then you wonder why you have so few
customers! That's bound to make business poor.

STROM (*quickly*): Well, at least I've got you. And as long as
you need someone to do your dirty work, I'll make out.

MARKURELL (*suddenly*): Where is Johan?

STROM: Out chasing after the girls, of course.

MARKURELL: You're a liar! He promised not to step out the
door.

MRS. MARKURELL: He was supposed to go out to a dance with
some boys and girls.

MARKURELL: Dance! The night before the examination! And
you let him? Is *that* being a good mother, woman? Is *that*
as far as I can depend on you? But I'm warning you that
if things go badly tomorrow, it'll be *your* fault. Remember
that!

STROM: The headmaster said that Johan would probably make
out all right . . .

MARKURELL (*excitedly*): When did he say that?

STROM: Just a little while ago. He said Johan would probably make out all right if you'd put Markurell in a straitjacket and leave him in the ice house to cool off.

MARKURELL (*hisses*): You lie! That's how much I can depend on you—even though you're supposed to be my friend! You torment me because you can't understand the feelings of a father . . .

STROM (*crushed, angry*): So . . . o . . . o? I can't? Even though I happen to have a son of my own?

MARKURELL: Yeah . . . an idiot!

STROM (*nearly choking with hatred*): And yours is a no-good, spoiled brat!

MARKURELL (*furious*): Watch it, rattlesnake! You just can't stand anybody else's having a son who is clever and intelligent and not mentally subnormal. You can't understand fatherly feelings, because there is a difference between one father and another, and between one son and another. Just remember *that!*

STROM (*gritting his teeth*): Don't worry! I don't ever forget stuff like that! Believe me!

MARKURELL (*sulkily*): I believe myself and nobody else. Well, except the boy, of course. But not *you,* barber! And not *you* either, red-headed female over there by the bureau! What were you doing in my safe?

MRS. MARKURELL (*very coolly*): Pooh—there was nothing wrong with that, was there?

MARKURELL: Wasn't there? That all depends how *I* feel about it. And so you promise to put yourself out for him. But when it comes down to cases, you send Johan instead. Because you thought that would work better. And maybe it would have— if I hadn't known you were behind it. But I could see that— I've got eyes in my head. I hear everything and see everything!

STROM (*who has pricked up his ears during the last exchange and listened attentively to all that was said*): You should never depend too much on the testimony of your eyes, Markurell. Sometimes a person can live in ignorance of what's right before his eyes day in and day out. Just for example, can you tell me right offhand what color his hair is?

MARKURELL: The judge's hair? It's black, of course.

STROM (*pretending surprise*): So far as I know, nobody even mentioned the judge! Huh-uh . . . I mean Johan's.

MARKURELL (*somewhat bewildered*): Johan's hair? What . . . what . . . why do you bring that up?

MRS. MARKURELL (*rising from the bureau where she has been rearranging stuff in the drawers, interrupts curtly*): Don't pay any attention to that barber's snide remarks. You know how queer in the head he is.

STROM (*blandly*): It's a good thing to start people thinking; sometimes it makes them less conceited.

MARKURELL: Aw . . . asshead! Johan's hair. Let me see . . . well . . . it must be about like mine. (*Strom laughs shrilly in a high falsetto.*)

MARKURELL: What are you laughing at, imbecile? Just think about how poor your business is . . . and you'll avoid laughing yourself to death! Let me see . . . maybe it's just a trifle darker.

STROM: Tee hee . . . now you're beginning to see. His hair is black as coal. Hee hee. I stand here and look at your wife's beautiful red hair, and at yours . . . which certainly isn't beautiful, but still red as a fox's tail. And so I reflect, "Nature certainly has her little whimsies!"

MARKURELL (*chuckling*): Ha ha! barber-whimsies, I'd call it! The devil with what color the hair is, as long as there's good brains under it, and good will that you can depend on—and believe me—he's got *them!*

STROM: Right! He promised not to go out the door tonight, and so he jumped out the window instead. Father can depend on me, he says . . .

MARKURELL (*smiling*): Did he say that? Hee hee hee . . . such a . . . such a . . .

STROM (*exploding*): Rotten-spoiled brat!

MARKURELL: Watch yourself, barber! If you don't, I'll close up your barbershop; and after that you can make your living by going around and exhibiting your idiot son for money!

STROM: Thanks for that lovely thought and that wonderful suggestion. I never forget things like that, Markurell!

MARKURELL: You'd better not. And don't forget to come early tomorrow morning with shaving gear, shears, hair oil, face creams, and whatever else you've got . . . for both Johan and me, so we'll look decent. And you're to clip our nails and manicure . . .

STROM: Trim the claws of Markurell—that will be a pleasure and a privilege.

MARKURELL (*walking toward door, left*): Don't be ridiculous! Although it's easy enough to see where your poor son got his feeble wits. I'm going into the dining room and have a bite, so now you can really yap about me! (*Exits left, slamming door*)

STROM: He slammed the door. That means he's listening at the keyhole.

MRS. MARKURELL: You shouldn't provoke him, Strom. It's bad enough already these days. Nothing but "Johan this" and "Johan that" all day long. Sometimes that God-awful father love of his actually nauseates me.

STROM: Now that's strange, Mrs. Markurell. Ordinarily it would make a mother awfully happy.

MRS. MARKURELL: Well, you'd better get on your way now. It's late. Good-bye.

STROM (*moving toward right*): Yes, well, good-night, Mrs. Markurell. Tch, tch, tch, just as beautiful as you are virtuous —maybe even more beautiful. (*Shouting toward left*) Good-night, Markurell. I'll come in the morning and try to make you look human. (*Exits right*)

MARKURELL (*entering from left with a huge slice of bread and butter in one hand and a sausage in the other*): Go to hell, Strom! And don't forget the hair oil and the rest of that fancy stuff. (*Eating, to Mrs. Markurell*) Listen, woman, I've got a little business to take care of, so I'll sleep down here tonight. So you won't have to wait up for Johan. Because I'm going to do that myself. And he's going to get it when he comes . . . you can be sure of that!

MRS. MARKURELL (*with an ironic smile*): Yeah, yeah . . . I can be sure of that. (*She nods and goes out. Markurell sits down at the desk and draws forth a large sheet of paper upon which he has already written something. He reads, scratches himself behind the ear with a pencil, and talks to himself.*)

MARKURELL: Ha . . . humph . . . hoo ha . . . About how much should I make it? Hum, hum . . . Markurell's gift, free and clear, at 6 per cent . . . will yield 1,200 a year . . . promising youngsters . . . To commemorate Johan Markurell's passing his examination with honors . . . (*He meditates a moment; then, looking at the clock, rises angrily.*) That's just too damn much! A person does the best he can for him . . . and he jumps out the window. I'll just quit worrying about the no-good loafer, since he doesn't give a damn about me. I mean it! (*He begins to undress, crawls*

*under the blanket after opening the sofa, which is already
made up, muttering meanwhile.*) Besides that, it's—hard to
know—just what would be the proper thing in this case—
lobster with mayonnaise—or smoked salmon . . . (*He turns
out the light. A moment's silence. Then the little tapestried
door opens, and Johan enters in his stocking feet, shoes in
hand, cautiously making his way across the floor.*)

MARKURELL (*sitting up violently and shouting*): Whazzat? Is
it you, Johan? Where in the world have you been?

JOHAN: Dancing.

MARKURELL (*complainingly, wailing*): Dancing—dancing—
the night before the examination! That's how much I can
depend on you!

JOHAN: Don't forget to wake me . . . can I depend on you?

MARKURELL: Who the hell else do you suppose you could depend on? Go to bed now.

JOHAN (*patting a kiss on the old man's head*): Pleasant dreams,
papa dear! (*Exits*)

MARKURELL (*groaning*): Oh oh oh . . . wonderful, isn't it . . .
to be a father . . . at 6 per cent. Let me see . . . Yep . . . p
. . . that'll be 1,200 . . . in commemoration of my son's—or
should I say *beloved son's*—aw . . . no . . . that's laying it
on too thick! (*After a tremendous yawn, he snaps off the
bed lamp.*) Wake . . . depend on me . . . my boy.

CURTAIN

ACT II

SCENE I. Outside the school gate

As the curtain rises, a wall appears immediately behind it, a large gate in the middle. From right and left the examinees enter in little groups. Disposing themselves here and there at random, they exchange various greetings.

VOICES: Hi, fellas, how do you feel? Do you know what time Latin comes? Where are we supposed to wait? I wonder if we'll get chem before recess. Your servant, Petterson. What time is it? Have you got butterflies in your stomach? Ugh, Boy! . . . I'm shaky. Aw, the heck with you . . . me, too . . . etc. etc.

(The large gate, center, opens, and the caretaker steps out. The boys sitting on the steps jump to their feet.)

VOICES: Good morning, Mr. Caretaker. Come on, please, give me a kick in the pants! Me too! Me too! Give me one too!

CARETAKER: With pleasure! Line up in a row. Hindside to.

(The boys all line up above the steps. The caretaker, hopping and bustling, kicks their behinds in order.)

VOICES: Ooooooooooh! Not so hard! Aw, please . . . harder . . . harder! That's good . . . splendid, splendid . . .

CARETAKER *(panting from his exertions)*: Silence! Here come the headmaster and the examiners.

(The boys hastily arrange themselves in proper groups outside the gate. From the right, the headmaster enters, followed by the professor and the cathedral dean.)

HEADMASTER: Mornin', lads.

BOYS (*all together*): Mornin', head—master! (*Headmaster through gate*)

PROFESSOR: Good morning, gentlemen. Lovely day.

BOYS: Good morning, professor—awfully lovely day.

A SINGLE, WHIMPERING VOICE: Awww—fly lovely! (*Professor through gate*)

DEAN: Good morning, my dear young friends!

BOYS: Good morning, dean, sir!

DEAN: God's glorious sun shines so brightly that one cannot help but be joyful in heart.

BOYS: Awfully joyful!

SINGLE VOICE: Aw . . . w . . . wwfly joy—ful . . .

DEAN: A blessed day. I wish you luck, my young friends. (*Dean through gate*)

BOYS: Thank you, dean, sir.

SINGLE VOICE: Bless the old geezer for wishing us luck!

VOICE: Hold me up—I'm going to faint! Here comes Barfoth in a high silk hat . . .

VOICE 2: And black gloves. Ugh! He's on his way to our funeral. (*Running over to the caretaker, he presents his posterior to him.*) Kick me again—please kick me once more!

BARFOTH: Good morning, dear louts.

BOYS: Good morning, dear teacher.

BARFOTH: Where is your heart, lout?

VOICES (*one at a time*): In my throat. In my stomach. In my boots . . .

BARFOTH: Correct! The class passes in anatomy. Are all the wretches assembled who are to be handed over to the Inquisition today?

CARETAKER: All wretches present, praise the Lord, sir.

VOICES: Oh no . . . Johan isn't here yet—Markurell.

BARFOTH: Bingo! Everyone here except the wretch-in-chief! That's all we needed—that the archlout should be absent. Caretaker, go and call his unfortunate parents—forward march, my dear little friends! (*Exits through gate, followed by the boys.*)

CURTAIN

SCENE 2. Main room at the inn

At a small table in the middle of the stage, Strom is shaving Johan. Markurell watches attentively. The phone in the office rings continuously.

JOHAN: Pa! Papa! Can't you hear how the office phone is ringing?

MARKURELL (*nervously*): It's not for us. Sit still, boy, so Strom doesn't cut you!

JOHAN: He musn't do that! Today I've got to think of my looks, so that the girls will say, "Too bad that handsome boy has to be so dumb he couldn't pass the examination!"

MARKURELL (*agitated*): Don't talk nonsense . . . nonsense . . .

JOHAN: Father . . . think of me between 11:00 and 11:30 and keep your fingers crossed. That's when we have chemistry. Father . . . think *awfully* hard about me . . .

MARKURELL (*still more agitated*): You . . . you said that you wouldn't get any question in chemistry.

JOHAN: I said I *shouldn't*. But Billberg is getting old and absent-minded. Maybe he'll get me mixed up with Louis

de Lorche or some other chem shark. (*Phone rings again.*)
There goes that phone again. It's *my* guess that it's about me.

MARKURELL (*exits through large door*): I'll answer it . . .

JOHAN: Have you got me all fixed up now, Strom? Hair parted
perfectly? Right now I have a feeling that we were supposed
to assemble at half-past . . .

STROM: It's already a quarter to . . .

MARKURELL (*bursting in*): Johan! Son! It was from Barfoth!
You're going to be late!

JOHAN: Well, what do you know! I guessed right! Hope I
can keep it up all day . . .

MRS. MARKURELL (*entering through large door, left*): Johan!
You're going to be late!

MARKURELL (*screaming*): Out of the way, woman! Does the
boy have to have a hen party right in the doorway? Give
him a buss on the neck if you have to, but don't muss his
hair!

STROM: Now there's a father who takes care of everything!

MRS. MARKURELL: What do you mean? Isn't he *my* boy?

MARKURELL: Nix! Today he's *mine!*

JOHAN (*on his way out*): Farewell, father; farewell, mother;
farewell, snug haven of my childhood! Now we run the
Marathon . . . (*Rattling off*) Marathon . . . ancient Greek
district in Attica . . . Miltiades, 490 B.C. And above all, gov'-
nor, don't forget *apo-ca-ta-sta-sis,* or the reunion of souls,
at 4:30 on the school grounds if God so wills . . . peace be
with you . . .

MARKURELL (*excited and moved*): Look! Look at him dashing
across the terrace . . . (*At one of the windows*) Look how
he runs . . . look, he can really run!

STROM: Yeah, just think! Only eighteen years old, and runs
like a lad of twenty . . .

MARKURELL: Shut your mouth! (*Moved*) Look . . . and still he takes time to wave at me. (*Opens window and shouts*) Good-bye, son! Your father will be thinking about you. I'll be down at the school. I'll be there, I say . . .

MRS. MARKURELL (*out the same window, shoving her husband aside*): Run, Johan, run!

MARKURELL (*furious*): Don't hold him back, woman! If he gets there too late, it'll be all *your* fault. Look! Look! Now he's turning and waving again. Good-bye, good-bye! (*Waves*)

MRS. MARKURELL (*angrily*): Quit shoving! He's waving just as much at me!

MARKURELL: Pah! . . . not at all! (*Shutting the window*) Why don't you get out in the kitchen and make sure the baskets are ready and the girls in clean uniforms? On your way! (*Mrs. Markurell leaves through small door, right.*) Listen now, Strom, you're going to help me out a bit with . . .

STROM: Am I? Doing what?

MARKURELL: Helping me serve a real swell, high-class smörgåsbord to the honorable examiners.

STROM: What are you going to do? Set up a stand under the elms in the schoolyard?

MARKURELL: Nix! But in the faculty room.

STROM (*astonished*): The faculty room? During the examination? And are you going to dress up in a clown suit or make up in blackface, and do a tap dance?

MARKURELL (*hisses*): Shut your trap! They've got to eat during the recess, as you perfectly well know. Do you expect those big-shot examiners to eat sack lunches? That'd really be something, huh? Nix! But smoked salmon, and a cold bird with Burgundy . . . *that'll* really put them in a good mood. That's *real* examination food! And you're going to help me, you miserable scarecrow, because your brother is the care-taker. You'll have to work on him—fix it up so we can get in . . . and you'll have to look halfway civilized. You can borrow my tux—for a tux is always a tux whether it's on a clothing-store dummy or a scarecrow. Besides, some of my glory will reflect on you! I've got something real swell in my hind pocket, see? A donation . . . if you know what that is. It's not bribing or palm-greasing, or anything like that. You merely give—feel free, help yourself! Salmon, fowl, three kinds of wine, and the donation . . . help your-self . . . all on the up-and-up. And if they flunk Markurell's son after that, his royal majesty's government ought to ap-point guardians for them, the imbeciles! Well . . . will you come along?

STROM: I'll go along, my dear Markurell. It ought to be both diverting and instructive to witness your downfall. (*Walks toward the window*)

MARKURELL: Downfall, you said? Tee hee . . . Markurell's downfall. Yeah, you can bet that would really please certain people!

STROM (*looking out window*): Yeah . . . certain people. Come over here and take a look out the window. In a minute you'll get a look at one of your victims.

MARKURELL: I don't have victims—I have *clients*. People that I help . . .

STROM: To destruction. She's coming this way . . .

MARKURELL: Who? I wouldn't even see the Lord himself to-day—no, blessed God, forgive me—our Lord, of course, but not anybody else.

STROM: It's Mrs. de Lorche . . .

MARKURELL (*upset*): The countess! No, no, no! I don't want to see her—not today. She's come here to beg for the judge.

That's for sure! But look—I don't want to say either "yes" or "no" to her. Not today, at least. Tell her I've gone downtown. But remember I'll hear every word you say! (*Rushes out through small door*)

STROM: I don't doubt it! What a man! Who can hear so much and learn so little! (*Someone taps at large door, left.*)

MRS. DE LORCHE (*stepping in*): Good morning, Mr. Strom. Is Mr. Markurell in?

STROM (*bowing*): Good morning, your ladyship. Ahhh, I don't know just how to answer. He himself says that he's not in. Your ladyship will probably have to wait a little while. He has gone into seclusion on account of his guilty conscience—if that brick-red monster *has* a conscience.

MRS. DE LORCHE (*smiling*): You dare say things like that about the omnipotent! What if he should hear it?

STROM: Don't worry—he'll hear it all right (*Pause*) Your ladyship is out early today.

MRS. DE LORCHE: I walked part way to school with my boy. It's supposed to bring good luck.

MARKURELL (*bursting in*): Luck! Luck! Now why couldn't my old lady have gone part way with Johan? But no—she's lazy . . . and ignorant . . .

MRS. DE LORCHE (*pretending surprise*): Why, Mr. Markurell, do you always stand behind doors and eavesdrop instead of greeting an old friend?

MARKURELL: Strom, get out into the office and sit by the phone. Barfoth was supposed to call. Good morning, Countess. But we are *not* friends—not us. No . . . not now any longer . . .

MRS. DE LORCHE: Oh dear, dear, dear—*we*, who have had so much in common!

MARKURELL: The boy, yes, Johan. Your ladyship has been just like a mother or an aunt or something to him and taught him fine manners. But what about yesterday? When you had the examiners up for a wonderful dinner? Did you invite *him*?

MRS. DE LORCHE: But my dear . . . It would scarcely have been proper to invite a student.

MARKURELL: Yeah, I know that, too. But I don't give a hoot about propriety. That is, if I've got anything to gain. Otherwise I can be proper, too. And today people are going to find that out. Anyhow . . . won't you sit down? (*He dusts off a chair with the corner of the huge bartender's apron he has tied on over his dress trousers.*) Can I offer you something? Fruit juice? We have five kinds of extrafine juice. Coffee? And we have fresh creampuffs for tonight's celebration. The graduation party is to be held here, you know. Very well—nothing, then. You were just now lecturing me about propriety—now listen to this. Your ladyship has come here to beg for the judge. Is *that* proper for a fine lady?

MRS. DE LORCHE (*sadly, but not without dignity*): Mr. Markurell, you understand my husband's situation. And you also understand that, in this particular case, I cannot be finicky about propriety.

MARKURELL: Yes, I understand. And it distresses me to see such a sweet, refined lady so . . . so . . . in such a . . . Are you sure you won't have something? And look—this is not a matter of sentiment—between the judge and me, I mean. It's business! People say I fish in troubled waters. Your ladyship can inform them that I fish in any sort of waters—where there are fish to be caught.

MRS. DE LORCHE: A beautiful credo, Mr. Markurell.

MARKURELL: Your ladyship . . . you know that I'm a father. You know my son. Now I ask you—have I any obligations to such a boy?

MRS. DE LORCHE: Many . . . and, above all, the obligation to leave him an honored and respected name.

MARKURELL: Yes, yes. I know that old song by heart. (*Goes to large door, left, and shouts*) Hey, Strom! Come here a minute. I keep the barber for a pet—a bloodhound and a parrot combined, so to speak. Isn't it so, Strom . . . that you usually tell the truth?

STROM: When it's convenient—for me.

MARKURELL: Tee hee! He's deceitful and vicious, but not stupid! And there are a few truths he'd just as soon speak out. Listen, Strom, what do the people in this town call me?

STROM: I can't say—not when there's a lady present.

MARKURELL (*laughing contentedly*): Hear that, your ladyship? For example, Strom, do they call me a *skunk?*

STROM: That would be unbelievably mild . . . a compliment.

MARKURELL (*laughing even more heartily*): That'll do, barber; get back to the office. And be sure to get into that tuxedo. (*Strom slinks out.*) No, you see, your ladyship, I haven't got any good name to bequeath my son, but to make up for it I'm going to give him something a darn sight better than a good name . . . money! Money, my dear countess! Not little crumbs, you understand. Not just a few savings bonds, but a real pile! There is nobody on earth who wouldn't rather have money and a bad name than poverty with a good one!

MRS. DE LORCHE: Oh, shame . . . shame . . . that's not true.

MARKURELL: Our countess' voice just got a bit trembly, seeing as she knows darn well that it *is*. If Markurell's son is poor, he's a bum; if he's rich, he's a gentleman! But if you really believe the opposite, you can console yourself with the fact that your son bears the highly respected name of de Lorche . . .

MRS. DE LORCHE (*slowly*): And what if that name isn't so highly respected any longer . . . after this . . .

MARKURELL: It won't be! Depend on it! But that's the judge's fault—not mine. He asked for it; he left himself wide open. *I* don't leave myself open. Not any more! Ever since I was knee high to a toad, people used me for a whipping boy. But I finally learned how to strike back. The barber said to me one time, "Markurell, you haven't got a friend in the world —you're all alone." And he hit it right on the nose! It's true. But is it *my* fault? I was just an ordinary little chick, and wanted with all my heart to be one of the flock. But they drove the ugly one away—with beaks and spurs. So I scrambled up—with my own wings, and my beak, and my spurs—until I got to be cock of the walk in Wadköping. Number one in the pecking order, as they say. But absolutely alone—except for the boy. If I didn't have him I wouldn't have anyone.

MRS. DE LORCHE: Markurell . . . we are both alike in some ways. I also have a son, my Louis. And if I didn't have him, then *I* would be utterly alone. (*More animated, without bitterness*) And Markurell . . . listen to this. We have still another similarity. I'm not worried about propriety either—when my boy is concerned. Otherwise I wouldn't be sitting here like a beggar in your doorway.

MARKURELL (*extremely embarrassed*): Now . . . now . . . now . . . my dear countess shouldn't talk like that. It's not fair to say that to me. You are a mother, and I am a father. So far we're alike. However, I'm not the father of the judge's son, but of my *own* son. Tell him that from me. And I don't

ask help from *anybody*. I don't need any. I have my Johan
—and nobody's ever going to take him away from me, damn
'em!

STROM'S VOICE (*through open door, left*): Markurell . . . you
mustn't swear!

MARKURELL (*with a start*): Wha . . . wha . . .

STROM (*entering, suavely*): Barfoth's on the phone.

MARKURELL (*alarmed*): What! Already? Have they had chemistry?

STROM: Hurry up. He can't wait.

MARKURELL (*anxiously*): Dear . . . dear countess . . . answer
it, please . . . I hear very badly over the phone.

MRS. DE LORCHE (*rising, and walking toward door*): All right,
I'll take the message for you.

MARKURELL (*humbly*): Thanks . . . thanks . . . thanks ever
so much. I won't forget it.

STROM (*cynically*): Are you going to offer her more fruit juice
and creampuffs?

MARKURELL (*yells*): Shut your mouth, rattlesnake! Tell me
. . . how did he sound?

STROM: Barfoth? Oh, he sounded exactly as if he was thinking,
"Old Moneybags Markurell thinks he's God Almighty, but
a little debt-ridden schoolteacher like me can set him back
on his haunches by merely calling him on the phone."

MARKURELL (*excited*): I've got to go down to the school! Right
away! Get a move on, Strom. Tell them in the kitchen. The
baskets, the lunch, the waitresses, the wines! Where did I
put the wines?

(*Exit Strom. Markurell, hurrying behind the bar, begins
to pull out various bottles from shelves and lockers. During
the following exchange, he packs them into a basket or two*

he has dragged forth from the far end of the bar and places
them on the counter. Mrs. de Lorche enters.)

MARKURELL (*anxiously*): Ah . . . ah . . . what did he say?

MRS. DE LORCHE: Oh, Barfoth told me to calm you down. Johan
made it all right.

MARKURELL (*exultantly, continuing to pack*): What did I say!
He's going to pass! Well, I put a flea in the headmaster's ear
this morning. And that's the sort of thing that takes hold.
Thank you, dear countess, for now there's nothing more to
do . . .

MRS. DE LORCHE: Mr. Markurell . . . I also had a little business
with you. We haven't said a word about that . . .

MARKURELL: Oh, yes . . . oh, yes—certainly we have. Look
. . . my little countess and I understand each other without
any words. It's about bonds and shares and things like that
—tiresome things—very disagreeable—nothing for a sweet
little thing like your ladyship to bother with.

MRS. DE LORCHE: Consequently, Mr. Markurell, I have come to
the tiger's den in vain.

MARKURELL (*still packing*): Tiger's Den? Never heard of it!
But if it's a nickname for this dining room, come again, you
sweet thing. Come back this evening. Look—I need a dear,
gentle, understanding person to celebrate with—if everything
goes all right.

MRS. DE LORCHE (*bitterly*): If everything has gone all right, the
great Mr. Markurell won't need any dear, gentle, understanding person to help him celebrate.

MARKURELL: Need? No! As long as Barfoth said everything was
going all right . . .

MRS. DE LORCHE: My dear . . . I didn't get a chance to finish
telling you. He said that Johan made it to the examination all
right, but that he won't pass in chemistry.

MARKURELL (*who has now finished packing*): What? Chemistry? That's the headmaster's doings! He wants revenge on me. I understand other people just like I understand myself —they're all crooks! The same kind of stuff goes on in the schoolhouse as in the stock market. That nasty old Markurell's son—we'll take it out on *him,* because in the schoolhouse Markurell has nothing to say!

MRS. DE LORCHE: No, no . . . Billberg did the best he could for all the boys—but Johan was the only one in class that the chief examiner himself failed in chemistry.

MARKURELL (*taken aback*): The chief examiner himself? Smooth customer, eh? Well, now I'm going to show him something else. (*Runs to the small kitchen door and shouts*) Shake it up, out there, so we can get going! (*To Mrs. de Lorche as he runs across the stage and disappears, left*) I've got to put on my coat. Be right along.

(*Mrs. de Lorche moves toward the door to leave, but pauses as she hears the kitchen door opened up with a bang. In comes a little caravan consisting of: [1] a little busboy dressed entirely in white, carrying a huge covered silver tray; [2] a trim little waitress dressed in black with white apron and cap. She is carrying two huge baskets; [3] ditto, carrying one basket; [4] a tall kitchen boy entirely in white and wearing a high cook's cap. He carries a magnificent decorated cake of several layers. Last comes Strom, dressed in Markurell's tuxedo, which is a good deal too wide for him as well as too long in the sleeves.*)

STROM (*tucking up his long sleeves, to countess*): You've got to admit that this will be a magnificent sight as it crosses the schoolyard—barber, waitresses, busboys, baskets, and (*pointing toward large door from which Markurell is just emerging*) Markurell!

(*Markurell enters, in frock coat and carrying a vase. His coat is unbuttoned and his hat perched on one side of his head. After quickly inspecting his troop, he takes the wine basket from the counter and hands it to the girl who has only a single basket*) You take this one, my dear. (*Straightens the kitchen boy's tall cap, thrusts his nose into one of the baskets, and inhales deeply*)

MARKURELL (*delighted*): Wonderful! First class! On your way now, boys and girls. Sing something so you can keep step. I'll follow right behind. A five-crown bonus apiece if you don't break any dishes. Keep an eye on them, Strom, and talk sense to your brother so he'll let us in. Let's go!

(*The caravan trudges away in goosestep, singing a marching song. Mrs. Markurell, who has entered during Markurell's last remarks, stands smiling at the display. Markurell has run ahead to the cashier's cage, rummaged about, and finally found a heap of napkins. Thrusting one into his pocket, he goes over to his wife.*)

MARKURELL: If it's got anything to do with food or Johan, you can depend on that old lady of mine! (*Turning to the countess*) Ah, yes. Thank you, and good-bye, dear countess. And welcome back to the Tiger's Den this evening. (*Lifting his hat and waving it, he bursts forth in a loud voice*) We march over dew-sprinkled hills, tra-la-la! For we'll go to see the tiger in a bunch, tra-la-la. Yes we'll go to see the tiger, we'll go to see the tiger, we'll march to see the tiger in a bunch, tra-la-la! (*Exits singing*)

CURTAIN

SCENE 3. Faculty room at the school

Large door in background, window at right. Near foot-lights a smaller door. Caretaker Strom, in an agony of fear, paces from window to door, from door to window. Gives a start, cowers unhappily, and folds his hands.

CARETAKER: Well, here they come, as the sheep said of the wolves. (*Darting over to the door and opening it, he peeps out and gestures for silence. The troop from the inn enters with barber Strom in the lead. Markurell is not with them. Whining*) Walk quietly—on tiptoes, for cat's sake!

CARAVAN (*whispering*): Softly on tiptoe—softly on tiptoe. (*Quickly and silently they set the faculty table with all the delicacies, running about helter-skelter, all on tiptoe.*)

STROM: How long till morning recess?

CARETAKER: Only seven minutes. But, my dear brother, what's going to happen when the headmaster finds his dignified faculty room changed into a saloon? That's not going to be good. He'll never stand for it.

STROM: Yeah, I know—but look, that'll be *his* problem. If he's got good sense, he'll let Markurell have his way. And if he hasn't got good sense, then Markurell will have his way anyhow!

CARETAKER: Where *is* Markurell?

STROM: Talking to Barfoth. You see, Barforth is going to bring the examiners in here. He's like a beater at a big-game hunt.

CARETAKER: That's the limit! Is Barfoth in on the deal with Markurell?

STROM: Tell me, brother dear, is there anybody in this town who is *not* in on a deal with Markurell? . . . regardless of whether he knows about it or wants to be! If Andersson wants to drive Pettersson out of business, he makes a deal with Markurell and ruins Pettersson. But at the same time Pettersson makes a deal with . . . who? With Markurell, of course, and ruins Andersson. Andersson and Pettersson . . . they can be just anybody at all. But Markurell . . . *he* is always Markurell!

CARETAKER (*with grudging admiration*): Yeah . . . that guy . . . the devil himself couldn't get the best of *him*.

STROM (*supervising the table setting, answers absentmindedly*): Yeah . . . maybe so . . . maybe so, I know he's the biggest and most powerful man in town . . . but you know the old saying, "The bigger they are, the harder they fall."

(*The caretaker grins. Markurell glides silently in through the door, then pauses to cock an ear outside. He is evidently excited, but in complete control of himself. Going quickly over to the Stroms, he stares at them as if saying, "What are you two babbling about?" The brothers, with embarrassed expressions, avoid meeting his glance. Swiftly and silently, Markurell immediately turns to the table and gives it a final touch. Then, with a gesture of dismissal which includes the entire kitchen crew, he hisses.*)

MARKURELL: Disappear! Into thin air! (*The servants, who have followed his movements anxiously, dash out the door as soundlessly as possible, the last one shutting it. Markurell, now standing between the brothers and turning first to the one and then to the other, gestures toward the table and exclaims with a satisfied air*) Yessiree, Strom! Now the most exalted visiting examiners and the rest of those guys can come in whenever they feel like it. And if this doesn't turn out to be a class-A cultural banquet . . . then, so help me Hannah, I don't know what culture *is!*

(*Voices from without. At a signal from Markurell, Strom opens the door. Markurell, napkin over arm, steps a little to one side of it. As Barfoth ushers in the examination officials, the caretaker sneaks out through the door and closes it after himself. At sight of the festive table, the theological dean makes a gesture of astonishment, and the professor looks somewhat grumpily pleased. Barfoth's eyes pop wide open as he looks first at Markurell and then at the table with its huge centerpiece of flags, ribbons, and flowers.*)

BARFOTH: Lift up your eyes, gentlemen, and observe the power of magic . . . which far surpasses that of reason.

PROFESSOR: What have we here? . . . ahem . . . ahem . . . lunch in the faculty room . . . very original idea, but very practical.

DEAN: A superb idea! (*Turning to Strom, who stands nearest him*) Well, and who have we here? Isn't it the barber who shaved us this morning?

STROM (*bowing*): I always shave the honorable examiners. My brother is the school caretaker . . . so it sort of runs in the family.

DEAN (*genially*): Oh, well, then we know each other.

STROM: Yessiree! It's part of my business to know the visiting examiners. You see, the students always come and ask me what sort of fellows they are . . . their characters, you know.

DEAN: And you can read a person's character?

STROM (*always softly and humbly*): I have to guess, you understand. You mustn't judge a dog by its hair, but you can judge a man pretty well by his bristles.

DEAN (*smiling*): Tell me then, my good man, what sort of character have I?

STROM: You ought to be extraordinarily decent and good-natured—the bristles were so soft—to be exact, like the down on a gosling.

PROFESSOR (*enjoying the other's misfortune, but good-naturedly*): Ha, ha, ha. That's where you got told off, dean! Gosling! You couldn't say that about me, could you?

STROM: No, certainly not. Your beard was coarse and curly—to be exact, like sheep's wool.

(*Now it is the dean's turn to laugh, whereas the professor looks a bit angry. But Markurell, who has listened to the repartee with rising displeasure, is even angrier.*)

MARKURELL: Shut your trap, Strom, and quit insulting the gentlemen!

BARFOTH (*who has been devoting himself to the delicacies on the table, exclaims ecstatically*): Oh, lovely board, that speaks so charmingly to eyes, to nose, to palate—whence came you? Moses conjured up quails in the desert. But Mr. Markurell has manifestly shot roasted pheasants in the schoolyard and caught smoked salmon in the drinking fountain!

DEAN (*smacking his lips with pleasure*): Yea, verily! Yea, verily! Our dear headmaster has prepared us a most agreeable surprise! Now we can eat our humble little meal in peace and quiet.

PROFESSOR: Humble! It would take the pastor of the richest congregation in the country to call this feast a humble little meal!

HEADMASTER (*entering from background, stops short in horror and indignation*): Wha . . . wha . . . what is this I see before me? The faculty table . . . of Wadköping School . . . turned into a lunch counter. Oh, Markurell, how could you do this to me?

(*Markurell smiles contentedly.*)

PROFESSOR (*exclaims delightedly*): A charming surprise, my dear colleague! You know—I had a hunch all the time that you had something up your sleeve.

DEAN (*approaching him with open arms*): My dear sir, you have written a glorious new chapter in the history of Swedish education. Culinary art in the qualifying examination . . .

(*While the headmaster accepts these unearned compliments, Markurell whispers something to Barfoth.*)

BARFOTH: Fall to, gentlemen, we have only a short time. But first let me introduce the *maître de cuisine* who arranged this miracle.

MARKURELL (*advancing quickly, shakes the dean's hand, smiles*): Thanks, thanks, just pitch in! Everything is first-class. (*He thrusts a plate into the dean's hand, and repeats the entire performance with the professor.*) It takes a lot of good food to support a head full of brains, heh, heh, heh. And just look here, dean; here is a cheese I've aged myself. Come, try some.

DEAN: He is like a father to us, our good innkeeper! Aaaaah! Exquisite! I can tell you, if those students were here they would get a real lesson in the physiology of taste.

PROFESSOR (*eating*): And in the chemistry of artistic cookery.

MARKURELL (*with badly feigned candor*): Chemistry . . . yeah . . . that old devil chemistry. The boys must have been tops in that? Just a moment . . . you must have a glass of Rhine wine with the salmon . . .

PROFESSOR: Just a few drops. Thanks. Aaaaah! Taking it all in all, it's a good vintage year.

MARKURELL (*delighted*): I could tell at once that you really understand that subject—it shows in your thick lips. Right you are! Liebfraumilch '87. You gentlemen don't get to drink *that* every day . . .

PROFESSOR: Not by any means! But by a good vintage I really meant the graduating class. However, it's not quite as good as Liebfraumilch '87 . . . at least not in chemistry. Pardon me, did I hear them call you Markurell?

MARKURELL: That's right. I'm the boy's father.

PROFESSOR: In that case, alas, I must feel sorry. That particular youngster handled the questions very badly . . .

MARKURELL (*giving a slight theatrical shudder, regards him with a mildly reproachful glance*): Oh, no. You must have got it wrong end to. The lad knows his subjects—I'm sure of that, since I paid for all those expensive books. But take a little more of the salmon, sir. It's superfine!

(*Barfoth, standing near Markurell and the professor in conversation with the dean, overhears what is being said. By motions and gestures, he induces the dean to listen.*)

PROFESSOR (*continues eating with great relish, but says stubbornly*): The gentleman's salmon is splendid; but the gentleman's son is poor—very poor—in chemistry.

MARKURELL (*extremely unhappy, tries to belittle the subject*): Chemistry . . . oh, well . . . chemistry . . .

DEAN (*stepping up to the table to refill his plate*): Don't let it bother you, Mr. Markurell. Chemistry is a subject of very little importance . . .

PROFESSOR: What's that? Chemistry of little importance?

DEAN (*with maddeningly serene authoritativeness*): Chemistry is, as a matter of fact, sheer humbug. Chemistry is the superstition of modern times.

MARKURELL (*exultantly shaking Strom, who happens to be near*): Chemistry is humbug! Did you hear that, old barberpole? Humbug!

PROFESSOR (*roaring out scornfully*): A theologian talking about superstition, ha, ha, ha!

MARKURELL (*dashing over to the headmaster, who has kept himself in the background, ill-humored and not eating*): Don't just stand there like a cast-iron deer while they're discussing science! Put in a good word: you won't regret it. Because look—I've got a surprise in my hind pocket.

(*The headmaster wrings his hands in despair. Markurell, friendly and trusting, turns to the professor again, just as the latter enthusiastically spears a fried half-chicken. The headmaster makes his way to the table and begins to help himself to food. During this scene Markurell, even when weighty matters are being dealt with, is always the attentive host, who in the middle of a conversation with one person can still hand a plate of food to another. Strom does his barkeeping very inefficiently, but is always around to pick up glasses and plates when necessary.*)

MARKURELL: Yeah . . . pooh! You couldn't expect a priest to understand chemistry. But if a lad is well-behaved and a credit to his father—then isn't that really the main thing, and chemistry secondary? (*He pours more wine.*)

PROFESSOR (*laughing good-naturedly*): Oh, well—we'll concede that. Besides, now that I look more closely at you, I see that I have probably made a mistake.

MARKURELL (*in happy surprise*): Let's have a drink on that! Let's have a drink on it!

PROFESSOR (*inhaling the bouquet of the wine appreciatively, studies Markurell's face reflectively*): I have obviously got the names mixed up. The youngster can hardly be *your* son, sir. He looked astonishingly like de Lorche . . . And he is certainly the illegitimate son . . .

(*The barber drops the tray full of glasses he has just picked up from the table. As it falls to the floor with a loud crash, Markurell hisses at him. The dean, who stands nearest*

*and whose attention is now fixed upon the bartender, ex-
claims in friendly surprise.*)

DEAN: Well I'll be blest! Isn't it the barber who shaved us this
morning?

PROFESSOR (*also somewhat surprised*): It is indeed! The jolly
fellow who entertained us with the local scandal. He's the
one who told us about the illegitimate son. What's the matter
with you, Barfoth? Why are you kicking my ankle? Did I
say something out of turn?

(*Barfoth, in deep anguish, has given him a warning from
behind. The headmaster, equally unhappy, pulls the dean
toward himself and whispers into his ear. Immediately there-
after, feeling weak in the knees, he goes to a chair and sits
down. Strom squints covertly, picks up the glasses, and disappears into a corner. Markurell stands isolated—physically,
but even more spiritually. Gathering from the others' embarrassment that something is wrong, but without the
slightest notion of what it is, he feels uncertain of himself.
After looking about, he goes over to the chair where the headmaster sits with his head in his hands, taps him playfully on
his bald spot, and asks in astonishment*)

MARKURELL (*wonderingly and amazed*): Sir . . . have *you*
heard that some lad in the class is supposed to be a by-blow
of de Lorche's? Who on earth could it be?

HEADMASTER (*raises his head and exclaims hysterically*): About
that . . . I don't know . . . anything!

MARKURELL (*indignantly*): Of course *you* don't! Mustn't say
anything against Carl-Magnus—he's sacred. But I can believe
every word of it . . . absolutely! I have never heard that he
has an illegitimate son, of course; but that is by no means the
worst thing on his record. (*Walking slowly toward Barfoth*)
Hey, Barfoth, have you ever heard . . .

(*Barfoth surreptitiously nudges the dean, who hurriedly takes a glass and says hastily but with his dignity intact*)

DEAN: The time is flying, gentlemen. Let us therefore thank Mr. Markurell most heartily for the friendly thought . . . (*This instantly interrupts Markurell's train of thought. The most important business of all, the donation, still remains to be taken care of. Gesturing for attention with one hand, he fumbles in his pocket with the other.*)

MARKURELL: Just a minute. The reverend dean mentioned a thought—now you'll hear about it. Take your glasses, gentlemen. (*Managing to fasten his pince-nez firmly, he reads solemnly*) I, Harald Hilding Markurell, hereby pledge to Wadköping School the sum of thirty thousand (*interrupting his reading he remarks seriously*)—it says twenty here, but *that's* niggardly. We'll have to change the figure. When I wrote it, I didn't know about this chemistry business. (*He chokes on the disagreeable word and the undefined apprehensions it arouses. Not until the headmaster gently takes him by the arm does he start up from his reverie, pull himself free, and continue in a loud voice*) Gentlemen, this is a donation.

PROFESSOR: Indisputably—it looks very much like a donation—

(*Markurell hands the documents to the headmaster, who has recovered his composure. Grateful for the change of subject, he speaks gravely.*)

HEADMASTER: But Markurell . . . Markurell . . . shouldn't the donation be announced later . . . when and if your son has passed his examination . . . with honor?

MARKURELL (*scornful, impatient*): Bah! Nonsense! What good would it do *then*?

(*At this unabashed cynicism a commotion arises. The headmaster, document in hand, sinks down upon his chair. The dean conceals his grinning face behind Barfoth's shoulder; the professor, champagne glass in hand, approaches Markurell laughing.*)

PROFESSOR: Skoal, Markurell! Damned if he doesn't want to bribe us right here in the faculty room. That's rich! Skoal, you old wag!

MARKURELL (*wounded by the frivolous tone*): Professor, if I had wanted to bribe you, I'd have gone about it a lot differently! Flunk the lad, then, if you feel like it. But if you do, the head of this culture factory is going to have to tell a lie in public once a year from now on! Bribery is an ugly business—but look, at least you could expect some ordinary gratitude from educated men . . .

PROFESSOR (*unaware that he has put his foot into it, speaks goodnaturedly*): Come come, now; don't take offense. As long as the lad who failed in chemistry is not our honored benefactor's son but the judge's little indiscretion . . . why . . . we're getting upset about nothing.

MARKURELL (*quietly*): No, sir, you didn't make any mistake. A serious occasion like this is no time for tricks and fibs. It *was* my son—my son—the one that you referred to. As far as I can see, it must be. Barfoth phoned and said that he—my boy—was the only one that did badly in chemistry . . .

PROFESSOR (*finally realizing that something has gone wrong, extremely embarrassed*): Actually . . . actually . . .

(*Markurell fixes his gaze on the professor, who turns a little aside and bends down to fuss with his shoelace. Markurell goes over to the headmaster, who sits bent forward with the document in his lap. Markurell snatches it, suddenly crushes it, runs his hand over his forehead, then smooths out the paper and puts it back. His glance wanders about the room. The headmaster avoids it. Then Markurell turns to the dean, who has been regarding him with the deepest sympathy. As their glances meet, the dean, embarrassed, turns toward the wall and studiously examines the old portraits of defunct bishops which adorn it. Markurell steps over to him.*)

MARKURELL (*slowly, laboriously*): Why . . . why do you turn away from me? Have you . . . also . . . heard something?

DEAN (*tormented and sympathetic, makes a gesture as though to embrace him*): Oh, my dear . . . dear . . . you must be in the grip of an evil spirit . . .

MARKURELL (*warding him off by grasping his wrists*): Evil spirits . . . yes . . . being a priest, you're probably well acquainted with them.

(*Markurell approaches Barfoth. At that instant the school-bell rings. The gentlemen prepare at once to leave the room, happy to escape the painful situation.*)

HEADMASTER (*holding the document in his hand*): Gentlemen, the time is flying. I wish to say, however, that even if certain irregularities attach to this donation, it still testifies to a magnificent generosity toward the school and to a most touching fatherly affection . . .

MARKURELL (*interrupting. His glance hardens*): Don't trouble yourself, Mr. Billberg. The bell has rung.

HEADMASTER (*hurriedly, relieved*): Yes, yes, of course . . . the bell has rung . . . duty calls. (*Exits backstage*)

PROFESSOR (*still groping*): Mr. Markurell . . . I . . . I am very happy to have made your acquaintance . . . I don't know whether . . . maybe I express myself badly . . .

MARKURELL: Not at all! The learned professor is happy to see me. I probably remind him of a hanged criminal. The professor has done his best—that's certain . . .

PROFESSOR (*extremely disconcerted*): I haven't time to explain right now . . .

MARKURELL (*coldly*): No, there isn't time. And it isn't necessary. (*Professor exits backstage.*)

DEAN: Dearest Markurell . . . you dear fellow . . . let me embrace you! My heart really . . . really . . . throbs . . .

MARKURELL (*as before*): I'm very happy. That you enjoyed the lunch.

DEAN: Lunch! Lunch! I am thinking of your magnificent gift to the school—and even more, of the noble sentiments that prompted . . .

MARKURELL (*who has been standing motionless in the same spot ever since the bell rang*): You're too late . . . For class. Good-bye.

BARFOTH (*walking heavily toward him, desperate*): My good friend . . . duty calls . . . thanks.

MARKURELL: Thank *you!* You tried your best. When you kicked his ankle to warn him. Even less than that can start a person thinking. You did your best.

BARFOTH (*distracted*): Dear . . . what else *could* I have done?

MARKURELL (*wearily*): Nothing at all. The only thing I can't understand is why you, too, don't say you are happy to see me. Just like the professor. It sounds so friendly-like. (*Barfoth turns without replying and exits backstage.*)

(*As soon as the others are gone, Strom emerges from his nook. Now that he has had his revenge, he stands there calm and unemotional.*)

STROM: Are we finished now, Markurell? Shall I clear the table?

MARKURELL: Yeah . . . we're finished.

STROM (*cynically*): You look unhappy, Markurell. Something on your mind?

MARKURELL: Uh-huh!

STROM: Oh. In that case, I won't disturb you.

MARKURELL: Thanks. And aren't you also going to embrace me and kiss me on the cheek . . . Judas?

STROM: No, thanks, I'll pass that up. Where are you going?

MARKURELL (*walking toward back of stage*): Don't know.

STROM: You walk so heavily, Markurell. As if you didn't have any more strength in your legs. Here, take my arm.

MARKURELL (*after a long look at his betrayer*): No, thanks. I can manage to drag myself . . . to where I'm going.

CURTAIN

ACT III

SCENE I. Main dining room at inn

Mrs. Markurell sits at the counter, which is piled high with glasses and silverware of the sort used only for especially grand occasions. She insists upon polishing it herself. As she rubs and scrubs, she sings a gay song. She is so engrossed in her work that she fails to hear the large door, right, open and Barfoth slowly enter. Pausing to listen silently for a moment, he steps forward into the room. Mrs. Markurell, hearing someone approach, turns toward the door.

MRS. MARKURELL: Well, well, what do you know? Already out taking your walk? Come in . . . come in! I know I look a mess, but a little thing like that shouldn't matter between old friends. It's only a few hours till we have to put on the graduation party, and I'm right in the middle of the worst part of the cleaning.

BARFOTH: And you're singing?

MRS. MARKURELL: It relaxes me. And besides, today I'm happy enough to bust. And thanks to *you!* My boy graduates today!

BARFOTH: Let's hope so.

MRS. MARKURELL: He will for sure! I always get a premonition whenever something real good or real bad is about to happen —and today my hunch tells me it's something extra wonderful. Just think—to have a boy so far along . . .

BARFOTH: So far along that he is about to go out into the world and leave his mother alone . . .

MRS. MARKURELL (*a trifle harshly*): Well, that's the way it goes in this world. The boy can't spend his whole life hanging onto his mother's apron strings. To say nothing of his father's! (*Jokingly*) You know, I'm an awfully unnatural mother . . . I'm really a bit jealous of Johan . . . sort of. Just think, Barfoth, isn't it strange the way things can turn out? When I got married to Markurell . . . well . . . it certainly wasn't for love. You know that all right. There was a different reason. And then? After we were married? Since then, it's been a bit of this and a bit of that, but mostly just so-so. Quarrels and hard words, you know. So you'd expect that by this stage of the game I'd be completely fed up with my old man. (*Pauses*) I know you're a learned man and all that— but now I'm going to tell you something that maybe all your learning can't explain.

BARFOTH: Go ahead!

MRS. MARKURELL: Well, you've noticed, of course, that most people dislike Mr. Markurell . . . that is, if they dare to show their feelings . . . yes, they actually hate him. I've hated him too, for that matter—and I'll admit it frankly to an old friend like you. But the more I've watched my husband —on the sly, so to speak—the more I've come to understand that way down underneath, he is a very kindly and gentle person.

(*Barforth laughs.*)

It's true! I said it, and I'll stick by it! Even though he's laid a hand on me more than once.

BARFOTH (*shocked*): He *has?*

MRS. MARKURELL: Don't faint, gran'ma. I'm not so feeble but what I can raise my own hand once in a while, too. As far as that goes. But I have gradually come to understand that he is wise and fair. He has helped lots of people—Carl-Magnus among them, for that matter. Coarse and crude on the surface, and as ugly as the very devil—but underneath it all, first-class merchandise! And after you've watched and understood . . . then you can forgive a lot. And that's why I'm a bit fond of him—the red-whiskered ogre!

BARFOTH (*suddenly resolute*): And what if he won't forgive?

MRS. MARKURELL (*missing the point*): Forgive? Oh, no . . . not him. He just isn't forgiving by nature. But he's man enough to set the whole town back on its haunches! I can tell you that! When I see all those elegant aristocrats running up here to beg from him . . . then I get a sort of stuck-up feeling. She . . . you know, the judge's wife—the countess, God help us—she was up here this morning to beg. And it sure did my heart good when she didn't get anything.

BARFOTH: Woman! don't exult in your fellow creature's misfortune! Your own may be waiting just outside the door.

MRS. MARKURELL: Bah! My back is stout enough to take both the good and the bad. And so is Markurell's. In spite of all the mean things you say about him, he's a real he-man, he . . .

BARFOTH: Not today.

MRS. MARKURELL: Pooh! He's a bit childish if it's got anything to do with the boy. I know *that* well enough . . . and it's made me mad many a time! And just think! There was a time when I prayed God on my knees that the man might show something at least approaching ordinary decency toward the child I was carrying in my . . .

BARFOTH: But why on earth shouldn't he?

MRS. MARKURELL: Oh, how can you ask? You were around yourself at the time—and you're not so dumb! Besides, you're not the only one that knows how it was.

BARFOTH: Unfortunately . . . that's the worst of it! I have found out . . . that I'm not the only one who knows it. I found *that* out just today.

MRS. MARKURELL: Today?

BARFOTH: At the school. Peddling gossip is a terrible thing, I know; but when we Wadköping natives indulge in it, we at least know when to keep our mouths shut.

MRS. MARKURELL: Thank you so much—all you two-faced, treacherous rats! Sitting here and babbling, "My, but that boy looks like his father!" Why did you have to do *that?* Why did you do it?

BARFOTH: Not I! *I* never did!

MRS. MARKURELL: Maybe so! But the others! Only yesterday, the barber sat here and spread his nasty insinuations . . .

BARFOTH (*who has been wandering nervously back and forth before the windows at the back of the stage keeping a watchful eye out*): Here he comes! On the terrace!

MRS. MARKURELL: Who?

BARFOTH: Barber Strom. But he's alone!

(*Strom enters, carrying Markurell's coat and hat over one arm.*)

BARFOTH (*anxiously*): Strom, where is Markurell?

STROM: *You* tell *me!* He left his clothes at the school.

MRS. MARKURELL: Left his clothes at the school? Why, what's happened?

STROM: What happened is . . . to make it short . . . that Markurell . . . has got it into his head, as they say, that Johan is not his son . . .

MRS. MARKURELL (*suddenly tossing aside the candlesticks she has been polishing, rises, and turns upon Strom*): Have you been shooting your face off, you dirty tattletale? You damned rattlesnake!

STROM (*cringing in fear*): No, no, no! What sort of pleasure do you suppose I could get out of repeating gossip that everyone in town already knows? The natives keep still because they know Markurell; but, you see, these outsiders didn't know his . . . that was the bad thing about it . . .

MRS. MARKURELL (*beside herself*): You beasts! Do you know what you've done? You've ruined my whole life—you filthy, miserable scum!

BARFOTH (*still at the window, anxiously*): Quiet! Quiet! Here he comes.

MRS. MARKURELL (*dashing to the window*): Where? I don't see him.

STROM (*whispers*): Look how he walks . . . look how he drags himself along . . . look how his head wobbles . . . like on a gallows bird.

(*Markurell walks past the window. His step is heavy, and he actually wags his drooping head slowly from side to side as though he wished above all to avoid seeing what is in front of him. Glancing through the window by chance, he pauses an instant. His eyes, though wide open, seem to see nothing. Nevertheless, the three in the dining room cringe involuntarily. Markurell walks on and disappears.*)

MRS. MARKURELL (*walking from the window as if in a trance*): Oh, my big, strong, magnificent man! Look what you've done to us, you beasts . . . you lice . . . you rats . . . who couldn't even look at a real man without stabbing him in the back . . .

BARFOTH (*sorrowfully, humbly, but with dignity*): Curse us, dear! Don't spare us! But remember also . . . that it was not our tongues that deceived him in the first place . . .

STROM (*who has crept over to the large door*): He's going into the office.

BARFOTH (*uneasily*): We musn't leave him alone.

(*Mrs. Markurell starts uncertainly toward the door. Alarmed, Strom makes a detaining gesture.*)

STROM: Don't go in there . . . he might do something violent.

MRS. MARKURELL: Let me go. I'm going in to him.

BARFOTH AND STROM: Alone? . . . not alone!

MRS. MARKURELL (*calmly, slowly*): Yes, alone! I don't think either of *you* dares to come along. And I wouldn't advise you to, either. Give me his coat and hat!

(*Strom hands her the garments. She exits through the large door.*)

CURTAIN

SCENE 2. Markurell's office

Markurell stands in the middle of the floor with hanging head and wavering glance. Someone knocks at the large door. Instead of answering it, he tiptoes to the small door, locks it, and removes the key. The knocking is repeated.

MARKURELL (*dully*): Come in. The door's open.

MRS. MARKURELL (*entering with the clothes over her arm*): Why didn't you come in and say hello?

MARKURELL: Give me time.

MRS. MARKURELL: You forgot these clothes at the school. (*She lays them on the sofa.*) How did it go?

(*Markurell walks absent-mindedly over to the sofa, picks up the topcoat and puts it on. Then he puts the hat on his head.*)

MRS. MARKURELL (*uncertainly*): Are you going out again? (*With an attempt at playfulness*) Of course! to meet Johan! The examination will be over any minute now.

(*Markurell gives her a sidelong glance, then slowly removes the garments and replaces them on the sofa.*)

MRS. MARKURELL (*unsteadily*): Uh . . . well, how do you suppose the boy made out?

MARKURELL (*slowly begins to tidy up the room—straightens out the papers on the desk, lays some things away in the drawers, and locks them, etc.*): Ask Barfoth. Or the barber. I saw you through the window.

MRS. MARKURELL (*with another attempt at cheerfulness*): You see everything, don't you?

(*Markurell goes over to the sofa a second time and puts on his coat and hat. As he buttons the coat with scrupulous care, he speaks.*)

MARKURELL: No, I'm blind as a bat! Even an old fogy of a professor can see better than I. (*He finishes buttoning his coat, and painstakingly dusts it, or rubs away at a nonexistent spot on his sleeve.*) He said . . . one of them . . . he said to me . . . the one who failed in chemistry is not your son . . .

MRS. MARKURELL (*with a final attempt at cheerfulness*): Oh, good! Then Johan passed!

MARKURELL (*after looking at the floor for a moment*): No, he didn't pass. (*Again he unbuttons his coat, removes it, and carefully replaces it and the hat on the sofa.*) The professor meant something different. He meant . . . (*Instead of finishing the sentence, he goes over to the door, locks it, and removes the key.*)

MRS. MARKURELL (*tensely*): What are you up to? Why are you locking the door?

(*His movements are heavy and without any trace of aggressiveness. His voice takes on a helpless, whimpering tone— the voice of a man struggling with an insoluble problem.*)

MARKURELL: I don't know . . . they say . . . do *you* know anything about it? that some people claim that the boy . . . that Johan . . . my Johan . . . is an illegitimate son of the judge . . . poor in chemistry . . . Barfoth called and said that the boy . . . the professor said that de Lorche's by-blow was the only one . . . that was poor in chemistry . . .

MRS. MARKURELL (*covering her anxiety with pretended annoyance*): What's that you're mumbling about? I can't make out a word of it. Get hold of yourself, Markurell . . . Are you going out of your mind?

MARKURELL (*exclaims suddenly*): Yes! Funny . . . but not exactly to be wondered at . . . that I should go crazy! I've never noticed . . . it never occurred to me . . . that he looks like . . . have you ever noticed that he looks like . . . ?

MRS. MARKURELL (*calmly*): Like who? I can't answer until you tell me who . . . (*To avoid meeting his glance, she turns to the mirror and fusses with her hair.*)

MARKURELL (*morosely, ingenuously*): Carl-Magnus . . . de Lorche . . . of course . . .

MRS. MARKURELL (*still facing the mirror, sternly*): Open the door . . . you've locked it.

MARKURELL (*almost trembling*): First tell me . . . tell me . . . does he look like . . . very much like . . .

MRS. MARKURELL (*in sudden uncontrolled anger snatches up the mirror and holds it before her husband*): There! Just take a look . . . a good close look . . . does he look like *you?*

MARKURELL (*dejectedly*): No . . . ooo . . . not much . . . not at all.

MRS. MARKURELL (*with an attempt at banter*): Well . . . would *that* have been something to be happy about? . . . for him to look like *you?*

MARKURELL (*sadly and extremely ingenuously*): Oh, yes . . . for *me* . . . it would have been . . .

MRS. MARKURELL (*dashing the mirror aside, panting*): Whew, but it's hot in here! Get me a drink.

(*Markurell obediently goes over to the table under the wall cabinet, upon which stand a decanter, a bottle of soda water, several glasses. At first he reaches for the soda water, but after an instant's reflection opens the cabinet, chooses from among the various bottles, and pours a man-sized shot of brandy into a glass, to which he then adds water. He hands it to his wife, who has been too busy controlling her emotions to pay him any attention. She swallows half of the mixture at a single gulp, making a wry face.*)

MRS. MARKURELL: Whoo . . . ee! but that was strong! What did you put in it . . . brandy? I thought it was French wine. Oh, well . . . maybe I could use a bracer. Now tell me about the examination. How did it go?

MARKURELL: I don't know. I left. After they'd let that business about the boy slip out, they just stared at me. I just *couldn't* stay there any longer. Afraid I might do something crazy.

(*Mrs. Markurell, rising, walks toward the door, as if by chance. Markurell, watching her intently, moves toward the window in the same fashion.*)

MARKURELL (*heavily, but not threateningly*): Don't try the door. You're not getting out of here until I let you. I've got the key.

(*Mrs. Markurell turns slowly and takes a few steps toward him with a nonchalant dignity so exaggerated as to be almost absurd. She is still trying to maintain superiority over her husband and command over the situation. But at the same time her nerves approach the breaking point, the liquor begins to weaken her self-control.*)

MRS. MARKURELL (*jeering*): Well, well! Just listen to that! So-ho! you're trying to scare me! Look, it won't work. Least of all right after you've made a crybaby out of yourself in front of all those other people! Fancy that! . . . so they stared at you . . . probably couldn't believe you could be so utterly blind. I couldn't either, as far as that goes!

MARKURELL (*groping for words*): Did you really think that I knew . . . that I suspected . . .

(*At his transparent simplicity, Mrs. Markurell, who cannot handle her liquor, becomes heedless. She regards him with an expression of contempt.*)

MRS. MARKURELL: Did I think! I'll tell you what I thought! I thought that you were a *man*—a real he-man—who could take it as well as dish it out! That's why I was so happy that you were good to Johan. Don't ever forget—I told myself—don't ever forget that he is a good father to your son. And just for that, I even grew a little fond of you. And not so awfully little, either. But now that's all over! (*In her highly wrought-up state, she takes a turn across the floor, stops in front of her husband, puts her hands on her hips and jeers. She screws up her face and imitates him.*) Funny . . . but not exactly to be wondered at, huh? Does he look like his father? Ask anybody in town, and they'll tell you!

MARKURELL (*stammering*): His father . . . you mean . . . what do you mean . . . his father?

MRS. MARKURELL: Damned if I'll lie to you any longer! It's gone too far already! You've never figured that I was a good enough mother for Johan. But always sent him to the countess. So he could learn fine manners! Yeah . . . It would have made me laugh if it hadn't nauseated me to see you so stupid. Now I've said it! And it's not as if I haven't wanted to say it lots of times before now! (*Commands harshly*) Look here . . . no more monkeyshines! Unlock the door!

MARKURELL (*panting*): All right . . . right away . . . but I still don't see . . .

(*Showing off her arrogant composure, Mrs. Markurell has gradually moved a few steps away. Now she turns, facing him with folded arms, hardened and made insolent by the panic she struggles to hold in check.*)

MRS. MARKURELL (*brutally*): What is it you don't see? That you're not Johan's father? Everybody in town can see *that*!

MARKURELL (*completely bewildered for an instant*): Yes . . .

Anders de Wahl as Markurell in *Markurells of Wadköping*. The
Royal Dramatic Theater, Stockholm

Olof Sandborg as the Baron in *The Baron's Will*. The Royal Dramatic
Theater, Stockholm. Photograph by Studio Järlås

no . . . but who . . . I mean . . . then who *is* . . . his father?

MRS. MARKURELL: You really want to know? Fine! Who is Johan's father? Johan's father is (*pouring forth all her scorn*) the KING!

MARKURELL: Wha . . . wha . . . king . . .

MRS. MARKURELL: Such a stupid idiot! King Carl-Magnus of Wadköping! Now are you satisfied? He's a *real* man . . . Carl-Magnus . . . no matter if you bankrupt him *twenty* times! What a stupid ass you are to ask! Is *that* any way for a man to act?

(*Markurell stumbles from the window where he has been standing, and suddenly, as his anger rises, his muscles begin to flex. Snatching up the safe, he raises it up above his head, standing like Atlas with feet wide apart. Mrs. Markurell, paralyzed with fright, shrieks.*)

MRS. MARKURELL (*screams*): What are you doing? Are you going to murder me?

MARKURELL (*stalking toward her one step at a time with his heavy burden*): Say that you lied . . . just now. Then I'll let you go.

(*At this critical moment, Mrs. Markurell recovers her coolness and self-control. An imperturbability solid as granite replaces her jeering hysterics of a few minutes earlier. Recrossing her arms, she faces him without a trace of either fear or uncertainty.*)

MRS. MARKURELL (*firmly, but not defiantly*): No, Hilding. No, my dear. There's been enough lying already. I won't lie any more. What I told you just now . . . is the truth!

(*Undoubtedly it is Mrs. Markurell's marvelous poise that saves her, but the rarely used Christian name and the still rarer "my dear" also have their effect upon Markurell. He has lifted the heavy safe above his head; to secure release from his physical and spiritual tension, he has to throw it somewhere. But his lust for vengeance, his desire to crush her, has weakened, so he flings it down—but quite obviously to one side of her. As its door springs open, all the papers stored in it, including the debenture envelope we saw in Act I, fly out upon the floor. Outside the door, right, shouts and hammering from Barfoth and Strom, who are trying to break in the door.)*

MRS. MARKURELL: Take it easy out there! He's opening it himself.

(Drawing the key from his pocket, Markurell opens the door. Barfoth enters, but Strom stops in the doorway. When Mrs. Markurell approaches Barfoth, he is so relieved that he is about to embrace her. But she shoves him roughly aside and walks toward the door.)

MRS. MARKURELL: Out of my way! This guy over here *(pointing at Markurell)* is a pretty poor specimen all right, but not one tenth as miserable a specimen as you two! *(In the doorway she turns.)* And now I'm going to get into my Sunday best. *(Laughs)* There's going to be a party tonight—a party for the youngsters. Our troubles don't bother them a bit, bless their hearts!

(Strom, impelled by curiosity, steps into the room. He and Barfoth look about the disordered room in astonishment. Walking slowly over to Markurell, Barfoth pats his shoulder gently. Markurell looks up at him—but only for an instant— then his head sinks again.)

BARFOTH *(quietly)*: My dear friend, here you sit like Job among the ruins . . .

(Markurell nods slowly.)

STROM (*in a whining voice*): Oy, oy . . . what a mess! You were going to murder your own wife . . . weren't you!

MARKURELL (*without glancing up, heavily, ingenuously*): Yes, but it wouldn't have done any good. It wouldn't have changed anything.

STROM (*with ill-concealed spite*): And just look at the safe— his heart's delight all smashed up!

MARKURELL: *Everything* is smashed to pieces. The Lord has smitten me. Oh, that I might sleep forever and know nothing! Have you known about it very long, you two?

STROM: Well . . . people *will* talk. You ought to know . . . you've spread enough scandal about others, yourself.

MARKURELL: And I didn't know a thing. Never dreamed of it! He was so tiny . . . a regular little angel. I mean when he was first born. And handsome and well-built and bright . . . and oh, so lively! Could I have suspected he was anything but my own? Oh, Lord . . . soon I will lie in my grave a feast for worms, and vengeance will be thine . . . as it says in the good book. Couldn't you have waited until then? Ah, Jehovah, how can it give You any pleasure to smash me like an old chamber pot!

BARFOTH (*sternly*): Calm down! Now you are as overbearing in your grief as you were before in your joy.

MARKURELL (*suddenly, impulsively*): What wrong have I done? Which commandment have I broken?

BARFOTH: You have been a hard man, Markurell. Many a tear has fallen on account of you . . .

STROM (*loftily*): Yeah! It turns my stomach to hear you blubbering like that. Didn't the dear little countess herself come, that exquisite little lady, and humble herself before you and beg mercy for her husband? And how did you treat her? . . . tell us that!

MARKURELL: I was neighborly and polite to her. I even offered her a glass of fruit juice.

BARFOTH: If it weren't for your tears and your twisted-up face, I could believe you were joking! You offer a glass of fruit juice to a tormented little woman seeking help . . . and imagine you've done your whole Christian duty!

MARKURELL: Well . . . you can't really blame me for tending to business. It was for my boy's sake.

BARFOTH: Hear, hear! Always the same old story . . . for the boy's sake . . .

MARKURELL: He was the only person who ever cared for me. I never did anything out of meanness, but only to help my son. And now when it comes right down to it . . . I haven't any son!

STROM (*who has been bent over double trying to check a laugh which he can no longer control*): Hee hee! . . . no son . . . and nobody to use for an excuse.

BARFOTH (*outraged by the barber's malevolence*): Shall I toss this rattlesnake out the window?

MARKURELL (*weary, forlorn*): Let the viper sting! Besides, he's right. Who am I going to slave for now? I have tramped the treadmill, tireless as a blindfolded ox. But now when I have begun to see, nothing seems worth bothering about any more.

BARFOTH: Calm yourself! Nothing has changed. You care for this boy, and the boy cares for you.

MARKURELL (*springing to his feet*): Keep quiet! It's all over! Finished! (*Placing his hand on his breast*) There's nothing in here any more. But you . . . you butterflies! You say I've been hard on people! Why, I've been one of God's own angels! But now you're going to see some real hardness . . .

a fiend! I'll make everybody in Wadköping suffer for this day!

STROM (*devouring him with his eyes, morbidly fascinated*): Look, look! Now his real nature is coming out. Now you can see what really drives him . . . pure spite and malice!

BARFOTH: Markurell, you have brought all this on yourself. You uprooted all humanity from your heart. You cherished just one single person. And now you want to disown him, too! What will you become after that? A wild animal, a raging beast . . . ?

MARKURELL: After that? What else could you expect me to be? To me . . . he is dead! Dead!

STROM (*peeking through the window*): The guests are beginning to arrive. Wipe off your face. An innkeeper can't be blubbering just because he's lost his son . . .

MARKURELL (*puzzled*): Wha . . . what are you talking about?

STROM: He's dead to *you*, of course; I know that. That's easy enough for you to take care of. At his age a person isn't as thick-skinned as you. When he finds himself received coldly . . .

MARKURELL (*stammering*): Coldly . . . c-c-coldly . . . who by?

BARFOTH: By the one he loves . . . by you. You've just got to get hold of yourself! I see my colleagues coming. I'm going to go and find out how the examination went.

MARKURELL (*eagerly*): Yes, yes, yes . . . and come and tell me.

(*Exit Barfoth. Markurell peers cautiously out the window. Strom regards him with a sly expression.*)

STROM: Markurell . . . that donation you were so stuck-up about . . . I suppose you'll take it back again?

MARKURELL (*innocently*): That will depend on how things went . . .

STROM (*sneeringly*): Ha! Still worried about the examination? What's it to you? Why should that bother you?

MARKURELL (*leaves the window. Strom follows him with glittering eyes*): That's right. I can't even do that any more . . . not even worry!

STROM (*tiptoes up behind him, takes him by the coattails and speaks conspiratorially*): Markurell! I've been thinking about something! Could she have been lying?

MARKURELL (*staring stupidly at him*): Lying?

STROM (*seriously*): Women are like that. One time they'll say they're innocent, and another time they'll say they're guilty . . . anything at all, just so they can torment a man.

(*Markurell stares at him for an instant, then hurries to the door and begins to lock it. He stops as Mrs. Markurell enters in all her finery. Her expression, proud and happy, becomes a little teasing, but not at all unkind. Markurell's tension gradually relaxes. As she crosses the stage, Mrs. Markurell turns slowly like a mannequin to show herself off.*)

MRS. MARKURELL: We——ll? Don't you think I look elegant? I should think that both of my menfolk ought to be awfully proud of me. (*Tranquil and majestic, she glides out of the door, right.*)

MARKURELL (*dejectedly*): Oh, no! I can tell by her looks that it's true! That woman doesn't bother to lie to me any longer. (*Sinks wearily onto a chair*)

STROM: Right! and pretty soon nobody at all will bother to lie and crawl for you any more. And then you might even become a decent human being! And who will you have to thank for it? Perhaps poor, insignificant me. (*At the win-*

dow) But look! If it isn't the little countess coming here for the second time today? Where have you got the cream-puffs, Markurell?

MARKURELL (*as though waking up*): Wha——wha happened . . . ? You'll find out that they flunked the lad!

STROM (*provokingly*): So what? That's nothing to you.

MARKURELL (*becoming anxious*): She said she wouldn't come back if everything went all right . . . she said . . . (*giving a start*) what if *he* has heard something? What if *he* knows? Oh, Strom, be a good fellow, and go out and meet her . . . I don't dare . . .

STROM (*with a mocking grin*): You don't dare hear what's happened! Oy, oy, Markurell . . . what a worm you've turned out to be. But a thinking worm, so I'm fairly well satisfied. So long, then . . . and thanks for everything. (*Exits right*)

MARKURELL (*his anguish growing*): Oh, heavens . . . oh, Merciful One . . . I have been a wicked man! If only *he* doesn't know anything . . . know anything . . . I promise . . . I promise anything at all . . . whatever you wish, dear God . . . I . . . Markurell, in all humility, you understand . . . just so he doesn't know! It doesn't matter whether he won his cap or whether he flunked . . . you understand, good Lord, that I pray with a broken and contrite heart . . . (*Someone knocks at the door, right. Markurell is almost in collapse. The door opens, and Mrs. de Lorche enters.*)

MRS. DE LORCHE: May I come in?

MARKURELL (*worried and self-conscious*): The place is in . . . sort of a mess.

MRS. DE LORCHE: You might put it that way. It looks as if it had been struck by lightning.

MARKURELL (*embarrassed*): Well . . . ah . . . it was only . . .
I got a little mad at the old lady . . . at my wife.

MRS. DE LORCHE: Mr. Markurell, it isn't very nice of you to
call your wife "my old lady"!

MARKURELL: What brings your ladyship here again? You said
you wouldn't be back if everything went well.

MRS. DE LORCHE (*a bit hesitantly*): Yes . . . well . . . not
everything went well.

MARKURELL (*frightened*): Has he heard anything . . .

MRS. DE LORCHE: Yes. It was my son Louis. He said . . .

MARKURELL (*even more frightened*): He said . . . what? Out
with it!

MRS. DE LORCHE: First you must promise me not to be . . . a
little angry when you meet my Louis.

MARKURELL (*pacing about*): What did he say?

MRS. DE LORCHE: Oh, my boy said to your boy that you were
a . . . wholesale swindler, a regular big-time crook.

MARKURELL (*astonished, but uncomprehending*): Wha——?

MRS. DE LORCHE: The fact is that our two young gentlemen got
into a quarrel . . . over some of your business transactions.

MARKURELL (*a little calmer*): But why . . . why . . . over me?

MRS. DE LORCHE: Because you're a vulture that threatens half
the town—and especially Louis' father—with ruin.

MARKURELL (*increasingly calmer*): Oh, oh, oh.

MRS. DE LORCHE: Well, the whole thing would have had to come
out sooner or later—and it's better for you to hear it from
me than from somebody else. There has been a real scandal
in the schoolyard today—two of the examinees got into a
fist fight! It took the headmaster himself to separate them!
The guilty ones are your son and my son, who fought because my son called you a wholesale swindler and a crook.

MARKURELL (*almost joyfully*): So-ho? Really? You don't say!

Crook, too. But he didn't say anything else . . . anything worse?

MRS. DE LORCHE: Now you listen to me, Mr. Markurell; you're being presumptuous! Your boy figured that "swindler" and "crook" were quite enough, so he started swinging . . . a disgrace to the school, the headmaster, and us poor parents!

MARKURELL (*happily*): Phooey on the disgrace . . . since that's all there was to it . . .

MRS. DE LORCHE: Well, yes . . . actually that's the way I feel about it, too. Good Lord! One boy fought for *his* dad, and the other fought for *his*. I find the whole thing very touching.

MARKURELL (*brightening up*): Yeah . . . yes . . . so he actually fought for me . . . Johan, I mean . . . "swindler" and "crook," he said . . .

MRS. DE LORCHE: Yes, that's what he called you. But promise not to be angry with him for it!

MARKURELL (*magnanimously*): Wouldn't think of it! Shucks! You and I know very well . . . how young roosters flare up. That's nothing to get worked up about after a person has led a dog's life . . . has led a Markurell's life, I might say . . . for fifty years.

(*Music in the distance, an orchestra playing "In Those Good Old College Days"; Markurell starts up and listens.*)

MARKURELL (*becoming apprehensive*): Wha——what's that?

MRS. DE LORCHE (*happily*): It's the students, of course! The graduates are here!

(*Markurell stares at the door with increasing dread, then at Mrs. de Lorche. Suddenly he dashes over to the sofa and snatches up his coat and hat. He has only one idea in his head—to run away—to avoid meeting Johan. He wanders to and fro like a rat in a maze.*)

MARKURELL (*in a panic*): I've got to get away . . . away . . . before he gets here . . . I can't bear to meet him. I'll go up and hide in the attic . . . you tell him I had to leave on a business trip . . . I can't . . . face him.

MRS. DE LORCHE (*walking slowly over to him*): No, Markurell . . . you can, and you shall!

MARKURELL (*stops near a wall, throws down the garments, and bursts into sobs*): I'm choking! I can't . . .

MRS. DE LORCHE (*beside him, speaks gently, but very firmly*): You can, and you shall . . . for Johan's sake. You have no . . . no right to spoil his happiness. You say that you can't bear to look at him. Oh, dear, it's even worse that way . . . you can't avoid seeing him! Because you'll never be free from him. And the very worst of it is that you don't really want to be. No . . . not for all the world!

MARKURELL (*calmer*): Does your ladyship think that he . . . that he . . . knows . . .

MRS. DE LORCHE (*positively*): He knows absolutely nothing about anything!

(*Pause*)

MARKURELL (*reflecting for a moment*): It's certain that I made a promise just now . . . no, not to you, you dear little thing . . . but to . . . (*He points upward.*) Well . . . not in so many words, of course, but we two (*pointing upward again and then at himself*) understand each other without words, so to say—exactly like (*pointing at the countess and then at himself*) us two. (*He picks up the envelope of shares from the floor and hands it to her.*) And when you make a promise . . . you've got to live up to it. So give this to Judge de Lorche. He'll understand what it's about.

MRS. DE LORCHE (*taking the envelope and looking at him gratefully, speaks softly*): Thank you, Mr. Markurell. (*The music comes nearer. Buzzing and murmuring from outside*) And now . . . shall we walk out there together?

MARKURELL: Certainly. As long as I'm the head of the establishment, I'd better get out and receive the guests. (*A little awkwardly, he offers the countess his arm. They walk toward the door together, but just before they reach it, Markurell gently frees his arm from hers and guides her through the door, saying*) I'll be along in a minute; you go ahead.

(*Mrs. de Lorche, sympathizing, smiles gently and leaves. Markurell steals over to the garments he has thrown on the floor, snatches them up, and seems on the point of dashing out through the smaller door. At this instant Johan's voice is heard outside the large door.*)

JOHAN: Dad! Where are you? Dad! (*Johan throws open the office door. By now Markurell has tossed the garments aside once more and stands in the middle of the room with bowed head and clenched hands.*) Well! So *there* you are! Now tell me, old boy, is this any way to receive a beloved son? What's the matter with you? Don't you see the cap? The *cap*, hey? I made it. I graduated. (*Johan pats himself on the head. Markurell cannot manage to answer, but he raises his head and the clenched fists relax. He nods, and waves his hand just before his face like an overjoyed puppy.*) Why don't you say something? Aren't you pleased with me?

MARKURELL (*finally mastering his emotions*): Of course, of course . . . it's only that . . . that . . . I'm so . . . happy . . . tears of happiness, like they say . . .

JOHAN: Well, that's all right then. But *you* . . . I'm not so pleased with *you*. You didn't come down to meet me. And did you think about me at 11:30 as you promised?

MARKURELL: I had to do something else then, and it must have just slipped my mind.

JOHAN: I knew it! I could feel it in my bones! Golly, what a fidgety worry-wart of a father I've got! But it didn't make any difference. You see, old boy, I knocked *apocatastasis* for a loop. So now . . . now I'm going to give you a big hug anyway . . . and forgive you all your sins in a really filial embrace! (*He gives Markurell a great, boyish squeeze.*)

MARKURELL (*softly, without the least tremor*): Thanks . . . thank you for that . . . Johan . . . my son.

CURTAIN

Note: Alternate ending. The doors open, and a happy company of young fellows, Johan's classmates, crash jubilantly in, filling the air with congratulations and flowers. They release gas-filled balloons, which rise to the ceiling; confetti and serpentines swirl about Markurell's head, and the curtain falls upon the celebration.

Introduction to
THE BARON'S WILL

IN THE PROVINCE of Närke in central Sweden where Hjalmar
Bergman laid his imaginary city, Wadköping, he also placed
chateaux and manor houses, foundries and farms; and he
peopled them with his friends and his friends' friends as he
needed them in all the many novels he later came to write. As a
schoolboy he often accompanied his father, the bank manager,
on business trips from his home town, Örebro, throughout
the surrounding province. Being very properly brought up and
quiet, he disturbed no one. He merely sat silently in a corner
and blushingly answered "yes" or "no" to anyone who happened
to address him. This boyhood blush was a whimsical trick
played by Providence. The boy could not keep his fat cheeks
from turning blood-red if anyone spoke to him or pointed
a finger in his direction. It was thus a continual embarrassment
throughout his childhood, but fortunately it passed away with
time. The noisy guests were at groaning tables in the large
rooms lit up by candlelight, open fires, and torches outside the
windows. But meanwhile what was the silent boy in the corner
up to? Well, he was photographing. His brain was like a camera
whose film caught and retained everything he heard and
saw. In his phenomenal memory he stored up arguments, jokes,

and stories; and then for the rest of his life he drew upon this stock for everything he needed in his tales.

People have often speculated upon the question of whether these actual places served as models for those which the author himself created. Naturally he drew upon reality for most, if not all, of his novels and short stories. He transformed things so much that it is difficult if not impossible to say that this fictional place reflects that real place. But in the case of His Lordship Baron Roger Bernhusen de Saars, a living model has been identified—the author's own godfather, Baron Styrbjörn von Stedingk of Ekeberg Estate.

The godfather's mere appearance would have fascinated any boy with imagination—long, shapeless legs, an enormous torso, and a bald head without a single hair on it. Even in his nursery days Hjalmar and his little friends had a game they called "playing baron." With his belly thrust out and his legs spread wide, the fat little four-year-old strutted about snorting, snuffling, and swearing. He thought he gave a marvelous imitation of his magnificent godfather. The old gentleman's unconventional behavior, his offenses against the current mores and good manners, impressed and delighted the little boy, who himself had had a strict, old-fashioned bringing up.

In 1909, when the author was living in Rome, he felt the time had come to compose a sort of memorial tribute to his dead godfather. And he wrote a novel brighter and funnier than any he had written before that time. In it the Ekeberg Estate became Rogershus Manor, and Baron von Stedingk became Baron de Saars, even though it was impossible to recognize the original model in him.

The Baron's Will (*Hans Nåds Testamente*) was of great importance to the development of Hjalmar Bergman's comic talent. And he now perceived that bantering is an excellent way to meet and conquer difficult situations in life. Self-irony, a play on the behavior of oneself and others, became a means of turning aside dangers, treachery, and suspicions. But it was also a shield and a screen that cut off the view from outside. Presently he was joking at all times. And there is some reason to suppose that the author himself was genuinely happy with his Rogershus and its whimsical humans, whom the baron, in his irascible speech, referred to as "curlicues."

Before the novel about His Grace was written, it would probably not have occurred to anyone to use the word "curlicue" as a title of address. The Swedish word *krumelur* means a strange little drawing depicting nothing recognizable. ("What kind of 'curlicue' have you drawn there?" "What kind of an odd 'curlicue' is that?) His Grace was the first to use the word in this special way, sometimes as a nickname and sometimes as a term of abuse. It is apparent that the seed fell on good ground, for now, more than fifty years later, it is used both in speech and in writing precisely as Baron Roger de Saars used it.

The novel about His Grace was a great success. And since the novel was dramatized for the radio theater in 1929 and then rearranged for the stage, filmed twice, and rewritten for television, His Grace has become a particular favorite over much of Europe. The self-indulgent, tyrannical, thundering, and yet —deep down inside—so good-hearted old martinet has established a very solid popularity. He is one of the few really great comic figures in Swedish drama. "With *The Baron's Will* and *Markurells,* with *Swedenhielms* and *Joe and Co.,* Hjalmar Bergman has given us a series of comic characters that compare well with those of Molière and Holberg," wrote one critic after the première in Stockholm in August, 1931, nine months after the author's death.

The radio version was used as the basis for the stage version, one of the last things the author worked at. It was a large-scale version for revolving stage. Next there was a version for small theaters without revolving stages, then a version for small outdoor theaters, then one for large ones, a version for silent pictures, another for talking pictures, television—what next? Altogether, in seven different languages, the play has been performed more than six thousand times.

STINA BERGMAN

THE
BARON'S
WILL

TRANSLATED BY HENRY PERSON

Characters

HIS GRACE, BARON ROGER BERNHUSEN DE SAARS
MADAME JULIA HYLTENIUS, *his sister*
ROGER HYLTENIUS, *her son*
ABRAHAM DAHLGREN, *His Grace's lawyer and district judge*
VICKBERG, *His Grace's butler*
JOHNSON
TONY, *servant*
MRS. ENBERG, *housekeeper*
ERIC
INGRID
THE SHERIFF
THE SCHOOLMASTER
AN INSPECTOR
CHILDREN, VILLAGERS, *etc.*

Settings

ACT I
SCENE 1. *The lawn in front of Rogerhouse*
SCENE 2. *His Grace's bedchamber*
SCENE 3. *The lawn*
SCENE 4. *His Grace's library*
SCENE 5. *A mountain lodge*

ACT II
SCENE 1. *His Grace's bedchamber*
SCENE 2. *The lawn*
SCENE 3. *The small dining room*
SCENE 4. *His Grace's library*

ACT I

SCENE 1

The lawn in front of the main entrance to Rogerhouse. A beautiful, sunny day. An occasional birdcall, the sound of a fountain close by. All is peaceful and quiet. The reason: His Grace, Baron Roger Bernhusen de Saars, is having his nap. The world, in the vicinity of Rogerhouse at least, is silent.

To the right, leading from the drawing room, a short flight of stairs. Then a terrace, and then a few more steps down to the ground. At the left a rose hedge. Near this Vickberg, Tony, and Johnson, all seated in lawn chairs, are playing cards. Mrs. Enberg sits nearby knitting stockings.

Vickberg, the Baron's butler, is a thin man, sensible and dignified. Johnson has been marvelously good-looking in his time, but whisky and beer have washed all that away. Tony, an Italian servant, is small, taciturn, and melancholy. Mrs. Enberg is a large heavy woman, well padded with fat. Johnson has a stein of ale on the table beside him. Vickberg's watch lies open on the table before him.

Johnson begins the play with an utterance—characteristic with him—which will be rendered here simply as "ark-tooey." But it is really much more than that, especially when he is angry or excited. It is a splendid thing that begins somewhere deep in the throat and, after rattling round the vocal cords and amplifying itself in the various resonating chambers, comes out a marvelous expletive. Whenever "arktooey" appears, the reader is asked to apply his imagination liberally.

JOHNSON: Ark-tooey! Are we still sleepin', brother Vickberg?

VICKBERG (*looking at his watch*): We shall sleep twenty-seven minutes longer.

JOHNSON: It's Tony's deal. (*Tony deals. Silence*)

MRS. ENBERG: Good gracious, Mr. Vickberg. I hope you haven't forgotten the yogurt, and the strawberries, and the wine.

VICKBERG (*with pride*): Have I ever forgotten any of those things, my dear? Have I ever forgotten His Grace? Have I, Mrs. Enberg?

JOHNSON: Ark-tooey! Don't pay any attention to her, Vickberg. She's scared her yogurt is going to separate.

MRS. ENBERG: Please mind your own business, Mr. Johnson. When did my yogurt ever separate?

TONY: There's thunder brewing.

MRS. ENBERG (*a little frightened*): Oh? What makes you think so?

TONY: At least it's going to rain. It always rains when you can hear him snoring all the way out here.

VICKBERG (*seriously*): Heaven knows His Grace can snore!

JOHNSON: Ark-tooey! Snore? Nonsense! You mean *sin*. Heaven knows His Grace can *sin!* But I'm here to tell you that a man who helps bring a sweetheart like Ingrid into the world . . . well, he deserves to have a lot of his sins forgiven.

MRS. ENBERG: You should be ashamed. Everyone knows that Ingrid is an orphan, and that His Grace out of Christian charity . . .

JOHNSON: Now, now, now! Just because you're the widow of a minister, you don't have to go round telling lies. At least not here among friends. If Madame Hyltenius' chambermaid had been a little less easy on the eyes, then there wouldn't have been any Ingrid around here.

TONY: And it would have been awfully empty, for all of us!

JOHNSON: Especially for Eric, eh? (*He leans toward Tony.*) And if Tony had stayed at home in *la bella Italia,* he would never have met Reverend Enberg's widow . . . (*a gesture toward Mrs. Enberg*) . . . and then we wouldn't have any Eric around the place, either. Those two kids are practically related—they're both illegitimate!

VICKBERG (*severely*): Watch your language, Johnson.

JOHNSON: Yep, yep, I guess I should. Otherwise Mrs. Enberg'll start to blush. Well, one thing's sure, she's Eric's mother. And incidentally . . .

MRS. ENBERG: If Mr. Johnson didn't drink so much beer, we wouldn't have to listen to so much nonsense.

JOHNSON: Why shouldn't a fellow drink a little beer when it's practically . . . well, when it's practically forced on him? The only good thing Julia Hyltenius ever did in this world was to fix things up so I could lie around here and drink free beer the rest of my life.

TONY: How did she do that?

JOHNSON: Well, my brother from *bella Italia,* I'll tell you. When Johnson was young, he was a handsome devil. So he got to meet some of the highborn young ladies around the place. One of them was Miss Julia Bernhusen de Saars, His Grace's sister. Well there were hayrides, and she had to be lifted up and helped down, and she had to be . . . Hmmmmmmmmmmmm . . . And we both enjoyed it. Ah Julia, what a little slut she was.

VICKBERG (*shocked*): Johnson, I told you to watch your language.

JOHNSON: Aw, why worry about it this late in the day, we all know Julia. Anyway, when her old man found out about us two, he damn near had a fit. He ranted and roared. Johnson was to be thrown off the place. All hell broke loose. But then Johnson had a talk with the old Baron and said that if he had been willing to take advantage of her then it would have been just too bad for the little minx—Julia, that is. But he hadn't, and he said he wouldn't. So I got a pension for life. And free beer till I die. A few years later Julia climbed into the nuptial couch with Reverend Hyltenius, and that was just fine and dandy for the two of them, and for everyone else.

MRS. ENBERG: What an imagination! But you've got to admit that the Reverend's widow is a nice, good-hearted lady.

TONY (*to Mrs. Enberg*): You know she's *not*.

MRS. ENBERG: But Tony, that was only that once.

JOHNSON: Which once?

TONY: When she was here at Rogerhouse nine years ago, Ingrid and Eric were playing under the chestnut tree there and I was standing on the steps. She asked me who the brat was there playing with Ingrid. I had to tell her that his name was Eric Enberg, but she knew damn well who he was.

JOHNSON (*he laughs*): You should have told her his name was Eric "Tonyson"; that might have shut her up for once. Arktooey! She's always been like that. I remember how she went up in smoke when she found out her brother had fallen in love with a poor girl—sweet little thing she was, too. Julia fixed it up so the old Baron ran the girl out, and then she married Brother Roger off to Ulla Seidel. Ulla was as ugly as home-made sin, but boy—did she have money! She had more property than she knew what to do with. But there was damn little smooching and billing and cooing in that family. Fortunately the gracious Lady Ulla soon joined the company of the blessed in heaven, and His Grace entered the company of the blessed on earth. He met sweet little Mimi.

INGRID (*off*): Aunt Enberg! Aunt Enberg!

MRS. ENBERG: Here come the children. Now, Johnson, you keep quiet.

JOHNSON: Ark-tooey! Leave it to Johnson.

INGRID (*enters*): Aunt Enberg, Eric has to play tennis with me when I want him to, doesn't he?

MRS. ENBERG: It'd be better if he did something useful.

ERIC (*entering from behind the hedge*): Useful? Isn't playing tennis with Goldilocks useful? Though she could at least be polite when she asks.

INGRID (*pertly*): Why do I have to be polite, idiot?

ERIC: You're an idiot yourself. What do you think I am, your slave, huh?

INGRID: Do you think I'm afraid of you, huh?

ERIC (*grabbing her by the arm*): Ask properly, darn it!

INGRID: Let go of me, darn it!

MRS. ENBERG (*getting up and separating the two of them*): You sound like you've gone crazy, yelling so they can hear you all over the place. You'll wake up the Baron.

JOHNSON: If they could do that, I'd give them three cheers.

TONY: Ingrid, honey, let the tennis go for a while.

INGRID: No! 'Cause pretty soon it'll start raining, and then we won't be able to play.

MRS. ENBERG: Eric is going to have to ride into town to get me some more yarn. I haven't got enough to finish.

ERIC: Then Ingrid can ride Liza, and I'll take Fingal.

MRS. ENBERG: Ingrid doesn't have to go along with you.

ERIC: What'll she do while I'm gone?

MRS. ENBERG: Good Lord, what'll she do for a whole hour? Well, she could mend her stockings. She hasn't got a single pair that isn't worn through—holes as big as pancakes. She should do something useful.

INGRID: I'd like to, but I don't have time.

ERIC: Okay, okay, I'll go alone, but so help me, I'm going to run the legs off the horse.

VICKBERG: Just a minute, Eric. While you're there you can pick up some things I've ordered for His Grace's birthday tomorrow. Find out if the fireworks are ready, if the colored lanterns have arrived, if the baker has the order filled, if the schoolmaster knows what time he's supposed to show up, and if the pastor finally has his poem composed.

(Eric and Ingrid have been moving slowly toward each other making faces.)

ERIC: Come on, ask pretty. Then I won't have to ride into town alone.

INGRID: Sweet, dear, darling Eric, come and play tennis with me.

ERIC *(slipping an arm around her waist)*: Okay. Come on, Goldilocks!

TONY: I think Ingrid was right. It's going to rain.

MRS. ENBERG: What are you mumbling about?

TONY: I can hear the mail wagon way out on the main road. That's a sure sign of a storm.

MRS. ENBERG *(sighing)*: Nonsense. *(Short pause)* You know I don't know what to do with those youngsters. The boy is more than nineteen, and still hasn't done two cents' worth of useful work. Only runs after the girl. Where will it all end? Mr. Vickberg, don't you think it's terrible the way these kids have been spoiled? His Grace lets Ingrid boss him around whenever she feels like it. It's terrible to bring her up as though she were the young lady of the house.

JOHNSON (*playing a card*): A father's indulgence. (*He laughs.*)

MRS. ENBERG: Don't you think so, Mr. Vickberg?

VICKBERG: I meld sixty queens.

MRS. ENBERG: What's going to happen when His Grace passes on? What's going . . .

JOHNSON: Meld forty pinochle.

MRS. ENBERG: What's going to become of Ingrid then?

TONY: Meld a run in hearts.

MRS. ENBERG: Maybe you think her blue-blooded relatives are going to take her in and look after her? Maybe Madame Hyltenius?

JOHNSON: Fat chance!

MRS. ENBERG: I think Mr. Johnson is right. I don't like to be unkind, but what do you think would happen if Madame Hyltenius took over here at Rogerhouse?

VICKBERG: I've got the rest of the tricks. Might as well throw in your cards.

JOHNSON: There sure won't be any love letter for old Vickberg in today's mail. You know what they say, "Lucky at cards, unlucky in love."

MRS. ENBERG (*glancing toward the kitchen door, behind the house*): The mail's in the kitchen now, Mr. Vickberg.

VICKBERG (*getting up*): Excuse me, gentlemen, I have to quit. In fifteen minutes it'll be twelve o'clock. (*To Mrs. Enberg*) Is His Grace's tray ready?

MRS. ENBERG: Certainly. It's on the top of the icebox.

VICKBERG: I'll go have a look at the mail. (*Exit*)

MRS. ENBERG: Tony, I don't know why, but I feel uneasy.

TONY (*gently*): So? What now? Everything's so calm and peaceful.

JOHNSON: Yep! As long as the old boy's asleep.

TONY: Time goes by. Eric'll be a grown-up man taking care of himself pretty soon, and you and I won't have anything to worry about any more. Down deep inside His Grace is a good man. He'll give Eric a hand.

MRS. ENBERG: I don't know why I feel so uneasy.

VICKBERG (*running in, a letter in his hand*): Listen, everybody, something terrible has happened!

JOHNSON: Look at his hands shake!

VICKBERG: His Grace's sister, Madame Julia Hyltenius, is arriving at Rogerhouse on the afternoon train!

(*Pause*)

JOHNSON: I'll say one thing, the only thing that fits: Ark-tooey!

VICKBERG: She writes: To Butler Anders Vickberg. This is to inform you that Her Grace, Madame Julia Hyltenius, in view of her brother's seventieth birthday, will arrive at Rogerhouse by the afternoon train on the twentieth. She and her son wish to reserve the Gold Salon and four adjoining rooms. Mr. Vickberg is to see to it that the dogs are all tied up, that the bull is locked in his pen, and that no animals are running loose about the grounds during our stay at Rogerhouse. In addition Mr. Vickberg will tell His Grace, the Baron, the happy news of his sister's arrival. (*He looks to heaven for help.*)

TONY: Oy oy oy, now there'll be a storm for sure, and poor Vickberg is going to be right in the middle of it.

JOHNSON: Verily, it delighteth my soul. The Baron will show the woman the door, he can't stand the sight of her.

VICKBERG (*with great dignity*): It's true that the Baron has a violent temper, but he will behave like a gentleman. None of us will need to be ashamed of Roger Bernhusen de Saars.

(Off stage a large clock begins to strike twelve. On stage, pandemonium)

MRS. ENBERG: Mr. Vickberg, you'll be late. The clock's striking twelve already.

VICKBERG: Where's the yogurt, and the wine and the strawberries? Get a move on, woman, let's not go looking for trouble.

MRS. ENBERG: Hurry up yourself. I told you the tray is on the icebox.

(Vickberg dashes toward the kitchen, followed by Mrs. Enberg.)

TONY *(putting away the cards and chips)*: Poor Vickberg.

JOHNSON: I'm sure glad I don't have to be anywhere near the old boy right now! Brother Johnson's been around here long enough to know that now would be a good time to put five or six miles between himself and the old boy. So long, Tony, see you later.

CURTAIN

SCENE 2

His Grace's bedchamber. In the background, an immense canopied bed. To the right of the bed, a door with a tapestry in front of it. Right, in the adjoining wall, French windows; in this scene the curtains are drawn. Between the windows and the footlights, a large mirror mounted on wheels. To the left, another window, likewise with drawn curtains. Closer to the footlights, a small table and a chair. Vickberg, tray in hand, enters through the tapestry door, stops, and listens to His Grace's snores.

VICKBERG: Thank God he's still asleep. (*He puts the tray down on the small table, opens the curtains in front of the left window. Sunlight streams in. He then goes cautiously to the bed, opens the curtains, and unties the Baron's nightcap. The Baron is tall and thin. There is still, especially when he is angry, something of the old soldier about him in spite of his otherwise well-worn body. His face, though plainly showing that he drinks too much, nevertheless bears the unmistakable stamp of the genuine aristocrat. The great aquiline nose dominates it; the bald skull varies in color between blue and red. He is not handsome, but he is a genuine, old-fashioned aristocrat. Vickberg stands at the head of the bed, attempts to wake the Baron. He says formally*) Your Grace! (*Only a snore in reply*) My Lord and Chamberlain! (*No response. Then with the utmost dignity and as much volume as he can muster*) Your Grace, Baron Roger Bernhusen de Saars! (*No result. He then shakes the Baron gently by the shoulder, says softly*) Roger.

HIS GRACE (*wakes and sits up slowly in bed. Yawns deeply*): Aaaaaah! What say, schoolmarm?

VICKBERG: The clock has struck twelve, the mail has arrived, the yogurt is chilled.

HIS GRACE: So it's twelve o'clock again, is it? It's been that so damned many times it doesn't surprise me any more. (*Vickberg removes His Grace's nightcap.*) Vickberg, how old am I?

VICKBERG: Your Grace will be seventy tomorrow.

HIS GRACE: Uh-huh. Practically old enough to know better. (*Pause*) Vickberg! Our snuff!

VICKBERG (*opens his own snuffbox and holds it out to His*

Grace): Because of the celebration tomorrow Your Grace will most likely be the object of various visits and honors.

HIS GRACE (*after a splendid sneeze*): Prosit, Vickberg! That's good snuff you carry around. I wish to hell I knew how you can afford to buy such fine snuff. Why is your snuff so much better than mine?

VICKBERG: The groom has orders to bring home two kinds. I put the best in my snuffbox and the other in Your Grace's, because Your Grace always takes his snuff from my box.

HIS GRACE (*laughs*): Thump my back for me, schoolmarm. Damned if I don't believe you. I can see by your face that you're an honest man.

VICKBERG: Would you like to have your yogurt now?

(*Vickberg serves, and His Grace eats heartily.*)

HIS GRACE: Visits, you say? That'll be the schoolmaster and all his youngsters.

VICKBERG: Naturally, but besides them . . .

HIS GRACE: Let the kids come, but you have to promise to follow them around and spray every flea that hops off them.

VICKBERG: I'll take care of that. In addition, may I suggest that since it's not only His Grace's birthday, but Saturday as well, it would be nice to allow everyone the run of the place after twelve o'clock. His Grace might also treat them to beer, coffee, and sandwiches.

HIS GRACE (*a trifle angry*): Beer and sandwiches, eh? Why not soup and fish and filet mignon? Maybe I'm a cute little enchanted golden hen that lays golden eggs? Does Vickberg think I can lay golden eggs?

VICKBERG (*slowly, with studied irony*): If my Lord Baron and Chamberlain doesn't feel that he can afford the refreshments, his humble servant will gladly contribute his meager savings toward the celebration of the great day.

HIS GRACE: So ho! So you're a rich man, are you? (*He finishes the yogurt.*) Ah, that was a good yogurt. (*Drinks a little wine*) And the wine is just the right temperature. Kiss Mrs. Enberg for me. It'd serve you both right. (*He scratches his head.*) I don't understand how a bald-headed man's head can itch so much. What's the matter with you, anyway? You look unusually schoolmarmish today. Something bothering you?

VICKBERG: Yes, Your Grace. A letter has arrived from Madame Hyltenius, Your Grace's sister.

HIS GRACE: Damn! I know that witch is my sister, you don't need to remind me. Now we'll get up. Give me a hand. Easy now! Ai! Ai! Ai! Oops! There! Now we're standing on our own spavined shanks. Seventy years, you say. Is that so very old? It doesn't seem like it now. Let's take a look in the mirror. Give me my walking stick.

VICKBERG (*handing him the stick*): My Lord and Baron still seems to enjoy remarkable vigor.

HIS GRACE (*standing before the mirror in his nightshirt*): Hell, yes! Especially when I've got my walking stick to hold me up! (*Pause*) Look! There stands little Roger in the flesh— gray, bare-legged. Ish! Pah! Away with him! The scrawny, old billy goat nauseates me! Ugh! That I should have to get so ugly before I die. Take me away before I'm sick to my stomach.

(*Vickberg cautiously puts his arm around His Grace and leads him away from the mirror. Just as he is about to begin dressing him, Ingrid's voice is heard from out on the lawn.*)

INGRID (*off*): Play!

ERIC (*off*): Ready!

HIS GRACE: What's that?

VICKBERG: The youngsters are playing tennis.

HIS GRACE: They are? Let's sneak over to the window and watch
them. Quickly! And quiet like a pair of mice. Criminy, don't
move the old frame so fast you shake it apart.

INGRID (*off*): If Uncle is a nice boy, and if Uncle wishes, and if
Uncle hasn't got snuff all over his face, then I'm coming up
and give Uncle a kiss.

(*His Grace cups one hand behind his ear and listens. His
eyes sparkle, and his whole face lights up with amusement
and silent laughter.*)

HIS GRACE (*laughs*): Vickberg, tell her that my snoot's all
plastered with snuff.

VICKBERG (*leans out the window and announces stiffly*): My
Lord Baron and Chamberlain wishes to announce that unfortunately, he does have snuff on his snoot. Ahem!

INGRID: Messy old uncle! Shame!

ERIC (*off*): Play! I said play!

INGRID (*off*): Ready!

HIS GRACE: Ready? Yes, I suspect the little schoolmarm is
readier in *that* way than he is. Oh, well, someday they'll get
married and make a fine couple. The boy, the idiot, isn't
stupid. Rather, very talented. Now we'll get dressed, Vickberg. We're going to have a lot of fun today, a whole lot of
fun!

VICKBERG: Unfortunately, my lord Baron, I'm afraid it's impossible for us to have fun!

HIS GRACE: Oh, yes, we're getting up there in years. We have
to remember our age, is that it?

VICKBERG (*cautiously*): I must remind His Grace of the letter
from his sister.

HIS GRACE: You mean Julia? What's the matter with that sanc-
timonious old scarecrow now?

VICKBERG (*shocked*): My lord Baron!

HIS GRACE: Now, now, take it easy. You're getting school-marmish again. Whose sister is she, anyway? Yours or mine? What seems to be on her mind?

VICKBERG: Her Grace expects to arrive here on the afternoon train.

(*Silence*)

HIS GRACE: Does it say that in writing?

VICKBERG: Young Roger is coming also.

HIS GRACE: What? Who the devil is young Roger?

VICKBERG: The son of my lord Baron's sister. Apparently he has been named after his uncle.

HIS GRACE: Just like that! After his dear, rich uncle! So they're coming down to rummage around in the treasure chest, eh? The rats! Give me that letter. (*He pounds the table with his cane, roars.*) Give me that letter I said!

VICKBERG: Yes, sir, help yourself. (*Hands him the letter*)

(*The Baron reads the letter, breathing heavily from anger. From the terrace comes the voice of Ingrid singing a gay tune. His grace lets the letter fall to the floor. After pondering a moment he turns to Vickberg.*)

HIS GRACE: Vickberg, do you know who is going to be Roger Bernhusen de Saar's heir?

VICKBERG: Your sister and her son?

HIS GRACE (*quietly*): No. (*Then, seized by a fit of anger, he again pounds the table with his cane, roars.*) I'd sooner leave it all to a home for broken-down politicians, officers in disgrace, or actresses with shady pasts! (*Calm again*) What is it she's written? She's "coming to kiss me on the forehead and call down the blessing of the Almighty upon my declining hours." (*Ingrid begins a new song; Eric joins in. They move away, singing.*) Yes, they're declining, that I know. Vickberg, do you remember that once I was just as young as that

Paul Reumert as Swedenhielm, Sr., in *Swedenhielms*. The Royal Theater, Copenhagen

Scene from *Mr. Sleeman Is Coming*. Little Stage, Royal Dramatic Theater, Stockholm

rogue walking out there with his arm around Ingrid? No, not that young. I was never *that* young, dammit. But something like that. And do you remember that I had a girl, too?

VICKBERG: Yes, I remember.

HIS GRACE: You have a good memory—and so do I. Do you remember who ran to father and mother and told them all about it? (*Vickberg nods.*) Right! It was Julia. Vickberg, I tell you she's a witch out of *Macbeth*—and that's just how she's going to be treated. Do you know how to exorcise witches? No! You don't, schoolmarm. (*Rising to his full height*) But *I* do! (*Suddenly*) Where does it say in writing that Julia's son is to inherit Rogerhouse? Tell me that! (*Bangs his cane on the table*)

VICKBERG: No——nowhere.

HIS GRACE (*with another bang on the table*): You're wrong. It says here, in this letter, that she is bringing her son here to his beloved uncle and benefactor. So I am his *benefactor!* No, dammit!

VICKBERG: Your lordship possibly has given him a silver spoon . . . a birthday present . . . or a Christmas gift . . . or something on some occasion or other . . .

HIS GRACE: No, little Julia, this time you counted wrong. You call down all the blessings you want to on my declining hours, but you're not going to get paid any more for your trouble than the sexton, or his eminence the pastor. Vickberg!

VICKBERG (*at a little distance*): Yes, my lord Baron.

HIS GRACE: What's the name of that fellow who lives in town?

VICKBERG: The man who lives in town?

HIS GRACE: The one who robs me.

VICKBERG: The one who robs you?

HIS GRACE: Don't be so damned stupid. I mean my lawyer.

VICKBERG: Judge Dahlgren?

HIS GRACE: See that he comes out here immediately. I intend to make out my will.

VICKBERG: Wi——will?

HIS GRACE: In favor of my daughter, Ingrid.

VICKBERG: Daugh——daughter?

HIS GRACE: Who will be my sole heir.

VICKBERG: Is . . . is my lord quite sure?

HIS GRACE: What?

VICKBERG: I mean . . . that little Ingrid is his own . . .

HIS GRACE (*pounding the table*): Schoolmarm! How dare you! Get out!

VICKBERG (*frightened*): Immediately, your Grace. (*Starts for the door*)

HIS GRACE (*roars*): Wait!

VICKBERG: At your service.

HIS GRACE: Tell Mrs. Enberg that she's a fat—fat—rat! Her yogurt is runny, her strawberries are rotten, and her wine tastes like warm vinegar. She herself is a fat pack rat, and her boy is a damned blackguard who is going to be sent away at once. Out of this house. Clear off the place!

VICKBERG (*rushing toward the door*): Right away, my lord Baron.

(*He goes out.*)

HIS GRACE (*bellows*): Vickberg!

VICKBERG (*pops back in*): At your service, my lord.

HIS GRACE (*a bit embarrassed*): That . . . that about the boy. You don't have to say anything to anyone about that. That's between the two of us. (*Furiously*) Do you understand, schoolmarm?

VICKBERG: Perfectly, your Grace.

HIS GRACE: Then don't stand there with your mouth open. Get

out of here! (*Vickberg goes. His Grace shouts again.*) Vickberg!

VICKBERG (*back in*): At your service, my lord.

HIS GRACE (*calmly, grimly*): All of my old servants must leave. You, Mrs. Enberg, Tony, Johnson, and all the rest. I won't have a pack of old rats sneaking around behind my back.

VICKBERG: Where shall we go?

HIS GRACE (*coldly*): To the poorhouse. I'll have them build a special wing for broken-down servants who talk too much.

VICKBERG: Anders Vickberg thanks you most humbly for the gratitude shown him after fifty years' service.

HIS GRACE: Don't mention it. You may go, Vickberg. (*Vickberg goes out. His Grace stands silent a moment, then murmurs softly*) Vickberg . . . old friend . . .

VICKBERG (*pops back in instantly*): At your service, my lord.

HIS GRACE (*roaring*): Don't stand there listening at keyholes, you damned schoolmarm! (*He snatches the cane and throws it at Vickberg, who hastily disappears through the door. From a distance Ingrid is heard approaching, humming a little song.*)

INGRID (*off*): Uncle, are you alone?

HIS GRACE: Yes indeed, all alone.

INGRID (*off*): Shall I come up?

HIS GRACE: No, kitten, you can't. I want to be alone.

INGRID (*off*): Oh, you ugly old man, you're crazy. It isn't any fun to be alone. But if that's what you want, okay then. See you later.

HIS GRACE (*at the window*): So, there she goes—dignified and determined—in a terrible hurry. Dashing through the hedge —the leaves and flowers flying every which way. I suppose the boy is waiting for her behind the hedge. (*He laughs *softly.*) *She* certainly doesn't have to be alone. And once in a while she thinks of her uncle. That ugly old devil will soon be alone—absolutely alone. (*He bends over and tries to pick up his cane. After some time and very much effort he succeeds. As he straightens himself up again, the curtain falls.*)

SCENE 3

The lawn. A corner of Ingrid's skirt is caught in the rose hedge. Eric is behind the hedge.

INGRID: Eric, come and help me, I'm caught. Don't just stand there like an idiot.

ERIC (*helping her*): Stand still or you'll tear the dress to pieces. Then you'll get yourself paddywhacked!

INGRID: Ha ha! By whom?

ERIC: By me, of course. (*Ingrid gives him a petulant slap.*) Hey, one more of those and you can sit here in this hedge till doomsday. (*He kisses her.*) What would have become of you if I hadn't been here to take charge of your bringing up? With tender love and stern but just spankings . . . (*Another slap from Ingrid*) Hey! Have you gone crazy? I'll get you for that!

INGRID: Get me loose, that's all. It isn't fair to kiss me when I'm stuck in the hedge. Get me loose and then help me pick the thorns out.

ERIC: Then can I kiss you?

JOHNSON (*entering*): Ark-tooey! What th'—what's goin' on in the hedge? What're you doin', Eric, plucking a hen?

ERIC: No, it's only a baby chick, Johnson. But what are you
sneaking around for?

JOHNSON: I'm bidding a fond farewell to the dear old familiar
places.

INGRID (*now free from the hedge*): Dear, decrepit Johnson, do
you feel your last hour approaching?

JOHNSON: Me? No, no, not at all. But I am going back to my
refuge. Oh Zion, oh Balm of Gilead, oh peace beyond compare! In my little hunting cottage, high on Mount Ararat,
away from the tornado which is about to strike. I had a dream
just now while I was taking my afternoon nap.

INGRID AND ERIC: What was it about? Come on, tell us.

JOHNSON: Ark-tooey! Well, I was walking up hangman's hill,
and who should I meet but the Baron himself. I don't know
whether he had been hanged yet or not. But anyway he
stood there in front of me as if to block my way.

INGRID: Shame on you!

JOHNSON: Shame, yes. I was ashamed to see that the old Baron
had come to such an end. But I walked boldly past him on
up the hill. And that's just what I shouldn't have done, because next I ran into the devil himself. Was I afraid? No! He
beat me with his tail, but I just pushed him aside and went
on my way up the hill. Just as I was coming to the top, a
strange old lady came flying out from behind the gallows.
Says I to myself: You've faced His Grace, you've even faced
the devil, so you can stand up to his grandmother. But I
was wrong! As soon as I saw her face I turned tail and ran
for dear life till I woke up on the davenport.

INGRID: Why? Who was it?

JOHNSON: I'll tell you, my dear. The old woman I met wasn't
the devil's grandmother at all, but old lady Hyltenius herself.

ERIC: Who's that?

JOHNSON: Oh, you'll find out soon enough who she is, Eric boy. It's His Grace's blue-blooded sister. And when she shows up the best thing you can do is just to keep yourself out of sight. For Ingrid's sake if for nothing else.

INGRID: What?

JOHNSON: And you'll have to cut out all the smooching and a lot of other good clean fun.

ERIC: You don't for criminy sakes think I want to neck with the old woman, do you?

JOHNSON: Ark-tooey! No, hell no! But remember what I said. And if things get too tough, then come up and stay with me in the hunting shack. There reigneth heavenly peace.

INGRID (*laughs*): Let's go with him.

ERIC: Sure! We can stay up there till she's gone.

INGRID: We can stay up there a whole week. Just the two of us, Eric, you and me—

ERIC (*a bit embarrassed*): What about Johnson?

INGRID: We'll send him up to the other cabin.

JOHNSON: If we're going we'd better hurry. Because unless my eyes deceive me, the old lady and her son are coming up the road right now.

INGRID: Does she have a son? How old is he?

ERIC: What do you care? Come on, let's get out of here before she sees us. Do you hear me? Come on! (*He pulls her away.*)

INGRID: I want to get a good look at them. (*Johnson exits. Eric drags Ingrid off.*)

(*From one side comes a little cart drawn by a painted horse on wheels. Note: If the play is to be done with realistic scenery, then the painted horse need not be used. To give the play a story-book quality, it is often done with more stylized scenery. In such a production the painted horse goes well.*)

MME. HYLTENIUS (*who is in the cart. Her son Roger is driving*):
Hello, there! Can you tell me if there are any dangerous
animals running loose on the premises?

(*Madame Hyltenius is sixty-five years old. She has an overbearing appearance and a sharp staccato voice. She also has
a terrible temper which she can control only with the greatest
effort and then only when her own well-being is at stake. She
is very aloof toward the servants, and for that matter toward
most everyone. She can, though, as we shall see, at least give
the impression of humility in her brother Roger's presence.*)

JOHNSON (*entering*): No, unless Madame Hyltenius counts old
Johnson among the billy goats.

MME. HYLTENIUS (*acidly*): Well, well, my dear Johnson. Roger,
there you see one of your uncle's innumerable dependents.
Poor fellow, he looks so old and decrepit.

JOHNSON: Yea, verily. If I remember right, I was born the same
year as Madame Hyltenius.

MME. HYLTENIUS (*quickly*): I saw a young girl disappear over
there. Who was it?

JOHNSON: That was the daughter of His Grace and Madame's
ex-servant, Mimi. No doubt you remember.

MME. HYLTENIUS: Heaven preserve us. Drive on, Roger, drive
on.

ROGER (*a young law student, about twenty-five years old*): Just
a minute, Mother. Call her over, Mr. Johnson. I'd like to
meet my cousin.

MME. HYLTENIUS: Roger! Shame!

JOHNSON: All right. It won't do any harm. (*Calls*) Ingrid, come
here and meet your aunt and cousin.

MME. HYLTENIUS (*as Ingrid enters, coldly*): Good day, child.
How do you do?

INGRID (*curtsies*): I'm very well, thank you.

ROGER (*lays down the reins and starts to get out of the cart*): Easy, Dapple, don't run away. (*To Ingrid*) Cousin, it's a great pleasure . . .

MME. HYLTENIUS (*holding him back*): Stay here and drive!

ROGER: But Mother, don't be silly. All I want to do is meet my cousin.

JOHNSON (*muttering*): I'll bet that's all.

(*Eric enters, looking angrily at Roger.*)

MME. HYLTENIUS: Who is that young man?

JOHNSON: His name is Eric. He's the son of Tony and Mrs. Enberg.

MME. HYLTENIUS: Oh, has Mrs. Enberg remarried?

JOHNSON: No, no. She still remains true to the memory of her dear, departed husband.

(*Roger bursts out laughing. Eric gives Johnson a shove and says*)

ERIC: Shut up, Johnson!

MME. HYLTENIUS (*snorting*): Well, we have certainly arrived at Rogerhouse. One scandal after another, and each one worse than the one before. Drive on, Roger. In the name of God, drive on.

ROGER (*to Ingrid*): I'll see you later, Cousin. (*Cart with Mme. Hyltenius and Roger out*)

INGRID: I didn't think the old lady was so bad. And her son was very nice and well-mannered.

ERIC: It was pretty obvious what you thought.

INGRID: But there's one thing I don't understand, Johnson. If my uncle is my father, as everyone says, why do I have to call him "Uncle"?

JOHNSON: That's something I can't answer, honey.

INGRID: And if Tony is Eric's father, why doesn't he call him "Dad"?

ERIC: That's none of your business.

INGRID: I know, but it seems like a crazy way to do things.

JOHNSON: Come on, are you kids coming with me or are you staying here?

INGRID: You two go on ahead. I've got to get a toothbrush and some pajamas and some other things.

ERIC: Cripes, but you're particular all of a sudden. Do you really have to have all that stuff?

INGRID (*with a toss of her head*): Yes, I do! (*She goes.*)

JOHNSON: Come on, Eric. Men are clean by nature, they don't need nightshirts and toothbrushes and all that stuff. (*From inside the house a bell rings—shrill, persistent, prolonged.*) That's the old man ringing for Vickberg. Hell's bells! It sounds like a fire alarm. Come away with me, lad, and let Rome burn. (*Both exit*)

CURTAIN

SCENE 4

His Grace's library. At left a large sofa. Also a table and two high-backed chairs. To the right a window. Door at the back. His Grace, in a Prince Albert, stalks around the room with a bell in his hand and rings. And rings! And rings!!

HIS GRACE: Vickberg! Vickberg! Where in hell are you?

(*Vickberg comes in.*)

Schoolmarm! My cane, the snuff, is my fly buttoned?

VICKBERG: My lord Baron is dressed perfectly. (*A change in tone*) Your sister, Madame Hyltenius, arrived just now.

HIS GRACE: Oh, she did, did she? Now listen to me. Has the judge arrived too? (*Vickberg nods.*) Good. Until I have finished talking with him, I am blissfully unaware of my sister's presence. *L'arrivée de ma chère soeur m'est tout à fait inconnue.* Do you get the point? (*Vickberg nods.*) Good. Now march out and bring in Judge Dahlgren.

VICKBERG: As you wish. (*He goes out.*)

HIS GRACE (*to himself*): Fi donc. (*He laughs. Sits*) *Senectus senectutis onus.* Old age is its own burden. You were right, Seneca old boy. But you're going to see that Julia isn't so young either. *Eo ipso morbus.* Yes, I feel it in my hind legs. But there's still one good swift kick left in them, and I'm going to put it right where it belongs.

VICKBERG (*enters, followed by Judge Dahlgren*): Please step in, the Baron is expecting you.

HIS GRACE: Well, well, well, my dear Judge Dahlgren. Thank you for coming so quickly.

DAHLGREN (*a man about fifty*): My dear friend, I'd have come if you called in the middle of the night.

HIS GRACE: Tut, tut. Spare me that, please. It's hard enough to see people in the middle of the day. But let's get down to business. I want to make out my will.

DAHLGREN (*with lively, but discreet, interest*): Yes, yes! When a person reaches your age, he must think about his responsibilities to . . .

HIS GRACE: Tut, tut. What has my age got to do with it? I want to arrange things for a few of my near and dear ones.

DAHLGREN: Oh, yes, now I understand. That is why young Roger has been asked to come here. He can thank you in person before you pass on. Ahem!

HIS GRACE: What in the name of . . . has *he* got to do with my passing on? Is he a gravedigger or something? *Ecoutez, mon cher*. My will is to be drawn up today and witnessed to-morrow on my birthday. Except for a few small bequests I shall leave everything I own to my daughter Ingrid. (*Pause*) So ho! Please sit down, my friend, sit down. Vickberg, pour a glass of cognac for the judge, some of our best Napoleon.

DAHLGREN: But my dear, kind friend . . .

HIS GRACE: Dammit, I'm neither dear nor kind, but I know what I want.

DAHLGREN: But Madame Hyltenius, your own sister . . .

HIS GRACE: . . . inherited an equal share of our parents' estate. It's not my fault if she's frittered away most of it.

DAHLGREN: But she arranged your marriage to Ulla Seidel. You have her to thank for the greatest part of your fortune. Don't forget that.

HIS GRACE: How in the name of God could I ever forget that? She trapped me into that marriage. Today I'll show her my gratitude by willing everything I own to Ingrid. Need I express myself more clearly?

DAHLGREN: No, no, no. But one other thing. You must be aware that if this young, inexperienced girl, this mere child, in-herits one of the largest fortunes in this part of the country, she'll be the target for all sorts of marriage proposals.

HIS GRACE: I have chosen her husband.

DAHLGREN: I beg your pardon? You've chosen her husband?

HIS GRACE: Yes! She is going to marry Eric Enberg, my house-keeper's son. What say to that? Then bring on the Hylteniuses, my friend. What's the matter, Vickberg, your knees are shaking. Sit down next to the judge, you need a drink too.

VICKBERG: Please, excuse me. Thank you, but excuse me. I think it would be best if I went to Madame Hyltenius and tried to prepare her for this. I think it would be best for my lord Baron's health, and perhaps . . . I think it would be best to tell Her Grace that my lord Baron is drawing up his will.

HIS GRACE (*calmly*): Just as you say, Vickberg. (*Vickberg goes. To Dahlgren*) You look like you'd seen a ghost. Don't worry, you get the same fee no matter who inherits the place.

DAHLGREN (*a little offended*): I must say that this is all a bit too much. Do you intend playing Providence?

HIS GRACE: Yes. I intend to put on our Lord's robe. I'm sure he'll understand my good intentions. Anyhow, I'm not being at all impulsive. During these past few years I've sat there in the window and listened to the youngsters talk—buzz, buzz, buzz. Just like a beehive when the honey is the sweetest. Winters I've sat here and pretended to sleep. I heard this— and that—and the other. Sometimes about myself, and some- times the remarks were scarcely complimentary. But that doesn't matter. The point is I know those two youngsters inside and out like I know the palm of my hand. I'm not playing Providence blindly. First of all I'm going to send the boy abroad to round off some of the rough edges.

DAHLGREN: Excuse me, my dear friend, but I'd rather know as little as possible about your plans. Madame Hyltenius will be after me trying to find out everything I know. I want to be an unmarked slate, innocent as a new-born babe. I'm a practicing lawyer, and as such I work for my clients' best advantage. Let it go at that.

HIS GRACE: Excellent. Now let's get the will down on paper.

(*Mme. Hyltenius hurries in from the back, followed by Roger. She comes in under full sail, doesn't notice His Grace and the judge sitting in the high-backed chairs.*)

MME. HYLTENIUS (*angry*): This is just about the limit! He

should have come out to greet us on the stairs. Instead the old fool is sleeping.

ROGER: Easy, Mama, take it easy.

MME. HYLTENIUS: He can't treat *me* this way, the heartless old beast. (*As the judge clears his throat and rises, Madame Hyltenius catches sight of her brother sitting calmly in his chair. She's furious, but controls herself at once, puts on her sweetest smile, speaks in a tone fairly dripping with amiability.*) Rooooo . . . oo . . . oooggerr! I thought you were in your bedroom.

HIS GRACE: So it would seem.

MME. HYLTENIUS: I just couldn't stay away another minute. Brooo . . . oother!

HIS GRACE (*embarrassed*): Hello, Julia.

MME. HYLTENIUS: My dear brother, let me look at you! Oh, you've changed so much during these nine years. You know it's been nine years since I was here at Rogerhouse. Poor dear, you look like an old, sick eagle.

HIS GRACE: Thank you very much. And you look like a stuffed goose right out of some museum. A bit ragged here and there, maybe even a trifle moth-eaten, eh?

MME. HYLTENIUS: Oh you darling, joking to the last. Even while you make out your will.

HIS GRACE: Precisely. That's why I'm just bubbling over with good humor.

MME. HYLTENIUS: Roger, now do be serious for a moment. Vickberg said that you might be making out your will. I rushed in as soon as I heard it.

HIS GRACE: I don't doubt that for an instant.

MME. HYLTENIUS: I want to ask just one thing of you. When you make out your will, don't give a thought to me or mine.

HIS GRACE: Wha——wha——what say?

MME. HYLTENIUS: It would hurt me terribly to feel that I, your only sister, had in any way prevented you from exercising an absolutely free choice.

HIS GRACE: Well, don't worry about it.

MME. HYLTENIUS: Or if the memory of our childhood games and youthful fancies . . .

HIS GRACE: Don't worry about it, I said, that's all forgotten.

MME. HYLTENIUS (*unable to control her anger*): And have you forgotten our parents, too? Our dear, beloved parents.

HIS GRACE: It's damned unlikely that a man would forget his parents, especially if he was thirty years old when they died. But have *you* forgotten that it was you who caused the break between father and me?

MME. HYLTENIUS: Oh, Roger, don't carry grudges. Remember only the pleasant things. Look, here is your nephew. He looks very much like you used to.

HIS GRACE: Poor lad, he has my sympathy.

MME. HYLTENIUS (*to young Roger*): Kiss your uncle.

HIS GRACE: No, dammit, I won't have menfolks slobbering over me.

ROGER: Hello, Uncle, how do you do. You know they call me "Little Roger."

HIS GRACE: Damned if he doesn't drip syrup, all six feet of him.

ROGER: Mother has always held Uncle up as a model for me to pattern myself after.

MME. HYLTENIUS (*moved*): I have, it's true.

HIS GRACE (*blowing up*): No, dammit to hell, that's going too far. Me, a pattern? A pensioned-off soldier, and a chamberlain in disgrace. A landed proprietor who never sets foot on his land. A rich man who lets his lawyer rob him without saying a word . . .

DAHLGREN: My dear friend, I think you owe me an explanation . . .

HIS GRACE: Shut your mouth, pettifogger! So ho, I'm an ideal for the young, am I? Me, with bourbon in my toes, champagne in my knees, cognac in my nose, and Scotch in my eyes. Me, who sleeps eighteen hours out of twenty-four and eats and argues the other six. Me, a model for your boy, my dear Julia? Then I must say he'll make a marvelous heel in his time. And no one can accuse me of doing anything wrong by cutting such a nincompoop out of my will! Vickberg, my dressing gown!

MME. HYLTENIUS (*implores*): Roger.

HIS GRACE: Let me go, or something terrible is going to happen.

MME. HYLTENIUS: Don't push me away, you brute.

HIS GRACE: I'm sorry, but I have diarrhea, and unless I leave at once there's going to be an accident. It's one of the consequences of a dissipated life. (*Starts for the door*) Vickberg, hurry. Hurry! (*His Grace and Vickberg out*)

MME. HYLTENIUS: Such manners! Such utterly scandalous behavior!

ROGER: But, Mother, everyone gets a pain in his stomach once in a while.

MME. HYLTENIUS: Keep your cynical remarks to yourself. What makes me boil is the way he received us. And, on top of it all, this incredible falseness, this deceitful cheating—the will.

ROGER: But, Mother, you said yourself we didn't want anything.

MME. HYLTENIUS: I told you to keep your cynical remarks to yourself. Even a child could understand that I meant precisely the opposite.

DAHLGREN: My dear Julia, please calm down. The will isn't even written yet, much less signed. And even when it *is* signed, witnessed, and recorded . . . well, my dear, we'll take that calmly too. For everything human is changeable; not least of all our dear friend Roger Bernhusen de Saars.

MME. HYLTENIUS: But how are we going to get that senile wretch into a more sensible frame of mind? He's a beast I tell you, he's a beast.

DAHLGREN: First of all, it would be best if young Roger stayed at a distance as much as possible. Old bulls and young bulls always fight over the . . . er . . . stall, as the old proverb says. Ahem! Coarse, but expressive.

ROGER: That's fine. I'm happy to give up the pleasure of the old fellow's company. There are more interesting people around here.

DAHLGREN: Next, and most important, my dear Julia, patience! Your warm, true, sisterly patience toward your brother's faults. Sisterly love, Julia, sisterly love can work miracles. Don't you think so?

MME. HYLTENIUS (*calm again*): Yes, Judge Dahlgren, I do. You see I'm really very shy and sensitive—and it's hard for me to express myself clearly. But I am consumed with sisterly devotion for my dear brother. Thank you for understanding me, Judge. Now please excuse me. I'll get him some paregoric and a towel to wrap around his poor, little tummy.

DAHLGREN: You might also get a glass of sherry.

MME. HYLTENIUS: Of course, Judge Dahlgren. I know who I'm dealing with, rest assured. We shall meet again at suppertime. Until then I shall remain faithfully with my poor brother. (*Exit*)

ROGER (*sitting on the window seat*): I feel a little sorry for the old devil. When mother gets through doctoring and plastering, he'll feel worse than he did before. Mind if I smoke?

DAHLGREN (*nods permission*): Listen, my boy. If the old man actually should make Ingrid his heir . . .

ROGER: He wouldn't do that. It's just a whim. He'll forget it by tomorrow.

DAHLGREN: I'm not so sure. The old boy seems to have thought a good deal about it. But if he should make her his heir, why shouldn't you . . . (*Pause*)

ROGER: Why shouldn't I what?

DAHLGREN: Court the girl. Get engaged! Marry her!

ROGER (*he perks up*): Ingrid? Hmmm. I suppose I could. She's not bad looking.

DAHLGREN: Fine! Now you understand, get to work. You have a rival, though he doesn't amount to much. The Enberg lad.

ROGER: You mean Eric, that long drink of water? (*He laughs.*) Boy, what an honor! The rival of a servant boy. (*He whistles.*)

DAHLGREN: Think it over, but don't be too long. A girl as sweet as that and three thousand acres of land are not to be lightly thrown away.

ROGER: No, they're not. But there are other things to think about. What about my position and my career? No matter how nice she is, she's still a bastard, though a bastard of the highest degree, so to speak. (*He glances out of the window.*) Wait a minute, someone was there listening to us. (*He leans out of the window and looks.*) Sure enough, a skirt just disappeared behind the bushes there. (*Back in the room*) It doesn't make any difference, just so it wasn't Ingrid herself. Anyhow, bastard or not, she's very nice. I think I'll let career and position go hang for a while and give the girl a rush. See you later. (*He goes.*)

CURTAIN

Scene 5

Tanning Cottage, a small hunting shack, with bunks against two of the walls. In the corner a small fireplace; some traps; hunting trophies; a few housekeeping utensils, etc. Johnson is on his knees before the hearth blowing at the fire. Eric is making up the bunks. In the distance Ingrid is singing.

ERIC: Hurry up with the coffee, she's coming up the hill. (*He throws aside the pillow he has in his hand and rushes out the door.*)

JOHNSON (*goes on blowing on the fire, muttering to himself*): Lo! A miracle of the Lord! The fire took hold as mean and reluctant as old lady Hyltenius herself. So the little lady is going to sleep here tonight, not that there's anything wrong with it. Where innocence slumbers, little angels keep watch. Imagine that, Johnson finds himself in with a host of angels. Well, even in a band of heavenly protectors, he can be counted on to do his part. Mrs. Enberg'll have a fit when she finds out, and Madame Hyltenius . . . Ark-tooey! I won't even think about that right now. If I did I'd start reciting the general confession of sins—backward!

(*Eric and Ingrid enter.*)

INGRID: Say! Look what a fine housekeeper Johnson is, so neat and clean. And look at the meal he's cooked up! Boy, am I hungry!

JOHNSON: Dig in, dig in!

ERIC (*eating*): How come you're so late? It's almost the middle of the night.

INGRID: I was looking for a couple of books to read. Something sort of funny happened. I was going by the window of uncle's library . . . and . . . (*Slaps her leg*) Have you got mosquitoes out here?

JOHNSON: Maybe one or two. Do you want to go back to civilization and get some mosquito netting?

INGRID: No, no, I can't do that. Well, anyway, the judge and young Roger were sitting in the library talking.

ERIC: And you stood there and listened, you ill-bred brat.

INGRID (*with a huge sandwich*): What's a bastard?

JOHNSON (*chokes*): It's hard to say. Maybe a misshapen dog, one who hasn't got a father or mother. What they call a mongrel. (*Brief pause*)

INGRID (*unhappy, bewildered*): But he said that about me.

ERIC (*angry*): What? What did you say? Who?

INGRID (*on the verge of tears*): Roger Hyltenius.

ERIC: What did he say?

INGRID: He said I was a bastard, but of the highest degree.

JOHNSON (*quickly*): Oh, well, that's something else again. In the highest degree. Sure, that's something extra elegant. Usually reserved for royalty.

(*Eric picks up his shotgun and starts for the door.*)

INGRID: Eric, where are you going?

ERIC: Down to Rogerhouse.

INGRID: But what are you taking your gun for?

ERIC (*furious*): Don't worry, I won't use the gun unless I have to. I'll take care of him with my fists. (*Johnson jumps up and quickly takes the gun from Eric. Then he plants himself, feet wide apart, in front of the door and says quietly*)

JOHNSON: Easy there, lad. Nobody is leaving here right now.

ERIC: Get out of my way, Johnson!

(*Eric jumps at him, but Johnson is too quick. He floors Eric with a well-executed shove and shouts*)

JOHNSON: Now don't go gettin' all lathered up! How crazy can you get? Run off down there and get you and your mother in trouble just to give that damn fool a going over.

ERIC: I'll fix him.

JOHNSON: Good! But do it some dark night when there aren't any witnesses. Fill his behind with buckshot, if you have to, but disturb the peace of the household? No, lad, you'll have to leave that alone.

ERIC (*scrambling up from the floor and charging at Johnson once more*): Get out of my way!

JOHNSON (*tosses the boy into the upper bunk*): The devil himself is riding you, you fool. Now blow off a little of that steam. Simmer down, simmer down. Now you lay there on your bunk, and I'll lay here on mine, and the door key will lay in my pocket.

(*He locks the door and puts the key in his pocket. Stops for a moment at the window*)

INGRID (*goes up to Eric*): Johnson, Eric is bleeding.

JOHNSON: Just a little bit of a bloody nose. Cold water is all it needs. (*Ingrid dips her handkerchief in a bucket of water and gently wipes Eric's face.*) Yes, sir, that's one of the ways of all-wise Providence, young roosters always get the nose-bleed. Peaceful folk like me never get so much as a scratch. Well, good night now, you two. If I start snoring, dream of Napoleon and the proud ship *Waterloo*. She sank with all hands and a mighty roar at the outer entrance to inaccessible, fair Helena.

INGRID (*has finished taking care of Eric's nose, now begins to take off her dress*): How you can talk!

JOHNSON: It's true. I read it in a book. (*Looking out the*

window again) Look, there goes a family of elk—papa, his wives, and his children. Yes, yes, good old papa elk. The prettier the horns, the more the wives. (*Lies down on his bunk*) Now I'm going to cork off and go to sleep.

INGRID (*creeps into the bunk below Eric and says softly*): Eric, are you all right?

ERIC: Uh-huh. (*Pause*) How about you?

INGRID: I'm fine. (*Pause*) Give me your hand. (*Eric puts one hand down over the side of the bunk so Ingrid can reach it.*) Promise me one thing—that you won't do anything stupid in the morning. (*Eric tries to take his hand back.*) No you don't, not till you promise.

ERIC: All right, but . . .

INGRID: No buts, just promise.

ERIC: Oh, all right. Anything if you'll stop chattering like a damned magpie.

INGRID: Thank you, my sweet, lovable, little Sunday School boy. (*Pause, then tenderly*) Eric, I love you.

ERIC (*overjoyed. Bursts out*): Ingrid.

(*Johnson puts an end to all this with a tremendous snore.*)

INGRID: Heaven help us. Pull the blanket over your head, Eric. There goes the *Waterloo*. (*She creeps in under the covers, Eric lies back down. Pause. The lights go down and come up again to denote the passage of several hours.*)

(*A cautious knock at the door. Johnson stops snoring and listens. A second, sharper knock. Eric and Ingrid sit up and listen too.*)

JOHNSON: Who's there?

ROGER (*outside*): Is Ingrid here?

INGRID: It's Roger.

ERIC (*jumps out of his bunk*): Open the door, I want to talk to him.

(*As Johnson goes toward the door, Eric tries to get hold of his shotgun, which is lying on Johnson's bed. But Johnson is too fast for him. Johnson gets hold of the gun and keeps it while he unlocks the door. Roger enters.*)

ROGER: I hope you'll pardon the intrusion, but I'm looking for Ingrid.

ERIC: What do you want with her, fancy pants?

ROGER (*turning to Ingrid, who is now fully dressed*): Ah . . . ah . . . Tony noticed you outside the library window. He thought, well he thought you might have been upset by what you heard . . .

INGRID: Upset? Why shouldn't I be upset?

ROGER: But the whole thing was a misunderstanding. We weren't talking about you, Ingrid.

INGRID: You weren't?

ROGER: No, of course not. But anyway I humbly beg your pardon, and promise never to say things like that again.

INGRID (*deprecatingly*): Oh for heaven's sakes.

ROGER: Then we're friends again?

ERIC (*furiously*): Get out of here before I throw you out!

JOHNSON (*stepping between them*): You'd better get out. Cool, night air is wonderful for hot heads. (*He pushes both boys out the door. Rumble of thunder. Johnson listens, then turns to Ingrid.*) Ingrid, do you hear the thunder out there? That's the Lord's voice in the desert, and the lightning in his finger is pointed at you.

INGRID: But why?

JOHNSON: Just a warning that you shouldn't raise a tempest in the boy's heart.

INGRID (*pertly*): Which boy?

JOHNSON: Oh-ho, so that's the way it is. You're so fickle and loose now that you ask "which boy."

INGRID: I am not loose. You ought to be ashamed.

JOHNSON: All that bum had to do was come up here and ask you to forgive him.

INGRID (*again pertly*): He's not a bum.

JOHNSON: Okay, he isn't. And he's not a scoundrel, either. So we'd best split the difference and call him a lawyer.

INGRID: Well, that's what he is. And he's a good one, I'll bet. Eric isn't anything. He's not even civilized. All he wants to do is fight. I wonder what they're doing out there.

JOHNSON: They're smooching! If you think Eric will forgive you for forgiving that fellow just because he snip-snap kiss-me-quick says he's sorry for something that Eric can't forgive and that you shouldn't . . .

INGRID: Criminy, criminy. Please be quiet. I thought I heard them.

JOHNSON (*a little anxious over what might be going on*): Listen, Ingrid, let's get a cup of coffee ready for them when they come in. But there isn't any fresh water. Take this pail and run and get some, huh?

INGRID: But it's so far to the spring.

JOHNSON: I'll send one of the lads after you so you won't have to carry it alone.

INGRID: Okay. But tell him to hurry. (*Takes the pail and goes*)

JOHNSON (*muttering*): Yeah, he'll hurry all right. But which one it'll be only time will tell. Whichever one of them hasn't got the daylights pounded out of him . . . (*Stops, listens*) Wait a minute. Things couldn't be so bad that they've settled their differences without a fight. No, not Eric, he's got a temper like an Irishman! (*Glances out the window*) Oh, oh, here they come. What? Well I'll be damned. Peaceful and quiet like shepherds. Modern youth, ark-tooey!

(*Roger and Eric enter.*)

ROGER: I don't understand why you won't accept my apology. Though I don't know why I should worry about it. I'm perfectly satisfied with Ingrid's forgiveness, which was granted me *in amplissima forma,* if you know what that is.

ERIC (*shakes his fist in Roger's face*): Do you know what this is?

ROGER (*calmly*): The right front paw of *homo sapiens*—the rational man. Though in this case we'd perhaps best leave out the "rational."

JOHNSON (*delighted*): Boys, boys, I'm going to pump the spirit of reconciliation into you. Let's have a little life around here. (*He shoves them together.*)

ERIC: I don't care whether Ingrid forgives you or not. *I* don't!

JOHNSON: So, I've got to be the peacemaker. (*He shoves them together again.*)

ROGER: All right, I'll leave without your pardon.

ERIC: Yeah. So you're yellow, too, you rat.

ROGER: Enberg, take that back.

ERIC: Coward, rat, they both fit.

JOHNSON: Sure, sure they do. Accurate indeed. But now listen to an old man's advice. Take off your fine jackets. Better now, than later.

ROGER (*infuriated*): Johnson, talk some sense into this boy. He's off his head.

JOHNSON: What? Talk sense to Eric just when the party's getting lively? Not on your life. Come on, boys, spit on your hands and get on with it. Better let me have your hunting knife, Eric. You know how it is. A fellow gets mad, and then it's best not to have anything sharp close by.

(Takes the knife from Eric's pocket in spite of Eric's attempt to prevent him)

ERIC *(furious)*: Are you scared to fight, you sissy?

(Roger takes a boxing stance and punches away vigorously at Eric.)

JOHNSON *(throughout the fight)*: Wham! Not bad at all, law student. Good one! I think our Eric is getting himself a thrashing. Wow! Just look at that lawyer fellow. I never knew they learned anything really useful in college. Oh-oh, now Eric is getting warmed up. Look at him go. I'm glad I got his knife away from him. Look at those eyes, as red as fire. That means the lawyer will be out cold in one minute.

INGRID *(off, calling)*: Eric! Roger! Where are you?

JOHNSON: Come on, boys, whale away, and let's finish it. The girl's coming and that—as the preacher said when he saw people in his church—will be the end of a pleasant Sunday. *(Roger goes down.)* Good going, Eric. That was a real haymaker. The circuit court just bit the dust at the hands of the peasantry.

ERIC: Cut it out, darn it, and bring a little water.

JOHNSON: Whooo, it's so bad it needs water, does it? Good. Never mind, I'll get it, I'll get it. *(Exit)*

ERIC *(Roger lies on the floor, groaning)*: Here, take my arm and try to get up before Ingrid gets here. Come on, be reasonable, take my hand.

ROGER *(groaning)*: I think I've twisted my ankle.

ERIC: Here comes Johnson with some water.

JOHNSON *(entering with the water bucket. Ingrid is close behind him)*: He got a little nosebleed.

INGRID: What? What happened?

ROGER *(with forced casualness)*: I stumbled and scratched myself a little. I think I turned my ankle, too.

INGRID (*going to him*): Does it hurt?

ROGER: Not at all. (*He tries to put his weight on the ankle. It's no good. He lets out a cry.*) Ouch! (*He tries to cover up.*) There! It doesn't hurt at all.

ERIC: There's no use lying to her, she knows darn well we've been fighting.

JOHNSON: Oh, come now, there hasn't been a fight—perish the thought! Never even thought about it. We've been having a match. They're called championship matches by educated people because fights are vulgar. And now that they're called matches they're very elegant and proper. You see what education has done for us.

(*Ingrid has been fussing over Roger. Eric is annoyed.*)

ROGER: Thanks, Ingrid. But now your hanky is ruined.

INGRID: Johnson, don't just stand there and look. Go on down to Rogerhouse and bring the surrey and Blackie.

JOHNSON: Will do, princess. This'll wake them up down at the house. (*He goes.*)

ERIC: What can *I* do?

INGRID (*after a moment's silence. Coldly*): You? You can make yourself scarce. Don't show your face around Rogerhouse again till I've left for school in the fall. I don't want to see you any more, you hoodlum.

ROGER (*delighted through his pain*): Ingrid, you can come to the ocean with mother and me and spend the summer. Ouch! Blast it!

INGRID: Wonderful! We'll go boating and swimming together. Eric and I used to go swimming in the lake, but now he can take Johnson along and fish for perch instead.

ERIC (*up to Ingrid*): So! Just like that, huh? The old brush-off. Good-bye forever, and all that. Well, we'll see . . . (*Eric picks up his shotgun and starts to go.*)

INGRID (*frightened*): What are you going to do?

ERIC: With your gracious permission, I'm going to take my gun and get out of here. Are you afraid I'm going to take a pot shot at your boyfriend there? Oh, no, duchess, I'm not that far gone. Keep your lover! And have fun!

INGRID (*furious*): Lover! I'll get even with him, just watch. (*Raises her voice and moves up to the door*) Roger, it's so wonderful here. Come and sit beside me.

ROGER: Ouch! If I only could.

INGRID (*whispering*): You idiot, pretend! Pretend!

ROGER: Okay, I understand. (*Raises his voice*) Ingrid, here with my head in your lap I feel as if I were in heaven.

INGRID (*whispering*): He deserves this. (*More volume*) What a summer we're going to have together! It'll be . . . it'll be . . . an experience I'll remember my whole life . . . beloved! (*Whispers*) Say something poetic, stupid!

ROGER: Kiss me, darling . . . Your lips glow like pearls.

INGRID (*a suppressed laugh*): Yours glow like raw beefsteak. Now come on, we'll kiss. (*Roger makes an effort to get over to her.*) No, no, in the air, you idiot. (*Loud*) Roger, you're the second man whose lips have touched mine, but what a difference! Such ardor! Such warmth and passion! (*Almost shouting*) That first one was just a silly schoolboy. Ah, bliss! Let no one ever disturb our dream of love! (*She opens the door wide, and sends smack, smack, smack out into the darkness toward Eric.*)

CURTAIN

ACT II

Scene i

His Grace's bedchamber. The drapes are all open. A dresser or a clothes rack stands at the left. His Grace stands at the window, half dressed. Vickberg is helping him on with his clothes.

HIS GRACE: Damn, Vickberg, now they're all here! Look, the driveway is jammed with people all the way out to the main road.

VICKBERG: I believe my lord Baron has shed a tear.

HIS GRACE: Of thankfulness, eh? Fell on your forehead, eh? You're welcome to it. It was only a pearl that dripped out of my nose. Look at the cows, tearing across the fields scared out of their wits by all the racket. You know what I'd like, Vickberg? I'd like to see sister Julia straddled on one of those cows and have it gallop her all the way into Stockholm. (*He laughs.*) I can see her now, riding across the bridge just at the changing of the guard. (*He laughs again.*)

VICKBERG: My lord shouldn't laugh so impiously. Remember, the bird that sings in the morning . . .

HIS GRACE: . . . will go through a hawk's arse before night. I know, I know. But if Julia has her way, I'll end up there anyway. Which uniform shall I wear—Colonel or Royal Chamberlain?

VICKBERG: I suggest we take the one you can get into.

HIS GRACE: Very sensible. Bring one of them here. (*Vickberg*

brings out a uniform. His Grace continues as he and Vick-
berg struggle to get him into it.) Well, well, I seem to still
have my figure. The pants hang beautifully, eh? Do they
have to be buttoned, too? Criminy, don't be so rough.
Couldn't we just borrow Mrs. Enberg's apron and hang it
in front? (*A knock at the door*) Somebody's knocking.
(*Calls*) Who is it?

MME. HYLTENIUS (*off*): Hurry now, Roger, the tenants are
crowding onto the front lawn.

HIS GRACE: That's fine, Julia. Go down and treat the men to snuff
while they wait.

MME. HYLTENIUS: But Roger, even the gentry are beginning to
arrive.

HIS GRACE: Tell them to go to hell!

MME. HYLTENIUS: And the pastor has arrived.

HIS GRACE: He can show them the way!

MME. HYLTENIUS: Roger, don't you have any respect for anyone?

HIS GRACE: Yes, for old women who keep their mouths shut.
I adore them like saints. Vickberg, open the window so I
can hear the music. (*Vickberg opens the window. Music
and confusion. Then silence as His Grace appears at the
window. As if at a signal, the crowd begins to sing "A
Mighty Fortress Is Our God." His Grace straightens up
and stands at attention. When the song is finished, he says
quietly, moved*) So, so, there they are, my own people: big
and little, farmers and smiths, mothers and husbands, girls
and boys. I've watched them grow up like plants in the
earth, like chicks in one big nest. If an old man's prayers are
of any use, may all go well with you in this life. God bless
your work. God bless your rest, and your children. Damn!
If I don't think Mamselle Vickberg is beginning to bawl.

VICKBERG (*who has stood stiff and straight behind His Grace, deeply moved*): That was the first time in many years that I have seen my lord Baron stand at attention.

HIS GRACE: Oh Lord, give me a shot of cognac, it looks like there's a hard day ahead. (*Vickberg brings a glass of cognac on a tray.*) Ah! Wonderful! What are all those banners out there in the yard?

VICKBERG (*as he looks out*): The one on the left there with the blue ribbons is from the "Save-the-Children Temperance League"; the one next to it is from "The Reformed Drunkards' Temperance Association"; and the one over there on the right is "The Ladies' League for Christian Temperance" . . .

HIS GRACE (*interrupting*): Yes, yes, it makes me very happy that the people don't booze it up. I'd join one of those associations myself, but I've heard those crazy curlicues are even prejudiced against cognac, whisky, and other light refreshments. (*Another knock at the door*) Who's there?

MME. HYLTENIUS (*off*): It's your impatient little sister, who's burning with desire to see you.

HIS GRACE: Just a minute, Julia, just a minute. Hurry up with this monkey suit, Vickberg. As old as she is, Madame Hyltenius is burning up with desire. Rip the coat up the back if it's too tight!

(*Vickberg has been struggling to get the Baron dressed and at the same time trying to keep an eye on what is happening in the yard. Now he stands at the window.*)

VICKBERG: Here come the schoolchildren, my lord. They're all carrying little banners they made themselves.

HIS GRACE: For heaven's sake, don't start bawling again. I'll make you a present of my late-lamented wife's gold thimble if you can manage to squeeze me into this tunic.

(*Vickberg struggles to get His Grace into the coat.*)

Ah! Damn! You did it! (*Pause*) How does it fit?

VICKBERG: As well as can be expected, your Grace, as well as can be expected.

HIS GRACE: A man can't ask for more. I feel like a knight in armor, eager for battle, fit for the fray. Let Madame Hyltenius in!

MME. HYLTENIUS (*enters, dripping sugar*): Brother, my beloved brother, may God's blessings . . . (*interrupts herself*) . . . but you poor dear, you look like a scarecrow!

HIS GRACE (*angry*): Wha——what? You have the gall to come sailing in here to say . . .

MME. HYLTENIUS: . . . that you look like a scarecrow. But there's nothing unusual about that. Come, take my arm, and Vickberg will take your other arm, and together we'll lead you out to the people.

HIS GRACE (*snorting*): What say? Lead me away? Am I dying?

MME. HYLTENIUS: You are certainly in a very delicate condition, and too much excitement isn't good for you. Besides, why should you have drawn up that bizarre will if you hadn't felt a premonition of death?

HIS GRACE: Oh yes, Ingrid? Where the devil is she? Where's Eric?

MME. HYLTENIUS: Well, I can tell you. They spent the night up at the hunting lodge. Just think, Roger, spent the night.

HIS GRACE (*genially*): My dear Julia, night occurs regularly once every twenty-four hours, and a person's got to spend it somewhere.

MME. HYLTENIUS (*a little angry but still under control*): And it doesn't seem strange to you that your own . . . hmmmm . . . well that she chooses to stay away from your celebration. Seems very inconsiderate to me. Shocking!

HIS GRACE (*perhaps a little hurt*): Tut-tut. Kids are kids. Still it seems like she could at least have come and said hello.

MME. HYLTENIUS (*scornfully*): Well, you see, she doesn't know anything about the will yet.

VICKBERG: May I offer an explanation, your Grace? Yesterday Tony heard that someone here in the house had insulted her by calling her a bastard.

MME. HYLTENIUS: That's terrible. Whoever it was should be punished at once.

VICKBERG: It was Roger Hyltenius.

MME. HYLTENIUS: How dare you!

VICKBERG: Ingrid ran away up to the hunting lodge with Johnson and Eric. When Roger found out she'd heard what he said he went after her to apologize.

HIS GRACE: You know, I rather like your son, Julia. God be praised he doesn't take after either you or the late lamented Reverend. More after *me*. I suppose Eric will defend Ingrid's honor, and young Roger will have to defend himself. Nothing like a good fist fight to liven a day up.

MME. HYLTENIUS: Fist fight? You don't mean that Eric, that servant boy, would attack my son?

HIS GRACE: In ancient times two boys and one girl meant exactly one thing: a battle to the death. But don't worry too much about it, times have changed. So now let's go. Throw open the portals, Vickberg. Let the people's homage be vigorous, but brief!

MME. HYLTENIUS: Open both doors, Vickberg. I'm going to appear at my brother's side.

(*First His Grace, then Madame Hyltenius, and finally Vickberg exit through the door at the back of the stage. Music is heard.*)

CURTAIN

SCENE 2

In the courtyard just outside the main entrance to Roger-house. Music. A great crowd is gathered in the yard. Included are the schoolmaster and several of his pupils, and the local police inspector, who acts as master of ceremonies. The doors of Rogerhouse open, and His Grace appears, Madame Hylten-ius at his side. He graciously acknowledges the cheering. Music ends.

HIS GRACE: Good morning, good morning, my good friends. 'Morning, Inspector.

INSPECTOR (*takes a step forward and begins his recitation*): Upon his seventieth birthday . . .

HIS GRACE: God in heaven, am I that old? Yes, yes of course, I know it only too well. Let's skip all that. Load your guns, boys, then aim and fire. That's all that's necessary when an old soldier approaches the pearly gates.

INSPECTOR: To our beloved Master, Chamberlain and Colonel, Knight Commander of the Royal Sword, Order of the North Star, Order of Vasa, Knight of the Prussian . . .

HIS GRACE: Vickberg, stop him. It'll take him an hour to get through all that.

INSPECTOR (*confused, but struggles valiantly on*): Everything must be done the right way. Listing honors or spreading manure, it doesn't make any difference. It's got to be done right. (*He turns to the crowd.*) All together now, three cheers for our beloved master, Colonel and Chamberlain, Knight Commander . . .

HIS GRACE (*puts his hand over the inspector's mouth so that nothing but gurgles come out*): It's a hell of a thing when a man has to lead his own cheer. All right now, all together, hail to the old man of Rogerhouse. And if it's absolutely necessary, long may he live. (*An orderly cheer, then a fanfare*) Well hurrah-ed. Very good. (*He turns and indicates that he would like to go back into the house.*)

MME. HYLTENIUS (*holding him back*): No, no. Wait, Roger, now it's your turn.

HIS GRACE: What say? My turn to cheer?

MME. HYLTENIUS: Naturally you're going to say a few words.

HIS GRACE: Yes, yes, indeed I am. (*Clearing his throat*) Dear friends and faithful servants, my heart is overflowing, as they say . . .

INSPECTOR: No, no, no! It isn't his turn yet. It says here in the program, and the minister wrote the program, that the children come next. Then it's the Baron's turn. Come on now, children, and do your bit. One, two, three! (*The schoolmaster's six children line up before His Grace with their home-made banners in their hands. At the count of three they begin to sing "Happy Birthday to You." They finish the song together, but the youngest child, Anna-Marie, goes back to the beginning and starts again alone.*) Schoolmaster! Take Anna-Marie away. She won't stop as long as she has an audience.

SCHOOLMASTER: Come on, number six, that's enough. (*Leads Anna-Marie off to one side and quiets her*)

INSPECTOR: Riflemen! Attention! Right shoulder arms! Ready! Aim! Your Grace, here comes the salute.

HIS GRACE (*in despair to Vickberg*): Vickberg, please massage my legs. They're beginning to cramp. This is never going to end.

INSPECTOR: FIRE! (*His Grace loses his balance and nearly falls down the steps. After studying his program, the inspector continues. To His Grace*) Now the Baron delivers his heartfelt thanks to one and all.

HIS GRACE: You are all kind and faithful people. God bless you all. Now Mrs. Enberg will see that you get something to eat. Besides that a ten-dollar bill for each man and a silver dollar for each child. Damn. Now I'm going inside. (*The people cheer and toss flowers toward His Grace.* They then exit to find the food. His Grace turns to go in, but remains standing in the doorway. He turns to Vickberg and says*) Vickberg, I've got cramps in my legs. I can't walk a damn step. Bring a chair. Why don't you massage me? (*A chair is placed behind His Grace. He falls into it. Vickberg begins to massage his legs.*)

MME. HYLTENIUS: Dear Roger, was it too much for you? The tribute was very impressive, but now you must rest.

HIS GRACE: Yes, thanks, now I'm going to rest until my eightieth birthday. We'll celebrate that here with a naval battle.

MME. HYLTENIUS: Always joking. Darling, you can rest till twelve o'clock. Then the bishop and the rest of the clergy will arrive; at twelve-thirty the school board and other deputations; and at one o'clock you are giving lunch for thirty special guests.

HIS GRACE: Vickberg, send word for them not to come. If they want to know why, tell them I've just come down with the hoof-and-mouth disease and that Julia has chickenpox.

MME. HYLTENIUS: Roger, what do you mean?

* If desired Swedish music and folk dancing can be introduced here. Vickberg brings a chair for His Grace, and he sits and watches. After the dance the scene goes on as written. [Author's note]

HIS GRACE: Precisely what I said. Ouch! Criminy, Vickberg, don't rub so hard.

MME. HYLTENIUS: But I sent the invitations myself. You wouldn't insult my guests like that.

HIS GRACE: If you've invited them, you'll have to entertain them. Vickberg, have the table in the large dining room set for lunch. Madame Hyltenius is entertaining, but not me.

MME. HYLTENIUS (*furious*): If you don't greet my guests, I'll leave.

HIS GRACE: Just as you please. Vickberg, call the carriage for Madame, and shut the door well so she doesn't fall out and come walking back.

MME. HYLTENIUS (*livid*): You beast!

DAHLGREN (*coming out the door*): Excuse me, am I intruding?

HIS GRACE (*motions for Vickberg to stop massaging. Vickberg gets up*): Quite the contrary, my dear fellow. Thank you, Vickberg, it feels much better now. Come, Dahlgren, we'll go to my room and have a bit to eat. Then we'll get at the will. May I take your arm? (*They go into the house.*)

MME. HYLTENIUS (*choking with rage*): Just wait! You can't treat me this way. Vickberg, did you hear him? He called me an old hen!

VICKBERG: I only heard him mention chickenpox, but I suppose that *could* affect old hens. What time does Madame expect to leave?

MME. HYLTENIUS (*after a moment's thought. Vehemently*): When do I expect to leave? Never! It's perfectly clear that I'm going to have to stay here and take charge of my poor, senile brother.

VICKBERG: It might be a good idea for Madame to have a little lunch first. You need to be in good shape, in very good shape, as Eric used to say, if you plan to take on His Grace.

MME. HYLTENIUS (*with confidence*): Why, Vickberg, you look as if just thinking about it frightened you. But then, of course, you're not a Bernhusen de Saars. As it happens, I am. (*She sails into the house followed by Vickberg.*)

CURTAIN

SCENE 3

A small dining room. His Grace and Dahlgren are seated at the table. Tony, in white gloves, serves them.

DAHLGREN: Madame Hyltenius will probably show up here any minute.

HIS GRACE: Certainly, my dear fellow. If she stayed away I'd be so shocked you'd have to send for the doctor *and* the parson. Whenever she thinks anything is up, she's got to stick her nose in it.

MME. HYLTENIUS (*enters quickly followed by Vickberg*): Is there room at the table for little old me? I was going to have lunch in my room, but it seemed so lonesome.

(*Vickberg has now taken over the task of serving. He has also put on white gloves. He lays another place for Julia.*)

DAHLGREN: A pleasure, my dear Julia. It's not good for men to eat alone.

HIS GRACE: And still worse for old women. Sit down, Julia, the guests can wait. (*Drily, indicating a platter of food*) May I help you to something?

MME. HYLTENIUS: No, thank you, I can help myself. I hope I'm not interrupting some important conference.

HIS GRACE: Important conference?

MME. HYLTENIUS (*carefully*): You said you were going to prepare your will.

HIS GRACE (*drily*): The will? Oh, that little trifle has already been taken care of. No, we were just talking about a very interesting subject: illegitimate children, our own and others.

MME. HYLTENIUS (*fighting for control*): You'll excuse me if I don't join in the conversation.

HIS GRACE (*laughs*): Look at her play innocent. You know, Julia can compete with a first-class encyclopedia when it comes to extensive and trustworthy information. The only difference is that she concentrates on the scandalous. There hasn't been a single affair in this part of the country in the last fifty years that has escaped her attention, whether it smelled of Chanel No. 5 or the haystack. (*Both men laugh.*)

MME. HYLTENIUS (*embarrassed, but giggles nervously*): Why, shame on you.

HIS GRACE: Of course, Julia doesn't gossip at all—*fi donc*—but she's as omniscient as God himself, and like Divine Charity her attention is always directed toward sinners.

MME. HYLTENIUS (*innocently*): Me? I can't even stand to hear about such things.

HIS GRACE: Yes, yes, of course, but life is no bed of roses, and sometimes a person has to do things he doesn't like. But what were we talking about, Judge?

DAHLGREN: We were talking about old Hanson.

HIS GRACE: Yes, of course. Julia, didn't he have a boy who . . .

MME. HYLTENIUS (*innocently*): How should I know?

HIS GRACE: Yes, he had a boy by the upstairs maid.

MME. HYLTENIUS: No, Roger, your memory is failing you. It was the governess.

HIS GRACE: Bravo! Skoal, Julia. (*They drink.*) Have a stuffed tomato. Didn't I tell you, Dahlgren? My sister's a reference book for the countryside's wild flora and fauna. A sardine, old boy. What happened to the youngster?

MME. HYLTENIUS: He was brought up in very modest circumstances by foster parents and then sent off to sea.

HIS GRACE: Vickberg, please pass the cheese. Didn't old Hanson take any better care than that of his own child?

MME. HYLTENIUS: What should he have done? Made him his heir? Oh no, Roger, Hanson didn't suffer from softening of the brain. Besides, there's more to this story than . . .

HIS GRACE (*laughs delightedly*): Listen now, Dahlgren, this'll be good. Vickberg, send Tony out and shut the doors.

VICKBERG: As you wish. (*Makes a sign to Tony, who leaves. Vickberg then closes the doors.*)

MME. HYLTENIUS: *Mon Dieu!* Well now, naturally, I don't *know* anything . . .

HIS GRACE: We know that, go on!

MME. HYLTENIUS: It seems that the governess had old Hanson completely fooled.

HIS GRACE: What do you mean?

MME. HYLTENIUS: Well, you know, old men and young girls. It's not really difficult to fool a man in this way if you go about it carefully.

HIS GRACE: What do you mean, Sister dear?

MME. HYLTENIUS: My, but you have a hard time catching on to anything today. I mean, naturally, that it can be difficult to determine just who the child's father really is.

HIS GRACE (*irritated*): Are you trying to tell me that a father can't tell his own child?

MME. HYLTENIUS: That's exactly what I was saying.

DAHLGREN (*beginning to think things have gone far enough*):
But, my dear Julia, it depends on many things. Why Hanson . . .

MME. HYLTENIUS (*interrupting*): There was a very handsome
young man, a forestry student, at his place the year before
the boy was born. He was the child's father. I know that for
a fact.

HIS GRACE: Listen to that, Judge. How would you like to have
her as a witness in a paternity case? She believes any story
she wants to, she never for one minute doubts it, and nothing
can make her change. Vickberg, more wine.

DAHLGREN: I think it would be best for me to change places with
her. She could do less harm as a judge than as a witness.

MME. HYLTENIUS (*innocently*): You should remember that
forestry student, Roger dear. He played Don Juan to the
whole countryside.

HIS GRACE (*a bit wearily*): Unfortunately, I have a poor memory
for forestry students, no matter how handsome.

MME. HYLTENIUS: He was here a great deal that summer, too.
That was the year I lived in the south wing. Just myself and
my maid—yes, you know who I mean—Ingrid's mother. I
saw Mimi and the young man together several times. Not
only I, but everyone else saw them, too, and of course we all
understood what was going on. You, Roger dear, were the
only one who didn't.

(*Vickberg, who has been standing with a small tray in
his hand, hurls it to the floor.*)

MME. HYLTENIUS (*jumping*): Vickberg, what on earth is the
trouble?

VICKBERG (*stammering*): I . . . I . . . happened . . . to drop
. . .

HIS GRACE (*cool and self-controlled, with great dignity*): Don't worry about it, schoolmarm, even I feel like smashing something. Who shall we drink to? The god of love? Ah, you rascal, you bombarded my heart most diligently for many years. And from those shots came both smiles and tears. But that was a long time ago. The old man is too far along in years to drink to you. But I will say this, my friend. Many a time you shot both sharply and well, but you never shot with poisoned arrows. (*He pauses a moment, squints, and contemplates his sister. Then suddenly*) How would it be if I drank to you, sister Julia?

MME. HYLTENIUS (*flattered, but still uncertain what he's up to*): Why, my dear, a toast to me *again*?

HIS GRACE: Yes, again. A good woman can't be honored too often.

MME. HYLTENIUS: Thank you very much. Skoal! (*She raises her glass.*)

HIS GRACE (*calmly returns his glass to the table*): Unfortunately you are *not* good. You are low-minded and common. You are nastiness itself. There is no reason on earth for drinking to you. (*He rises.*) Instead I shall drink this toast . . . (*he is standing head high, glass in hand, as though talking to himself*) . . . to my daughter Ingrid and her blessed mother, my dearest, most beloved Mimi. (*He slowly drains the glass and then throws it to the floor, where it shatters.*) No one shall ever drink from that glass again. No matter how it sounds, that toast was sacred to this cynical old man. Vickberg, give me your arm. Judge Dahlgren, Julia, I hope you will excuse an old man for leaving so abruptly. (*Steadied by Vickberg's arm, His Grace leaves the dining room. After a few seconds Madame Hyltenius explodes scornfully.*)

MME. HYLTENIUS: My, how touching. A cynical old man! He's cynical enough all right. Poor old devil, I feel sorry for him in spite of everything. He thinks he can do anything he wants. I'll show him he can't. (*Thunder is heard outside. Madame Hyltenius is afraid.*) Dear God! Ohhh! Thunder. Shut the windows. Why didn't someone say it was going to thunder?

DAHLGREN: You should have told us it was coming, you're the encyclopedia. Anyway you shouldn't worry about it. Lightning is just like love. You don't know you've been hit till you're out cold. (*Thunder again, louder and closer*)

MME. HYLTENIUS (*on the verge of tears*): Ohhh, dear heaven, forgive me my sins. Dahlgren, please hand me my smelling salts. Ahhhh, that's better. I'll show him who's boss in this family. (*Thunder, louder. Madame Hyltenius is paralyzed with fright.*) Ohhh, I'm a poor sinner . . . bathe my temples . . . born in sin . . . with cologne water.

(*Distant rumble of thunder, Vickberg enters.*)

VICKBERG: Oh, pardon me!

DAHLGREN (*helping Julia*): What is it?

VICKBERG: His Grace would like to see you. It's about the will.

MME. HYLTENIUS (*recovering quickly*): Go, Judge, for heaven's sake go!

(*Dahlgren exits.*)

MME. HYLTENIUS: I hope the thunder hasn't disturbed poor Roger.

VICKBERG: Not at all. His Grace has been occupied examining and signing his will.

MME. HYLTENIUS (*viciously*): He has, has he? How do you know?

VICKBERG: I have just had the honor of signing it as a witness to the fact that it was drawn up at his own request and that he was of sound mind and in full possession of his faculties. (*Madame Hyltenius bursts into shrill, mocking laughter.*) His Grace is now resting on the library sofa. He usually takes his nap in bed, but today he wanted to wear his uniform a little longer.

MME. HYLTENIUS: How touching.

VICKBERG: Unfortunately I must also inform you that your son Roger has injured his foot up at the hunting lodge. Johnson came to get a horse and carriage early this morning to bring him down.

MME. HYLTENIUS (*her mind on other matters*): He's always doing something like that. What does it say in the will?

VICKBERG: Forgive me, Your Grace, but I must go.

MME. HYLTENIUS (*starts to go with him*): I have a few things to say to him, and I'm going to say them right now.

DAHLGREN (*entering hastily*): Just a moment, Julia. You mustn't disturb His Grace now, not now. (*Vickberg exits quickly.*) This is no time for hysterical outbursts. The will is signed. The only chance you have of getting it changed is to be as agreeable as you can.

MME. HYLTENIUS (*pathetically*): He detests us.

DAHLGREN (*not unkindly*): I'm afraid he does detest you, Julia.

MME. HYLTENIUS: Me! He detests me, his own sister?

DAHLGREN: On the other hand, he seems to have a certain affection for his nephew.

MME. HYLTENIUS (*crossly*): The clumsy oaf has hurt his leg.

DAHLGREN: That doesn't make any difference.

MME. HYLTENIUS: Doesn't make any difference? My poor boy . . .

DAHLGREN (*his patience gone*): Stop interrupting me, damn . . . (*Control again*) Please, Julia, let me finish! I think I've found a way. I have induced him to strike out a provision in the will whereby Ingrid was required to marry Eric Enberg. It wasn't easy, but I finally managed it. (*He looks out the window.*) There's a carriage coming up the drive with

Roger and Ingrid in it. (*Interested*) And Roger has his arm round the girl. (*He pulls out a handkerchief and mops his brow.*) Perhaps this means that . . . well, that . . .

MME. HYLTENIUS: It means that he's twisted his ankle. (*She stops herself. Then her face lights up with excitement.*) But perhaps . . . (*sweetly*) . . . it's an affair of the heart!

INGRID (*rushing in*): Criminy, where is Uncle Roger?

MME. HYLTENIUS (*motherly*): Shh! He's asleep in the library, my dear little girl.

INGRID (*doesn't notice the tone*): Then I'm going to wake him even if I have to put a bee in his mouth to do it. Criminy, I'll explode if I don't tell him! (*She dashes out.*)

MME. HYLTENIUS (*more sweetness*): What a lovely child. (*Sweetness gone*) Though I'd like to . . . (*Back again*) Aren't you going to protect His Grace's blessed slumbers?

DAHLGREN (*mysteriously*): I'd be careful, Julia dear. In my opinion the next fifteen minutes will decide the whole question of the inheritance.

CURTAIN

SCENE 4

The library. His Grace lies asleep on the sofa, snoring gently. Ingrid enters and goes straight to him, takes him by one shoulder, and shakes him vigorously.

INGRID: Uncle! Uncle Roger! Uncle, wake up! You blessed old man!

HIS GRACE: Wha . . . who . . . is blessing me?

INGRID: I am, of course.

HIS GRACE: So ho, little mouse, and you have good reason to be happy. Two estates of five thousand acres each . . .

INGRID: Oh, be quiet. Who cares about your old estates? Uncle Roger, congratulate me.

HIS GRACE (*with pretended anger*): Now listen to me, you little imp. First, one doesn't say "Be quiet"; the correct thing is "Shut your mouth." And secondly, *you* should be congratulating *me*. Don't you know that today is my seventieth birthday?

INGRID (*tenderly*): My dear, ugly, old uncle, I forgot. But is that something to be congratulated for?

HIS GRACE: No, I guess you're right, sweetheart. Now why should I congratulate you?

INGRID: I'm engaged.

HIS GRACE (*delighted*): So ho, Eric has finally popped the question, eh? But that's no surprise to your old uncle! He's as omniscient as the Lord himself.

(*A knock at the door*)

INGRID (*calls*): Come in.

ROGER (*limps in*): Hello, Uncle Roger.

HIS GRACE: Well, well, look what the cat dragged in!

ROGER: I had a little fight with Eric.

HIS GRACE: Good for Eric. Dammit, I've always been fond of that boy.

INGRID: Shame on you, you ugly old man. You shouldn't talk like that to Roger.

HIS GRACE: Tut, tut. I really don't think ill of you, my lad. You're well behaved and honest and don't resemble your mother at all.

MME. HYLTENIUS (*sneaking in*): Yoo-hoo, may I come in?

HIS GRACE: Yes, yes, of course, Julia. Could I keep you out if I wanted to?

MME. HYLTENIUS: *Want* to keep me out? (*She giggles.*) Have you congratulated your nephew?

HIS GRACE: What? Do I have to congratulate him too? What for? For having gotten himself beat up?

MME. HYLTENIUS: Yes, in a way. That good-for-nothing little peasant only hastened things when he attacked my son.

ROGER: Mother, please don't talk like that.

INGRID: Yes, don't talk like that about Eric.

MME. HYLTENIUS (*imperiously*): Hold your tongues. Or, better yet, leave the room at once. I wish to speak to my brother alone.

ROGER: Come on, Ingrid. When she uses that tone, it's best to get lost as fast as possible. (*They exit.*)

HIS GRACE: What now? Are you going to give me a dose of castor oil? Well, out with it, what's on your mind?

MME. HYLTENIUS: My dear old brother, you sit here all alone summers and winters . . .

HIS GRACE: Don't worry about it, I'm not complaining. I've got my books here.

MME. HYLTENIUS: Oh, do you read much?

HIS GRACE: Never. But I examine them occasionally. When I find one of mother's bookmarks in *Corinne,* or when I find one of grandfather's snuff-smeared thumbprints in Montesquieu, I have all the company I want. Besides, I have Ingrid . . .

MME. HYLTENIUS: But, my dear, how long can you count on having her company?

HIS GRACE: Till I die, I hope.

MME. HYLTENIUS (*a trace of severity*): Oh, you old egotist. You think you can run life to please yourself.

HIS GRACE: Not while you're around. Otherwise I'd be having a pleasant nap.

MME. HYLTENIUS (*sharply*): Nevertheless, your power has its limits. Just today something happened that my late husband would have called the hand of Providence.

HIS GRACE: Your late husband is romping around heaven like a small child, singing "May she live a thousand years." I'm sure your dear departed husband wishes you a very long life.

MME. HYLTENIUS: You shouldn't make fun of the blessed dead. Besides that, you'd best be careful not to provoke me, Roger dear.

HIS GRACE (*delighted, he laughs*): But I give you permission to provoke me to the point of having a stroke, for the will is signed and sealed.

MME. HYLTENIUS: You think your will is stronger than the will of Providence. I know the will that was to deprive my son of his rightful inheritance is drawn up, but he'll be the master of Rogerhouse just the same.

HIS GRACE: He will, like hell!

MME. HYLTENIUS: Your daughter, Ingrid . . .

HIS GRACE: So ho, now even you admit she's my daughter.

MME. HYLTENIUS: I have never denied it. And now I know for sure.

HIS GRACE: Oh, I suppose Mimi appeared to you during your midday nap and gave you definite confirmation. What happened to the handsome forestry student?

MME. HYLTENIUS: I know it because I want to know it. I know it because Ingrid is going to be my daughter-in-law. She and Roger became engaged today!

HIS GRACE: What did you say?

MME. HYLTENIUS: My dear brother, are you having trouble breathing? I thought it very nice that they became engaged on your birthday. Now it's a *family* celebration! (*She laughs.*)

HIS GRACE (*after a long look at his sister*): Vickberg! Vickberg!

VICKBERG (*entering at once*): At your service, my lord.

HIS GRACE (*calmly*): Call Ingrid in here.

VICKBERG: Ingrid and Roger are just leaving for a drive.

HIS GRACE: Then Roger will have to go alone. Tell him to drive up to the hunting lodge and bring Eric here.

VICKBERG: Very well, Your Grace. (*He exits.*)

MME. HYLTENIUS: My dear brother seems to be showing some signs of energy. A wonderful sight. (*She laughs.*)

HIS GRACE (*calmly*): That laugh has tormented me ever since I was a boy. It's a vicious laugh, and you are a vicious person. I don't believe your husband needs to worry about meeting you again, at least in heaven.

MME. HYLTENIUS (*laughs again*): Well, my husband wasn't exactly a saint himself.

HIS GRACE: No. (*Pause*) A martyr!

INGRID: Uncle Roger, why can't I go for a ride with my fiancé?

HIS GRACE: So it's true, then, you are engaged to Roger? Rather sudden, wasn't it?

INGRID: Yes, but the boys got into a fight, and Roger got a little bit beat up, and Eric would have gone crazy with cockiness if I hadn't taught him some manners.

HIS GRACE: So you don't like Eric any more?

INGRID: Oh yes, sure I do, but he has such a terrible temper and he's such a *boy!* If we're at a dance, he says, "C'mon, shall we shake a leg a bit," or "Let's stumble around the floor a couple of times!" And then he says, "Just think how cozy and snug it'll be when we're all married, just you and me and our ten kids!" And every now and then he climbs on his high horse and asks me if I really love him or am I just pretending in order to get such a fine husband!

MME. HYLTENIUS (*laughs again*): He's just a child, you see.

INGRID: At first I only wanted to tease him a little, but then . . .

HIS GRACE: . . . Roger came along.

INGRID: Uh-huh, that's what happened. Are you angry with me, Uncle Roger?

HIS GRACE (*smiling*): No, kitten, you're so much like your dear, stupid little mother I couldn't possibly be angry with you. Now march on out of here. If you run across Judge Dahlgren, send him in, will you?

(*Ingrid nods and exits.*)

MME. HYLTENIUS: What do you want with Dahlgren, Roger dear? The engagement is none of his affair, as far as I know.

HIS GRACE: No, but as far as *I* know . . .

DAHLGREN: At your service, my friend, always ready to . . .

HIS GRACE: . . . to make a fast buck. Give me the will.

DAHLGREN (*taking it from his pocket and handing it to His Grace*): Here it is, Your Grace. Here is the precious document.

(*His Grace takes the will and calmly tears it to bits.*)

MME. HYLTENIUS (*gasping*): Roger, what are you doing? Tearing up your will?

HIS GRACE (*still calmly*): A little while ago it would have made you happy; now it seems to make you sad. The world is very changeable, Julia. Dahlgren, a girl who gets engaged only to tease her sweetheart is obviously incapable of handling her own private affairs, much less two large estates. (*Slight pause*) On the other hand Eric is serious and intelligent—oh, maybe a little impetuous, but what does that matter? I intend to make *him* my heir. (*Indignant, astonished exclamations. His Grace continues imperiously.*) Be quiet. I have not lost my mind. I will make him my heir on the condition that he marries my daughter Ingrid. If she refuses, she and Eric will receive smaller shares, and the bulk of my estate will go into a fund for old noblemen's widows. That's what I said, for old noblemen's widows. First of all, because I'm thankful that I'm not leaving a widow behind, and second, because I have been permitted to enjoy the blessing of being a widower for twenty-five years.

MME. HYLTENIUS (*all self-possession gone*): Dahlgren, can you still stand there and tell me my brother is in his right mind?

DAHLGREN: Tut. The point about the blessings of widowerhood indicates beyond a doubt that his mind is remarkably clear.

MME. HYLTENIUS (*furious*): This is an obvious . . . an obvious conspiracy. I detest you, Roger. I'm going to have you locked up in an asylum!

HIS GRACE (*calmly*): Won't you sit down, Julia? We can talk this over calmly and peacefully.

MME. HYLTENIUS: Me sit down? I'm leaving this house for good. Never again will I darken its doorstep! (*Storms out and slams the door*)

DAHLGREN: Should I see her to the carriage?

HIS GRACE: Lord, yes! I had no idea we'd be lucky enough to get rid of her that easily. Listen! Listen to her chatter out there.

(*Sounds from beyond the door indicate that Madame Hyltenius is phoning the sheriff. We hear her asking for a number, an occasional word. She hangs up. Doors slam.*)

HIS GRACE: She's not my sister for nothing. If she couldn't blow off some of that steam, she'd explode.

MME. HYLTENIUS (*as she enters*): Roger, in ten minutes the sheriff will be here.

HIS GRACE: What? What on earth for?

MME. HYLTENIUS: To arrest Eric Enberg for attacking my son. (*Pause*)

HIS GRACE: No, but Julia, that's the craziest thing I've ever heard. Call the sheriff just because a couple of kids get into a fight?

DAHLGREN (*laughs*): Julia, you're making a fool of yourself. You ought to go on the stage.

MME. HYLTENIUS: Go ahead and laugh. Eric attacked my son in a fit of jealous rage, and I can prove it. Johnson told me that he took a knife away from him.

HIS GRACE (*quietly*): Why, you old witch, you're so full of malice that green sparks come shooting out of your eyes. Julia, my dear, you're going to poison yourself with your own meanness.

MME. HYLTENIUS (*with quiet viciousness*): Yes, you old fool. I wish you all the bad luck in the world, you and your vulgar companions, you filthy old billy goat.

DAHLGREN: Julia, Julia, you were going to be agreeable.

MME. HYLTENIUS: No, I've had enough of that. I'm going to see young Enberg in the penitentiary.

HIS GRACE (*sternly*): All right, that will do! It's dangerous to have such a malicious person around the house; it brings bad luck. Vickberg! (*Vickberg enters at once.*) Listen! Madame Hyltenius has invited the sheriff to come here. Very well, that's her business. Set out some punch so she can entertain him. But now listen to this. I hold you personally responsible, on the pain of immediate dismissal, to see that Madame Hyltenius and her son leave on the evening train. We've got to get her out of here before anything else happens. (*A shot is heard in the distance.*)

DAHLGREN (*dashing to the window*): What in the world was that? Everyone is gathered round a carriage in the driveway. There goes Eric with a gun in his hand. Someone is lying in the carriage . . .

MME. HYLTENIUS: Roger, my son . . . (*She runs out.*)

DAHLGREN: Vickberg, look after His Grace. I'm going with Madame Hyltenius.

(*He leaves. His Grace stands paralyzed with astonishment, then suddenly collapses. Vickberg helps him to the nearest chair.*)

VICKBERG: Your Grace, Baron Roger . . . are you . . .

HIS GRACE: Thanks, I'm fine now. What do you think I am, some feeble old maid? But dab a little cologne on my forehead anyway. (*Vickberg fetches a bottle from a nearby table and bathes His Grace's temples.*) Thanks. That's wonderful. (*A knock at the door. His Grace half rises.*) Who is it?

VICKBERG (*goes to the door. A second later he replies uncertainly*): My lord, it's . . . it's Eric.

HIS GRACE (*weakly*): Let the ruffian in.

ERIC (*enters, speaks very quietly*): Baron . . . I have shot Roger.

HIS GRACE (*in a commanding tone*): Explain, and make it short.

ERIC: He met me on the road and offered me a ride home. I wasn't mad at him, I swear I wasn't. I'd thought it all over and decided that it wasn't his fault that Ingrid . . . that Ingrid . . . (*His voice catches in his throat.*)

HIS GRACE: Skip the part about the girl. You said you weren't mad.

ERIC: No, I wasn't mad—down-hearted, naturally, but not mad. I climbed into the cart, and we talked things over. Finally I said, "As long as she likes you more than she likes me, I'll clear out and leave . . ."

HIS GRACE (*doesn't understand*): What? What say? Are you two old buddies now?

ERIC: Yes, I guess so.

HIS GRACE: Well, I'll be damned.

VICKBERG: But, but . . . Your Grace sits here and doesn't even ask how your nephew is. He might be dead . . .

ERIC: Don't throw a fit, Vickberg. Roger only got a scratch on the shoulder.

HIS GRACE: May I respectfully request that Mr. Vickberg refrain from throwing a fit. Go ahead, Eric.

ERIC: Well, then . . . then what shouldn't have happened, happened.

HIS GRACE: The shot, yes . . .

ERIC: Oh, *that* wasn't anything. But Roger said something then. He said that because I had withdrawn of my own free will and all, he'd make it up to me. With *money,* you understand. (*He is furious by now.*) I could have killed him on the spot, but I controlled myself and kept cool. I just jumped out of the wagon and told the filthy rat to get going if he wanted to live any longer. And did he drive! I stood there in the road and watched him.

HIS GRACE: Completely self-controlled?

ERIC: Yes! Well . . . no. I did send one shot after him.

INGRID (*rushes in*): Eric, where is Eric? Oh, Eric, save yourself. The sheriff is here. Uncle Roger, save him. Madame Hyltenius says he's an assassin. The sheriff has taken out his handcuffs. Uncle Roger, you've got to hide him.

HIS GRACE: Vickberg, take her out of here.

INGRID: No! No, I won't go.

HIS GRACE: Vickberg, take her out!

(*Vickberg takes hold of her, but she gets away, knocking him over in the process. She runs to Eric and throws her arms around him.*)

INGRID: I won't let you go. I'll commit some crime so I can marry you and be locked up in the same cell.

MME. HYLTENIUS (*heard shouting outside the door*): Let me know as soon as the doctor gets here.

HIS GRACE: Eric, take Ingrid and go out the other way. Here comes my sister.

INGRID (*crying*): Uncle Roger, I love Eric.

ERIC: Come on, don't be so dumb. His Grace has got other things to think about. (*He takes her by the hand and they leave.*)

HIS GRACE: Vickberg, snuff, if you would be so kind. (*Vickberg offers him his snuffbox.*)

MME. HYLTENIUS (*enters, the martyred mother*): Roger, can you look me in the eyes?

HIS GRACE: Not at the moment, no. (*A sneeze is coming on.*)

MME. HYLTENIUS (*in a quavering voice*): Roger, you see before you a deeply wronged mother, who . . .

HIS GRACE (*a violent sneeze*): Julia, my dear, you're supposed to say *Gesundheit.* But before you say anything more, you're going to listen to what I have to say. For the time being, I've decided not to draw up any will at all. Today has been so lively and refreshing that it's made me ten years younger. It's also convinced me that I should give some additional thought to who my heir should be. Understand, Julia? (*She nods.*) Anyway, there's a good ten years in the old rooster yet.

MME. HYLTENIUS (*a changed person*): You shouldn't call yourself an old rooster, Roger.

HIS GRACE: Why not? There's still some play acting left to be done here. You just hold your tongue and remember the unwritten will. You had the unmitigated nerve to call the sheriff here to arrest one of my people, and just a boy at that. And now you're going to get just what you deserve for it.

MME. HYLTENIUS (*meekly*): Roger, now don't do anything you'll be sorry for.

HIS GRACE: Vickberg, bring in the punch and bring in the sheriff. Julia, you have nothing to fear if you just sit there quietly and nod and say "yes" to everything I say.

MME. HYLTENIUS: Of course, I will.

VICKBERG (*enters, followed by the sheriff*): Please step in, sir. His Grace is waiting to see you.

HIS GRACE: My dear fellow, how nice of you to come.

SHERIFF: Yes, I heard about what happened. Attempted murder, bloodshed . . .

HIS GRACE (*thumping the floor with his cane*): What on earth are you talking about?

SHERIFF: Why, Madame Hyltenius . . .

HIS GRACE: Oh yes, my poor, poor sister. She's been suffering all day with a severe case of "nerves."

SHERIFF (*slightly bewildered*): Oh, how sad. How very sad indeed.

HIS GRACE: The sight of her beloved brother, the old family home and the people on the estate—her one-time playfellows and their children . . . Well, it's been too much for a heart as sensitive and tender . . .

(*Madame Hyltenius coos a bit.*)

SHERIFF: Oh, that's too bad! Has she got heart trouble?

HIS GRACE: You see, her son attacked a youngster here. When the silly goose, I mean when my poor sister, heard about it she was afraid the lad that was attacked would try to get revenge, so it was best to put her son under your protection.

SHERIFF: I'll see that all precautions are taken . . .

HIS GRACE (*laughs heartily*): Excuse me, but now comes the funniest thing. Since the fight the two young roosters have made friends and sworn eternal brotherhood.

SHERIFF (*laughing boisterously*): Well, I'll be d——d—— (*a glance toward Julia*) . . . darned!

HIS GRACE: Yes, the whole thing is just an unfortunate mistake. (*Pause. Then confidentially*) There's something I should tell you. I wasn't going to, but we owe you an explanation for dragging you way out here. You see, when my sister was very young, she was kicked in the head by a horse. Ever since she's had these attacks of "nerves." There've been times when we thought we were going to have to put her away. Up to now, at least, that hasn't been necessary. So you see . . .

SHERIFF (*flattered at having been taken into confidence*): Sure, sure. We'll just forget about the whole thing.

HIS GRACE: May I suggest that we all take a glass of punch and drink to Madame Hyltenius. (*Vickberg distributes the glasses.*) To Her Grace, may she be cured of her affliction once and for all. (*They all drink. His Grace in amusement, the sheriff in all sympathy. Madame Hyltenius nearly chokes.*)

SHERIFF: Of course, of course. We'll just forget the whole thing. Sure, sure. Now I think I should be going. (*A look at Madame Hyltenius*) Trust me, sir, everything will be hushed up. Good-bye now to Your Grace . . . (*and solicitously*) . . . and to you, Missus. (*He bows, takes a few steps, bows again, out. Madame Hyltenius, whose monumental efforts at self-control have allowed only several nervous giggles thus far, now explodes.*)

MME. HYLTENIUS (*trembling with rage*): So it's come to this! You think so much of that young whippersnapper Eric that you humiliated me publicly.

HIS GRACE: No, it's come to *this*. You are so greedy that you would rather endure the humiliation than give up your chances of being mentioned in my will. I'm sorry, Ingrid will be my heir. And I rather think she won't be marrying Roger. (*He holds out his hand to her.*) Good-bye, Julia. The matter is decided, and time flies. Your train leaves at eight o'clock. Remember, Vickberg!

MME. HYLTENIUS (*ignores his outstretched hand and walks stiffly past him*): Someday you'll regret this. Farewell, Roger! (*Goes proudly out*)

HIS GRACE (*remains standing, his hand outstretched. Smiles wearily and lets it drop*): Farewell, Julia. (*To Vickberg, his tone changed*) Well, Vickberg, old schoolmarm, I did the right thing, didn't I? Now open the window and let in the summer evening. (*Vickberg opens the windows.*) I wonder if Eric will get into any trouble.

VICKBERG: Absolutely not, I'll take him under my protective wing.

HIS GRACE: Tell me, Vickberg, will you take the last Roger Bernhusen de Saars under your wing, too?

VICKBERG: Tut, your Grace, I did that many a long year ago.

HIS GRACE: Really? You know, I believe you did at that.

INGRID (*looking in at the window*): May I come in?

HIS GRACE: Look at that. Just like the devil himself. If you lock the door, she comes in through the window.

INGRID (*hops in. Goes to His Grace and gives him a hug and a kiss*): What a day! I'm so tired I'm nearly dead. (*She kneels by his side.*)

HIS GRACE: At *your* age?

INGRID: Come on, don't be sarcastic now. You haven't got any feelings, so you don't understand. But if Eric had been arrested, I never would have survived.

HIS GRACE: Me neither. We would have gone down in our graves together, you and I.

INGRID: You dear, ugly old man, I feel so sorry for you.

HIS GRACE: Why?

INGRID: Oh, I don't know. Yes I do. It's because you're so all alone.

HIS GRACE: Well, if everyone else goes, I still have Vickberg.

INGRID: Oh, that old wooden Indian.

HIS GRACE: Don't pay any attention to her, Vickberg.

VICKBERG: Wooden Indians are, by nature, rather hard of hearing.

HIS GRACE: Where's Eric now?

INGRID: He's playing pinochle with Johnson.

HIS GRACE: How prosaic and unromantic! Like Johnson I say, "Ark-tooey!" But I'll bet if you'd step out there on the lawn and warble a few notes he'd forget all about card playing and romance would come into its own.

INGRID: You won't be lonesome? (*His Grace shakes his head.*) Then I think I'll go out for a while. Good-bye. (*She leaves as she came, through the window.*)

HIS GRACE (*quietly*): In she flew, out she flew . . . Ah, yes . . . summer evenings and youth . . . these things we remember forever.

VICKBERG: I think it's time for bed now, my lord Baron.

HIS GRACE (*slowly*): Just as you say. Though one of these days the old man at Rogerhouse will have his fill of sleeping. (*Getting up*) Then you'll never wake him again. Everything will be over and done, and the curtain will come down. *Voilà tout!*

CURTAIN

Introduction to
SWEDENHIELMS

Martin Lamm, a professor of Scandinavian literature at the University of Stockholm, once wrote, "Sweden has had only two dramatists in a hundred years: the first, August Strindberg; the second, Hjalmar Bergman." And Dr. Erik Hjalmar Linder, Sweden's leading student of Bergman, writes: "The freedoms and the possibilities which Strindberg had created for drama were soon utilized by his younger colleague. This does not mean at all that he had simply become Strindberg's successor. But he could feel quite free from naturalistic theater conventions as step by step and under the influence of another's symbolic drama he felt his way toward his own dramatic form. Even his first play, the poetic drama about Mary the mother of Jesus, shows remarkable independence. He was only twenty when it was written, but even then he was looking beyond the great teacher, Strindberg."

If it can be regarded as an asset for a country's theater to have a classic tragedy, it is also an advantage to have inherited an immortal comedy. This is the case with France, which has been provided with a comedy repertory for three hundred years, thanks to Molière. Denmark has had Holberg's comedies to laugh at for almost as long. But Sweden lagged behind a few hundred years until it got its first classic comedy in 1925. The author was Hjalmar Bergman; the comedy is called *Swedenhielms*.

In early 1923 the director of the Swedish Royal Dramatic Theater turned to Bergman and tried to persuade him to write a comedy. Even before this, friends had asked him to write a farce in which he would transfer his narrative from Wadköping trolls. The author moved to Taormina, in Sicily, and there he wrote the comedy about the Swedenhielm family in ten days. The whole countryside seemed covered with snow, but it was really a great white sea of almond blossoms above the Mediterranean. There was sunshine both without and within—at least during the creation of the first two acts. But a comedy without "tragic" undertones was impossible for Hjalmar Bergman. If he was to write a realistic comedy, it would have to mirror life itself; and as everyone knows, life does not consist entirely of either sunshine or shadows.

In the third act, clouds of uneasiness begin to hover over the sunny Swedenhielms. Before the author restores the summer-blue comedy sky in the last act, several catastrophes threaten. The vision of a Nobel Prize flutters before the poor but brilliant family. First the vision dissolves into thin air; then it becomes a reality. This is one of the dramatic chain reactions. A second is set in motion by some forged promissory notes—an acid test for the family's incorruptible sense of honor. Like a detective story writer, Bergman plays a game with the notes: he lays down a number of false clues; he reveals the unexpected guilty party; and he re-establishes the honor of the Swedenhielms. These two lines of action give rise to a series of dramatic shocks so sudden and so abrupt they would have broken the back of the comedy without such a leading part as that of Swedenhielm. It is his personality that delights us in these violent shifts between light and darkness, between pessimism and optimism.

The play was given its première performances simultaneously at Stockholm and Göteborg in the spring of 1925. At that time one of the critics wrote, "Doesn't Mr. Bergman understand that in a comedy you're supposed to laugh and in a tragedy you're supposed to cry, and that you shouldn't do both at the same time?" However, the critic had to get used to it, for in all his later plays Bergman blended laughing and crying.

Engineer Swedenhielm is a witty and extravagant, somewhat absent-minded and egocentric old gentleman whose only wealth —according to him—consists of his honor. He is sometimes moving, sometimes a bit conceited. This man who worships honor is forced by circumstances to examine himself and thus to reflect when dishonor momentarily seems to threaten his own beloved family. Though the play is rather traditional in form, the dialogue and the plotting show such splendid invention that *Swedenhielms* has become Bergman's most often performed work. Translated into eleven languages, it has been performed in fourteen different countries, filmed three times, and produced on radio and television in Germany, England, and Sweden. It has surpassed the record of *The Baron's Will* by several hundred performances; and even now, more than forty years after its première, there is always some theater in Sweden or Germany still playing it. It has often been called the Swedish national comedy; and in it Bergman undoubtedly tried to create types of character which the public would recognize as particularly Swedish.

Swedes are generally said to be slow, shy, afraid of being different from the group, tightly bound by traditions and training. But deep down there is a Bohemian temperament which tries to assert itself. Sometimes it succeeds; and then it produces artists, personalities—original, charming people— always open to criticism, but always people that one gets along with and remembers. It can also produce some impossible individuals who merely provoke and annoy, but that is only when their worse selves get the upper hand. Most Swedes, I suppose, would like to release the gamin in their nature, but few are willing to try it without something that encourages them to abandon their reserve. They don't dare try it themselves, but they admire and love those who do dare; and it is probable that the affection for Engineer Rolf Swedenhielm shown by the general public is due precisely to the fact that he dares to be himself.

STINA BERGMAN

SWEDENHIELMS

TRANSLATED BY RAYMOND JARVI
AND ROBERT LINDQUIST

Characters

ROLF SWEDENHIELM, SR., *engineer*
ROLF SWEDENHIELM, JR., *engineer*
JULIA KÖRNER, *née Swedenhielm, actress*
BO SWEDENHIELM, *lieutenant*
ASTRID, *Bo's fiancée*
MARTA BOMAN, *Swedenhielm's sister-in-law and housekeeper*
PEDERSEN, *journalist*
ERIKSSON

The action of the play takes place at the Swedenhielm home in Stockholm. The time is 1924.

ACT I

The scene is a large room that is a living room and drawing room combined. There is some beautiful old furniture, evidently the remains of an ancestral home or of a great house. The carpets on the floor are somewhat worn. Two doors are to the right, and to the left a row of windows, almost hidden by heavy curtains. A double door in the background leads to the dining room, where the dining table can be seen. At the moment, however, it is piled with chairs, and a couple of charwomen are engaged in housecleaning.

Rolf Swedenhielm, Jr., is sitting in an easy chair, drinking his morning coffee and reading the newspapers. He has several of them and seems to be searching for some special item; when he finds it he studies it with great interest and some excitement, makes an exclamation, and throws the paper down. He does this with each paper.

Marta Boman enters. She is dressed for housecleaning. She comes up to Rolf and begins methodically to remove the cover from the chair on which he is sitting.

BOMAN: Get up.

ROLF (*without looking up from his newspaper*): Well, Auntie!

181

He's not getting the Nobel Prize! What do you say about that?

BOMAN: Get up.

ROLF: Do you have to take the cover off the chair when I'm sitting on it?

BOMAN: You don't have to sit in the chair when I'm taking the cover off. Get up.

ROLF (*rises*): Do I dare to ask for five, maybe six, regular, little sweet rolls to go with the coffee in this water?

BOMAN: Out in the cupboard. (*Continues taking off the chair cover*)

ROLF (*sitting again*): Thanks. But I'm not going out there. I'm a man, and should be able to demand a little table service, what with so many dreadful old women running about the house!

BOMAN: Go right ahead, demand.

(*Julia enters from her room. She wears a low-cut negligee. She shivers as she moves up to Boman.*)

JULIA (*affectionately*): Mutti! Dear sweet little Mutti! Coffee, please! Some hot, delicious coffee? Hmm?

BOMAN: The pot is on the stove, the mill is on the table, and the coffee's in the cupboard.

JULIA (*with a sigh*): Oh well. Thank you anyway. (*She shivers as she exits into the dining room.*)

(*Bo Swedenhielm is heard shouting from his room up right.*)

BO (*off*): Mummy! Mummy!

BOMAN (*smiles*): What is it?

BO (*off*): Hunger!—terrifying—unthinkable—hunger!

BOMAN: What'll you have, then? (*Pause; a touch of impatience*) What is it that you want, I said!

(Bo enters from his room. He wears pajamas and is brush-ing his hair with two stiff military brushes.)

BO: Shh! Dearest little Mummy, you know that I'm a man who thinks before he speaks.

(He stands in front of Boman, looking straight at her, thinking, brushing his hair. Finally he slaps the brushes together.)

BO: A sandwich with cheese, one with ham, another with sausage, one with anchovies, corned beef, and six tongue sandwiches. How's that?

BOMAN: You have illusions.

BO: And a big glass of milk.

BOMAN: A big glass of milk. *(She exits with the chair covers.)*

ROLF: Bo! He isn't getting the Nobel Prize!

BO *(his arms fall weakly)*: Oh, that's all I need! Are you trying to ruin my appetite?

ROLF: It's in every one of these daily atrocities. "In spite of the extraordinary contributions Dr. Swedenhielm has made to science—"

BO: What did I say ninety-nine times last spring? He isn't a professor, I said, he'll never get the prize. He's a self-made man. And furthermore, he's a Swedenhielm. People don't quite allow for us. We're not solemn enough, we don't have that certain facial austerity. There you have it—

(Intones suddenly from I Pagliacci)

"The argument I've told you; now I let the action itself speak!"

But I'd like to know what the Nobel Committee thinks I'm going to live on! Does it say anything about that in the papers?

ROLF: Here's a column and a half trying to prove that father's research isn't original. And, of that column and a half, exactly three lines are devoted to me. Three lines! And I've worked side by side with him for ten years! (*Gets up and begins to wander back and forth*)

JULIA (*comes in from the back, working a coffee mill*): What is it, boys? What's the matter?

ROLF: He isn't getting the Nobel Prize!

JULIA: Who?

ROLF: Father, of course!

JULIA: What a shame! Would he have gotten it, otherwise?

ROLF: Otherwise! What do you mean, otherwise?

JULIA: I mean—if there hadn't been any intrigue, etcetera, and so forth—

ROLF: Ham! Intrigue!

JULIA: Poor darling papa, oh but he'll be so very sad! By the way, have you heard how I fixed Axelin? Presto! Took the role right from under her nose—

ROLF: Ham!

JULIA: Well it's just what she deserved. Poor little papa! But if I score a really smashing success, then he'll surely be glad again. Don't you think so?

ROLF: Ham!!

JULIA: And I will be a success, even if it costs me all of my clothes allowance. Axelin shall burst at the seams with envy, I can promise you that. I simply cannot fathom how you boys can be so sad! Life is much too glorious! Oh, but you're both in such a terrible humor. Here I go around grinding and grinding, and no one has a single, friendly word for me—

(*During this, she has been walking around the stage; she is now in front of the dining-room door; she turns suddenly, bowing and smiling, first to the right and then to the left, then out with a flourish.*)

ROLF (*shouting after her*): Ham! Prejudiced, egotistical, frivolous little thing, never thinks of anyone but herself. "Smashing success!" But that I, after ten years of work, can be declared a failure in three lines! Tch! That doesn't mean anything! And on top of that they called me August. August Swedenhielm! It's absolutely infamous! Don't they have a directory of the aristocracy, these scoundrels? It is a total lack of attention—an absolute contempt for this apparently meaningless detail—which actually makes your blood boil! No—the press must be reformed, that is my *preterea censeo*. It must be ripped out of its materialistic dissipation—

(*During this speech Boman has come in from the back and placed a tray with sandwiches on a table; she has begun to leave, having taken several steps toward the back, when she is interrupted by*)

BO (*who cries*): Mummy! (*profoundly, but mildly reproachful*) Mummy, you are altogether a very, very great unhappiness. Here you come with six anchovies and I have never in my life named the word anchovies. I don't even know how to spell it!

BOMAN (*turning to Rolf*): Didn't he say anchovies?

ROLF: —and this would also be the perfect task for us Swedenhielms, for whatever they might say about us—we are idealists!

BO: And furthermore it is absolutely inconceivable that I should have said anchovies, for I hate anchovies. And you know that I am as uncompromising with what I hate as I am with what I love. Caviar I said, caviar, caviar—

BOMAN: You do have illusions!

(*Boman exits at the back. Both Bo and Rolf rush to help themselves to the sandwiches.*)

BO: Well, then, the old man didn't get the money. I guess the only thing left for us is to fear God and obey His commandments. But even this requires a certain amount of ready cash.

ROLF: That's easy enough for you to say—you with your half million!

BO (*brushing his hair with one hand, eating with the other*): *Putz weg!* Since I didn't get the Nobel Prize, I break off my engagement.

ROLF: What are you thinking of?

BO: My honor. A poor boy can't marry for money. It's sordid.

ROLF: Hardly! I'd sell my honor any day for a mere fifty thousand.

BO: And I don't think you'd attract any speculators. Women with very few scruples and outstanding political figures: their honor goes for a real profit, but honest people are forced to throw their own away for the rock-bottom prices.

ROLF: That's just it! Mean, ignoble mediocrity! It's this very pettiness that's pulling me apart. There's no doubt that I was born to achieve something. And, by God, I've already made discoveries, many discoveries—marvelous, brilliant things. But they've been—you might say—a little lacking, in terms of utilitarian value. And in any case I have also received something of the old man's implicit sense of grandeur, don't you think?

BO: Well, for my part, I've received more of the implication and less of the sense . . .

ROLF: Yes, things are, as a rule, woefully provincial in this country. It's depressing, it's aggravating—

BO: What do you find most upsetting?

ROLF (*with a sudden change in his voice*): Do you want to know? But you won't say anything to father?

BO: Of course not.

ROLF: Nor to Julia?

BO: Especially not to Julia!

ROLF (*half ashamed*): I have a . . . a rather shady set of creditors.

BO (*calmly*): Well, in this day and age, who the devil hasn't?

ROLF (*upset*): You mean—? No, you can't be serious!

BO: I'm quite serious.

ROLF: Have you been patronizing loan sharks?

BO: Oh, son of a wizard and an innocent, where else could I get the money for shoe polish, champagne, and other necessities of life?

ROLF: Yes, but this is outrageous, it's absolutely abominable! A little toddler who isn't even dry behind the ears! Guilty of recklessness that I, old man that I am, am ashamed even to mention—

BO: Shh—

(*Boman enters with new sandwiches.*)

ROLF: Have . . . um . . . have you heard that there isn't even going to be a prize this year? That's a good one, don't you think?

BOMAN: Well, you don't get the Nobel Prize just because you're crazy. (*Passes Bo the tray*)

BO: Mummy—my own poor mother died when I was born, didn't she?

BOMAN: What is it now?

BO: At that time you promised, Mummy, to be my mother in her place. Isn't that right?

BOMAN: Well, what is it?

BO: Well, when I ask you for caviar, why do you come in with cod roe?

BOMAN: Did you mean caviar?

BO: Ca—vi—ar!

BOMAN: Real Russian caviar?

BO: Real—Russian—caviar!

BOMAN (*stares at him, slowly but emphatically*): He's taken leave of his senses. (*Turns and goes*)

BO: Oh, well, it looks like we'll eat cod roe. Paltry, but good. How much does it amount to?

ROLF (*nervously*): It . . . it varies, here and there. It gets very tangled, when you stop to think about it. And it can't possibly get any better, after this—since the press has seen fit to strip me of both honor and merit. In three lines! Three lines! Tch! But that doesn't matter! Let 'em come!

BO: Who?

ROLF: Everybody! And all the rest of them!

BO: Who are you talking about?

ROLF: I don't know! Everybody who wants to hold me back— from—from achieving the pinnacle of success. But I salute them! Even if they were to drag our honorable name through the mud, I still will salute them. I have the devil's own humor, that's what I'll say to these gentlemen. And they'd better watch their step! Come on, let's empty a bottle of champagne.

BO: At ten-thirty in the morning?

ROLF: Just out of spite! Or else, let's go out somewhere. I have a strong desire to present myself—

(*Julia comes rushing in from the back, screaming and frightened—in a melodious and dulcet manner.*)

JULIA: Good God! He isn't coming after me, is he?

ROLF: Who?

JULIA: The blackguard! There's a reporter in the hall!

ROLF: Bravo! Bo, do me a favor—drive him out!

BO: Drive him out, righto! (*Going with a long stride and using the hairbrushes vigorously, he exits at the back.*)

ROLF: It's so typical of these vampires to come pushing their way into private homes—it could be the middle of the night, for all they care. Who went to the door?

JULIA: I did.

ROLF: In that outfit?

JULIA: Well, I went running, of course, as soon as possible.

ROLF: Then how do you know he's a reporter?

JULIA: That's what he said through the keyhole. I stayed just long enough to shake hands and give him a quasi smile à la Duse. After all, you can't be openly rude to the press.

ROLF: Ham! Just because a gossip monger wants to root around in your father's misery—

JULIA: Gossip monger! He was from *Dagbladet.*

ROLF: What's that? Umm. Well, if the fellow's that persistent, I guess I could spare him a few seconds.

BO (*enters*): He vanished into thin air.

ROLF: Vanished? Wasn't he insistent, demanding?

BO: Not in the least.

ROLF: My God! Call him back!

BO: What?

ROLF: Well, damn it, you'll never set the press straight if you just snub them.

BO: True! (*Goes to the window and opens it*) Pst! Pst! Hello! Hello! Good sir, young man—yes, exactly—you! Come back on the double! Pst! Pst! (*Closes the window*)

ROLF: Leave me alone. I need to collect my thoughts. And would you be so kind as to get yourself into something decent? Ham!

JULIA: Are you implying that theater people aren't respectable? I'll have you know: we're absolute prudes!

ROLF: The morning after, yes.

BO (*at his door*): And if you should happen to start talking about me, don't forget I hold the Swedish high altitude record.

(*He goes into his room.*)

JULIA: And throw in something about my part. You can say that Axelin fought like a beast! (*Throws him a kiss and exits*)

(*Bo sticks his head out of his room.*)

BO: And the King's Medal for marksmanship!

(*Julia sticks her head out of her room.*)

JULIA: Five costumes, don't forget. Five costume changes in three acts!

(*Rolf waves them into their rooms and sits at the secretary. The reporter comes in. As he comes through the door, one of the charwomen comes in, too. They hesitate, each waiting for the other to go first. Finally the reporter enters, followed by the charwoman. Rolf, in the meantime, has been making an effort to appear busy at the secretary. He looks over his shoulder and says, rather sharply*)

ROLF: Out!

(*Both the reporter and the charwoman stop. After an instant, the charwoman exits. The reporter, somewhat nervously, holds his ground.*)

REPORTER: Uh—did you mean me or—er, the lady who left?

ROLF: Kindly take a seat.

REPORTER: Thank you.

(*He sits near the door, but rises at once and bows.*)

REPORTER: My name is Pedersen, Valfrid Pedersen.

(*Rolf nods.*)

ROLF: Rolf Swedenhielm, Junior.

(*Pedersen resumes his seat.*)

PEDERSEN: Oh! Junior! Then it's not the engineer himself I have the pleasure of speaking to, only his son. I mean—I don't have the honor of speaking to your father—I'm speaking to you.

ROLF: Yes. You are speaking to me.

PEDERSEN: Oh, yes. Fine name, Swedenhielm. Now mine's Danish—but we've been here since great-grandpa—uh, he came to Sweden as a drummer boy.

ROLF: Really.

PEDERSEN (*self-conscious*): Er . . . yes . . . drummer boy . . . you know . . . one of those little fellows . . .

ROLF: Is that what you've come to tell me about?

PEDERSEN: Oh no, of course not. But you see, I'm not very good at this. It's my first interview.

ROLF: Yes, I see what you mean. Are you on the staff of *Dagbladet?*

PEDERSEN: No, but I hope to be.

ROLF: You really think you'll make it?

PEDERSEN: Oh, yes. I've got a heck of a lot of drive, once I know where I'm going. I read in the papers that Dr. Swedenhielm would receive the Nobel Prize in . . . ah . . . er . . .

ROLF: Physics.

PEDERSEN: Yes, you see, these technical terms are just impossible to remember.

ROLF: But every one of the morning newspapers clearly states that my father will not receive the Nobel Prize.

PEDERSEN: What did you say? I had no idea! But that'll certainly make my story even timelier. What do you know! I did have the right instinct, in any case.

ROLF (*curtly*): What do you wish to know?

PEDERSEN: Yes, tell me! What do you really think people want to know about such a man?

ROLF: Do you wish to have some general information about my father?

PEDERSEN: That would be magniminious! But wait a minute, I've got a book and a pencil . . . (*takes them out and strikes himself on both the right and the left vest pockets*) And here's the sharpener, and here's the eraser. All right: anchors aweigh.

ROLF: My father belongs to one of Sweden's oldest and finest families. One of our ancestors was a signatory to the Treaty of Westphalia and was, perhaps, the most important person at the Congress. His brother's son fought under Charles the Twelfth, and was perhaps his most able—

PEDERSEN: Pardon the interruption, but . . . who was the charming young lady who let me in?

ROLF: My sister, Julia Körner, perhaps one of the most outstanding talents in today's theater. In the very near future she will create an important major role—which a number of futile intrigues vainly tried to do her out of, and in which she will display a wardrobe of unprecedented luxury—

PEDERSEN: Say, that thing she was wearing, some sort of negligee, wasn't it?

ROLF (*annoyed*): Yes.

PEDERSEN: Ye Gods and little fishes, so sweet!—oh dear, then there was that Carolinian, perhaps the bravest of all.

ROLF: But it is in the scientific world that our family has done its best work. Perhaps Linné's most famous disciple—

PEDERSEN: Not so fast! Not so fast, please!

ROLF: Don't you take shorthand?

PEDERSEN: No, holy Moses, that's much too difficult. (*Writing*) "Perhaps Linné's most famous disciple . . ."

ROLF: . . . was named Swedenhielm, and my father is perhaps one of the greatest inventors of all—

PEDERSEN: Wait a minute. We seem to have a lot of perhapses. Perhaps the bravest, perhaps the most famous . . . It doesn't sound right, style-wise. Couldn't we just call him *the* greatest inventor of all time? And stop chewing the scenery—

ROLF: Why not? It's your responsibility.

PEDERSEN: You see, I think quite a lot about style. As a matter of fact, I'm a writer myself. You may have heard of me. Pedersen, Valfrid Pedersen?

ROLF: I'm sorry.

PEDERSEN: No—I've noticed that I'm not very well known. Believe it or not, it's not much fun being an author in Sweden!

ROLF: I can imagine.

PEDERSEN: If you only knew how it feels to be completely ignored!

ROLF: I have an idea.

PEDERSEN: Sometimes I wish that drummer boy had stayed in Denmark. And the critics! When they trouble to mention me at all . . . the Swedish press . . . sir, the Swedish press— pardon the expression, but they're a bunch of damned scandal- mongers!

ROLF: I share your sentiments and regard this so-called inter- view as ended. (*He rises.*)

PEDERSEN (*rising, beside himself*): No! Please! Just think what this means to me! It's my debut as a reporter, after all. I haven't found out a thing about your famous father. What's he like? Why did he decide to become an inventor? There must be something strange about him. My friends are always saying to me, "You must be a little cracked to be an author." And maybe this is something like that. No—please! Don't get angry again! I mean, there must be something that drives a man to become an inventor . . . ?

ROLF (*superior, gently ironic*): Yes. A powerful force. It's called genius.

PEDERSEN: Ah.

ROLF: And as far as my father is concerned, another drive: a sense of duty—duty to uphold a great family's proud tradition. Grandfather was mayor of Nora. A small town, his salary was small, his estate insignificant. My father is a thoroughly self-made man. His genius has had to fight against unbelievable economic and ethical difficulties. No one has ever worked as hard as he. They can steal the fruits of his labor, but they can never rob him of the honor he has won.

PEDERSEN (*writing so that his fingers tangle themselves into a cramp*): ". . . honor he has won"! Now that's what I call style. And that about genius was also tremendously well put, don't you think? It's—called—genius! You might say that about us authors, too. I mean, when ignorant people come and ask why we decided to become authors: "It's—called—genius!"

ROLF: Say whatever you want to!

PEDERSEN: Another thing. In my prose I generally use the word "father" because it has more solemn connotations, while in verse I use "dad" because I find it easier for rhyming. What advice do you have for me in this matter—

ROLF: I—I advise you to go!

PEDERSEN: Please—just a few seconds more! I mean, I haven't found out anything about *you*.

ROLF: Well, no one's interested in me.

PEDERSEN: Don't say that. You're the son of a famous man. That's always something interesting. Just a few words about you personally. Personally!

ROLF: Give him your blasted little finger, and he takes the

whole hand. But I guess I could say a few words about my insignificance. (*He sinks into deep thought.*)

PEDERSEN (*ready to write*): An only son?

ROLF: Yes . . . no . . . that is, I have a younger brother— one of those who's always in the clouds.

PEDERSEN: What?

ROLF: An aviator, you understand—a lieutenant—with a medal, gold or something—holds some sort of record—we can talk about him later.

(*Boman enters, followed by two old charwomen. They are carrying a stepladder. They go to the window, left. At the moment Rolf has his back toward them.*)

ROLF: What can be said about my modest person can't be summed up in just three lines, it's true—still, I'll be brief, since publicity is something I loathe—(*He turns, sees Boman and the other two at the window.*)

ROLF: What are you doing?

BOMAN (*calmly*): Taking down the curtains.

ROLF: Today?

BOMAN: It's the end of the month.

ROLF: But can't you see I'm being interviewed?

BOMAN: It's the end of the month.

ROLF: Auntie, once and for all, I forbid it.

BOMAN: It's the end of the month. (*She goes up the ladder and begins taking down the curtains.*)

PEDERSEN (*curiously*): Good heavens, is she a relative?

ROLF (*a bit unwillingly*): Don't pay any attention to her. She's (*he taps his forehead*) a little . . . (*Bitterly, but with regained tranquillity*) So. The press wishes to know something about Rolf Swedenhielm, Jr. You may say that I am— are you listening? You may say that I am the scientist who has made the most important—

PEDERSEN: We could go back to the perhapses again here. We haven't used them for quite a while. We could say, "Perhaps the scientist who perhaps has made perhaps the—"

ROLF: Three perhapses in eight words?

PEDERSEN: No, that *is* too many—

ROLF: —the most important research into the effect of alternating current on—

PEDERSEN: Stop! No terms, please. The public doesn't like that. Popular, popular, popular!

ROLF: To the point, then. My father's tremendous inventions would never have been possible without my unselfish and intelligent collaboration. For ten years I have worked faithfully by his side, and I venture to presume that his honor will not be detracted from by emphasizing my share in the work. In fact, without my help, he wouldn't be the world-famous genius he is today.

BOMAN (*who during this speech has dropped the curtains and slowly turned toward Rolf*): Now listen to *him!*

ROLF (*nervously*): What—uh—what are you talking about?

BOMAN (*calmly, but emphatically*): I suppose he's taken leave of his senses?

ROLF: If the name of Swedenhielm means anything at all, some of the credit is mine. Not that I want to belittle father's efforts, on the contrary—

JULIA (*enters from the right, she is now dressed*): Bravo! Bravo! Very generous of you, since father is a world-famous inventor and you're not known anywhere, other than possibly in the Opera Cellar.

ROLF: I'm not a histrionic exhibitionist! I don't display myself in the weeklies or the film magazines. I don't start any fashions, don't sell kisses for charity, don't pose on the local promenades, don't flirt with the press, don't arrange scandals and intrigues! But I work! Quietly. And my father, with all due respect—

BO (*enters from the right, in uniform*): It's ridiculous to compare yourself with father! I might as well try to say *I'm* the one who gave the Swedenhielm name its brilliance. My flight record on the Ystad-Haparanda route shouldn't be forgotten, should it, Mr.———?

PEDERSEN: Pedersen, Valfrid Pedersen. Unfortunately, however, I haven't forgotten it.

BO: Unfortunately?

PEDERSEN: Actually, I've never heard of it.

BO: There! You see how flying is encouraged in this part of the world. Believe me, it's not much fun being a Swedish aviator.

JULIA: You should try being a Swedish actress! That's the most ghastly, soul-destroying, heart-breaking business on earth, isn't it, Pedersen?

ROLF: *Mr.* Pedersen.

JULIA: Oh, we're already old friends. I think we understand each other, don't we, Pedersen?

PEDERSEN: Certainly! And how! You bet!

JULIA: For instance: I just got a role in a new play, a tremendous role, like this. (*Demonstrates*) It was nip and tuck between me and Axelin. You surely know Axelin. Isn't she fascinating?

PEDERSEN: The one with big blue eyes!

JULIA: Well, they're green now and several sizes larger. She fought like a beast to get this role. As far as I'm concerned, she could have had it, but intrigues don't always work. I can only say: let this role pass from me. It's killing me!

PEDERSEN: Is it *so* potent?

JULIA: Is it? Just listen! It's going to open in just fourteen days.

I have to create five complete ensembles in just fourteen days! Yes, I said create—we can't allow theatrical stereotypes on our stage. I have to search, grope, dream, suffer my way to perfection. And, when I'm finally sure that I've created something of value, sure enough, the play closes after one week. Then it has to be scrapped—it can't be used in a new piece. Isn't it just heart-rending?

ROLF: Then why scheme to get the part?

JULIA: Why? Because I have a sense of duty! Because I feel that I alone can do this role!

ROLF: Just the way Axelin feels, I'll bet.

JULIA: But she can't—not in just fourteen days. No, you can say what you want about theater people, but we have a sense of duty. I can, I will do this part, even if I have to live at the dressmaker's. But such is the life of a Swedish actress!

(*One of the charwomen enters with a bucket in one hand and several letters in the other. She puts the letters on the secretary and goes on to the windows.*)

ROLF (*walking back and forth*): In Sweden the unwanted child is, and always will be, the scientist. He doesn't want to be discussed, and he seldom is. He seeks no crass encouragement and as a result receives no encouragement. He despises publicity, and the public regards him as negligible at best. He loathes the press, and the press covers his life's work in three lines! So you see, Pedersen my boy, it isn't a bit pleasant being a scientist in this country. (*He nearly stumbles over the old woman's pail.*) Out of the way, you old frump!

THE OLD WOMAN (*offended*): It's no fun to be a scrubwoman either. In the better houses.

(*Rolf sits down at the secretary and turns to Pedersen.*)

ROLF: Is there anything else you'd like to know?

PEDERSEN: No, thank you, I think I've heard enough for today.

ROLF: Today? Isn't this going to be in tomorrow's paper?

PEDERSEN: Oh, no. These impressions must have time to settle.
In about two weeks I will have evolved a detailed picture of
a famous scientist's family life. One more thing: what re-
lation, exactly, is the lady on the ladder?

ROLF: Miss Marta Boman. My father's sister-in-law. She has
been mother to us ever since our own mother died twenty
years ago. But for that matter she very seldom says anything.

BO: Mummy, you're going to be in the newspaper.

BOMAN (*curtsies on the ladder*): Oh, heavenly days, that's
much too great an honor for me! (*Garrulous*) I can only
say, sir, that it hasn't always been very easy to satisfy Mr.
Swedenhielm. He is particularly difficult about food, and he
insists on his wine. However, I do suppose there are worse
gentlemen than he. You see, my dear sister and I were Cop-
persmith Boman's only daughters in Askersund, that is, if you
know who *he* was. No, I don't suppose you would. Well
it wasn't much of a match for Swedenhielm, although he
was poorer than our family. But just between you and me,
he's always been rather conceited. And I can say on perfect
knowledge, you'll understand I'm sure, there's a lot to do
in this house, lots to look after, lots to keep clean. Lots to
do and not much money to do it with. And if you had a
couple of boys like these, you'd also know what it costs
just to keep the youngest in uniforms and the other—

BO: Mummy! Mummy! You're ruining us! Who the devil
prompted you to say these things?

BOMAN: When you're going to be in the newspapers, you have
to tell the truth.

(*Pedersen acknowledges this and bows to Boman, who
curtsies.*)

PEDERSEN: I'm very grateful, Miss Boman. Now just one more

thing. Is there, by any chance, a famous dog or cat in the family?

ROLF: No pets.

JULIA: Yes, I have a fascinating canary. Would you like to see it?

PEDERSEN: Oh, that would be magniminious! You know, a serious and factual interview needs a poetic ending—for the reader's sake. And a little bird is, no matter how you look at it, a little bird!

ROLF (*with a letter in his hand*): I wonder what this is. It looks like father's handwriting.

BO: It is. Mailed in Gothenburg.

(*Julia has become aware of what they are saying.*)

JULIA: Papa? Has papa written?

ROLF: I don't understand.

BOMAN: If Swedenhielm has written a letter, it's all over with him.

JULIA: Quiet, Mutti!

BO: But he's supposed to come home tonight.

ROLF: If I know father, he's either sick, or he wants us to send him money.

BO: He knows we can't do that.

JULIA (*taking the letter*): Let me see. Poor papa. I wonder what's the matter.

BO (*taking back the letter*): If he had only left a return address. Now we can't possibly know anything.

ROLF (*taking the letter*): Not a word. I just don't understand. Why has he written? Why? And what does he want? He should have come home today, I'm positive. It's an absolute enigma!

PEDERSEN: Couldn't—couldn't you open the letter?

(*Silence. Rolf glares at Pedersen, as do Julia and Bo. Rolf*

*takes a letter opener from the secretary and slowly opens
the letter. As he reads, he becomes more and more grave.
He finishes, hands the letter to Bo without a word. Julia
snatches the letter from him and reads.*)

JULIA: Papa! He's dead! He's dead!

(*They look at each other.*)

ROLF: Why believe the worst? Why?

BO: Don't get excited!

JULIA (*sniffles*): He's taken his life!

ROLF: You're exaggerating—

BO: There's not a word here about— (*Sudden silence*)

JULIA: Then why should he write, "If we never see each other
again . . ." (*She takes the letter from Rolf and continues
reading.*) "If we never see each other again, my children,
forgive your old father, who always tried to do his best for
you . . ." (*Her voice gives way to sobs, and she sits down,
crying. Bo strokes her hair; Rolf stands in gloomy contem-
plation. Boman comes up to the secretary, takes the letter,
looks at it, and then wipes a tear from her eye.*)

BOMAN (*on the verge of tears*): Swedenhielm was sensitive, all
right.

JULIA: They drove him to it!

BOMAN: Though he looked strong enough.

(*Pedersen also wipes away a tear. Then he bows in turn
to Rolf, Julia, Bo, and Boman. Only Boman, with a little
curtsy, acknowledges his bow. He goes toward the door,
bowing to the charwoman as he goes. He turns in the doorway as if he were going to say something, but thinks better
of it. He bows once more to all of them and is about to go
when the front door slams and a voice is heard intoning,
without words, the "Toreador Song" from* Carmen. *It is
Rolf Swedenhielm, Sr. He is in high spirits. He marches in*

*as he sings, waving a small overnight case. He doesn't stop
for Pedersen, but walks right in. Pedersen bows as he passes.
Julia jumps up and runs to him.*)

JULIA: Papa!

(*Swedenhielm does not stop his march or his song. He
puts an arm around Julia and takes her with him as he moves
about the stage.*)

SWEDENHIELM (*putting words to the "Toreador Song"*): Good
morning, children; good morning, children; good morning,
children; good morning, children! (*He stops center stage.*)

SWEDENHIELM: Here am I; where are you?

JULIA: How could you bring yourself to scare us so?

SWEDENHIELM: Scare you?

JULIA: Did you write this letter or not?

SWEDENHIELM (*looks at the letter, a bit ashamed*): Yes, actually
I did. I was so damned miserable. You see, I realized that the
trip was all for nothing. Couldn't raise a penny! That newspaper campaign closed all the doors to me—and now even
the Nobel Prize got away. I realized that I had to let my
patents go. Sell them. Let others make a fortune on my life's
work. One can be miserable for less, my girl.

JULIA: Poor Papa.

SWEDENHIELM: And when you sit alone in a boring place: poor
food, a Lubeck ham that was no more Lubeck than Boman,
a Chambertin just as sour as she is, and not even one pretty
waitress to console yourself with. No, it's the devil's work
to keep your spirits up in those circumstances. I felt the
blackness of night over everything. I thought—it's best
if you disappear in one way or another, old wretch. I felt
it so strongly I didn't think I'd ever see my home again. Can
you imagine, that's just what I thought!

JULIA: Certainly I can imagine! But now you're happy again?

SWEDENHIELM: Now I'm happy, damned happy!

ROLF: Has something happened to encourage you?

SWEDENHIELM: No, nothing in particular.

ROLF: Did you get hold of some money?

SWEDENHIELM: Impossible! But, damn it, I can't spend my whole life sulking. I had enough of that yesterday. No, let them come! Let them take my patents, my furniture, my old slippers! They can rob—but they can't steal me, myself. And besides I've got a few assets that nobody can touch.

BO: You have! What?

SWEDENHIELM: Well, for one thing, I've got a tall, healthy, young villain of a son (*he goes up to Bo and slaps him on the back*), who's going to be a general someday, because there is no higher rank. And I've got a daughter who is a brilliantly gifted, beautiful, and refined actress.

JULIA: Yes, you do!

SWEDENHIELM: And then I have my first-born, my alter ego, my colleague, who carries half of the work load—and the other half as well—

ROLF: Don't make jokes!

SWEDENHIELM: —and whom I have to thank, if I have succeeded in bringing anything about—

ROLF: Oh, Father—I won't hear that kind of nonsense—

SWEDENHIELM: Well, there it is, and that's how it ought to be. The name of Swedenhielm will go up, not down. I have talent, but after me comes the one who's going to make it—the genius.

ROLF: Now I ask you! You ought to be ashamed! And on top of everything, in front of a stranger.

SWEDENHIELM: Yes. Who is it?

PEDERSEN: Pedersen, Valfrid Pedersen. Journalist.

SWEDENHIELM: Farewell, Pedersen, we shall meet at Philippi!
(*Pedersen doesn't understand.*)

SWEDENHIELM (*stronger*): Farewell, Pedersen!

PEDERSEN: But I was going to see the ca—ca—canary.

SWEDENHIELM (*shouts*): Farewell, Pedersen!

(*Pedersen disappears. During the last few lines Boman has resumed her place on the ladder.*)

SWEDENHIELM: And then I have Boman. Good God! Woman, what are you doing? Housecleaning again?

BOMAN (*busy with the curtains*): It's the end of the month.

SWEDENHIELM: So it is. But it's also the day Swedenhielm comes home from a hard and tiring journey. You knew that, Boman!

BOMAN: The calendar is dependable, Swedenhielm isn't. I'll take the calendar.

SWEDENHIELM: And I'll take a cane, and thrash you with an— (*He covers his mouth suddenly—then manages to control himself.*) Boman, I defy you! I will not let myself get angry! Absolutely not! It's a little bit of hell—but it's going to be a happy hell! Children: that person on the ladder there wants to keep us from enjoying ourselves in our own home. All right, we bow before superior forces. We'll go out. Have breakfast. Wherever you want! No luxuries, no extravagance! It can't be like that nowadays, blast it. Something simple, but exquisite!

BO: Caviar!

SWEDENHIELM: Imported Russian, of course!

JULIA: But Papa, have you got enough money?

SWEDENHIELM: Oh, money! If you scrape around in your pockets, you'll always find enough for a bottle of champagne!

CURTAIN

ACT II

*The scene is the same; the curtains have been taken down,
the carpets taken up. Some of the furniture from the dining
room has been brought in and arranged among the furniture
already there as well as possible—among other things, a
large settee, which stands with its back toward the footlights.
The doors into the dining room are closed.*

Several hours later.

*Rolf, Julia, and Bo are sitting in chairs from various parts
of the house. Rolf is smoking a cigar, and at the moment he
is at peace with the world. Julia is smoking a cigarette and
clearly shows signs of discomfort; she counteracts the cold
by throwing a nearby Siberian sheepskin rug over her
shoulders. Bo sits leaning forward with his head between his
hands, staring moodily straight ahead.*

*The silence is interrupted here, and at other points in this
act, by the sound of energetic scouring brushes coming from
the adjoining room.*

ROLF (*breaking the silence*): A light, little breakfast. What's to
be said about it? Rash? Well, it did get a little expensive. On
the other hand, there was value received. Not only the body,
but even the soul is stimulated to a stronger, quicker, more
agile operation. One learns not to underestimate one's own
potentials, one's abilities—which is a common mistake among
us Swedes. One's self-reliance is spurred. One views one's
opportunities in an entirely new light. No, even though
there's a bit of wantonness in the Swede's desire for festivity,

it has good moral grounds. I'm all for such a little breakfast, now and then.

JULIA: If only we weren't forced to freeze afterward.

ROLF: It's the clamminess of cleanliness, that's all.

JULIA: Why does Mutti have to scrub this place so often? It's never very dirty.

BO: Possibly because it's scrubbed so often.

JULIA: But how does she pay all these cleaning women?

BO: She sells your empty cold-cream jars. By the dozen.

JULIA: You're sweet today!

BO: I'm sleepy.

JULIA: Sleep! And refrain from committing these gross sins against your unfortunate sister.

BO: I can't. I'm too sad.

ROLF: He's waiting for Astrid.

JULIA: Oh, then I understand my poor, beloved little brother. Waiting for Astrid *is* dreadful!

BO: Be quiet!

JULIA: She's insinuating, intolerant, and incomparably un-lettered, uncultured, and incurably ignorant—not to men-tion the fact that she's awkward, awful, and appalling!

ROLF: Bo's thinking of breaking it off.

JULIA (*fallen from the skies*): What? Is he crazy? Why should he break it off?

ROLF: It's his doubting conscience.

JULIA: Breaking up with a girl who has a cold half million?

ROLF: Yes, and in some ways, I think he's right. The Sweden-hielm family is on the brink of disaster. Father's going to crash; I'm going to crash. Strictly speaking, it's not right to continue with an engagement which began under entirely different circumstances. The girl should have a chance to get out of it, at any rate.

JULIA: You're a pleasant one! A moment ago you looked so cheerfully on our situation.

ROLF: Yes, but now I begin to decline.

(*A solitary snore shakes the room. It comes from Sweden-hielm, Sr., who is asleep on the large settee. The children are startled by the noise.*)

BO (*enviously*): He isn't sad. He's sleeping.

ROLF: That's his strength. When boredom sets in, he goes to sleep. When he wakes up, everything is all right again.

(*The door to the dining room opens, and Astrid enters, finding her way through the furniture. She wears a magnificent fur coat. When she comes downstage, we see that she is in her stocking feet and that she carries her shoes in her hand. As she enters, Bo gets up to greet her. The other two remain seated.*)

ASTRID (*softly, just above a whisper*): What a friendly reception. The way Boman looked at me I didn't dare walk across her polished floor. It wasn't enough to take my overshoes off, so off these came, too.

(*She sits in Bo's chair. He takes her shoes and falls on his knees before her. He kisses her feet, puts on her shoes, kisses both of her hands, and rises.*)

ASTRID: And on my lips.

(*He hesitates, then kisses her.*)

ASTRID: Well, you all look very comfortable. Is that Papa sleeping under the tablecloth?

(*Bo nods.*)

JULIA: When we Swedenhielms are alone with each other, we always have a good time—even on cleaning days.

ASTRID: Thanks. (*To Bo*) Shall we go in your room and talk?

BO: They're cleaning there, too.

ASTRID: In Julia's then?

JULIA: Julia's there! (*She goes out with majestic poise.*)

ROLF (*rising*): My dear sister-in-law-to-be, today we Sweden-hielms feel like being somewhat sensitive. Oversensitive, too. Don't take offense. (*Exits at the back*)

ASTRID: What's wrong with all of you? The whole house is upside down. When I asked Boman, she only said, "It's the end of the month."

BO: What's wrong with us? Disaster!

ASTRID: More than usual?

(*Bo goes quietly up to the settee and bends over it. There is another snore. He turns to Astrid.*)

BO: More than usual. The old man's creditors have sent an ultimatum: "Your money or your life!" The Nobel Prize is out the window; the press campaign has closed the doors. He might as well try to hold onto the wind as try to hold onto his patents. To top it off, Rolf's private finances are hopelessly tangled, to put it mildly. Julia's up to her eyebrows in debts, and so am I.

ASTRID: Big debts?

BO: Awkward debts.

ASTRID: Well, I have money.

BO: But I don't. I'll probably have to resign my commission.

ASTRID (*after a moment*): Thanks! Then I'll break our engage-ment!

BO (*quiet, moodily*): Thanks.

(*Profound silence in the room; the scouring goes on with regular cadence in the adjoining room, and the silence is again broken by a snore.*)

ASTRID (*softly*): Come and kiss me.

(*He goes to her, hesitates, and then kisses her.*)

ASTRID: Why did you say "thanks"?

BO: Now . . . now I don't have to break our engagement myself.

ASTRID: Were you going to do that?

BO: Yes.

ASTRID: I see. Yes, that would sound nice. "He broke the engagement. Poor girl—"

BO (*interrupting angrily*): It wouldn't sound at all nice! Well, now it can be the other way around.

ASTRID (*after a pause*): Why do you want to do this?

BO: I'm not answering that.

ASTRID: Oh, yes, you are!

BO: Shh— (*Silence, another snore*) Do you really want to know?

ASTRID: Yes.

BO: It's unpleasant, but true: I'm not in love with you.

ASTRID (*after a moment*): Couldn't you think of something better than that? So you're not in love with me? Maybe you never were?

BO: Never.

ASTRID: Not a bit?

BO: Not a bit.

ASTRID (*softly*): Give me a kiss.

BO: No. (*He moves away from her.*)

ASTRID: Why did you ask me to marry you, then?

BO: Because—you have money. A cold half million would tempt anyone—

ASTRID (*vehemently*): Oh, damn you!

BO: Shh—

(*Silence, another snore, scouring.*)

ASTRID: Am I poor now?

BO: No, but I am.

ASTRID: And that's why you want to call it off? My sweet little darling, you're making yourself a bit ridiculous.

BO: Not at all. We always thought of Papa's patents as being worth a fortune, that is, a potential fortune. I wanted to get married, and naturally I looked for a wife who could at least pay for her own clothes and put something into the household budget. Economic equality, you see. It's a sound principle. Well, you're rich, you're pretty, chic, and you're a splendid girl. I thought an awful lot of you, and I still do.

ASTRID: Thanks.

BO: But what they call love—not a bit.

ASTRID: Couldn't we possibly marry without love? They say it can work out successfully.

BO: Impossible. I'm irrevocably poor. And a poor boy exploiting a rich marriage—that's a bit degrading. It's letting a wealthy young lady purchase herself a lapdog.

ASTRID: Such a darling lapdog—six foot three. Here, little Goliath! Come to the floor!

BO: I'm glad you can joke. But I *would* become dependent on you—take nearly everything from your hand . . . that's not for me. A man should support himself, at least. (*Suddenly angry*) All right, sit there and sneer. You think it's terribly old-fashioned, and it is. But that's nothing against the Swedenhielms—because we are damned old-fashioned!

ASTRID: Shh— Come and give me a kiss.

BO: No.

(*Silence, snoring, scrubbing*)

ASTRID (*her voice changes*): Well, maybe it's just as you say. You're not in love with me. Is that it?

BO (*with difficulty*): Yes—that's just what I said!

ASTRID: Are—are you in love with someone else?

BO (*after a moment*): I won't answer.

ASTRID (*stronger*): Are you in love with someone else?

BO: I won't answer

ASTRID (*after a moment, threatening*): Do you want me—to lose my patience?

BO: Just don't wake up the old man!

(*Silence, snoring, scrubbing*)

ASTRID (*whispering*): Come and give me a kiss.

BO: No, I said!

(*Astrid comes up to him and puts her arms around his neck; he tries to hold her away, but suddenly takes her in his arms, holds her tightly, and kisses her.*)

ASTRID (*tenderly*): You're very clever, my dear.

BO (*between kisses*): What do you mean?

ASTRID: I mean that your kiss betrays what your lips deny.

(*Silence. Rolf comes in from the dining room. He is in a hurry and doesn't notice that he is entering at an inopportune moment.*)

ROLF (*whispering, urgently*): Excuse me—excuse me—but something important has come up. I just got a letter. Bo, do you know a man named Eriksson?

BO (*disturbed*): Eriksson? I know lots of Erikssons. What is he?

ROLF: He's a— Well, I can't rightly say. Come in here a minute. Astrid will excuse you, just for a minute.

(*Rolf takes Bo by the arm and leads him off. Astrid turns toward the footlights and stretches herself, savoring the warmth of the kisses and releasing her happiness and her triumph in a smile. Over the back of the sofa Swedenhielm now lifts his head, over which the tablecloth hangs like a veil down to his shoulders. He frees himself from under the cloth and rises. Astrid turns around.*)

ASTRID: Well, then—good morning!

SWEDENHIELM (*crosses to her*): Good morning to the young— good evening to the old. (*He kisses her on the cheek, then takes her chin in his hand and looks at her closely.*) Well?

ASTRID: Well, what?

SWEDENHIELM: Did you two come to a decision?

ASTRID: Have you been listening?

SWEDENHIELM: Not much. When I snored I couldn't hear a thing, but between snores I picked up a word or two.

ASTRID: Your son's very bright, don't you think?

SWEDENHIELM: Perhaps not so terribly bright, but he's a decent, honorable boy.

ASTRID: Well, what do you think?

SWEDENHIELM (*after a moment*): I think he's right.

ASTRID: Right! To break our engagement? Maybe you gave him the idea?

SWEDENHIELM (*smiling*): No! When it is a question of honor, my boys decide for themselves. And thank God for that!

ASTRID: Is this a question of honor?

SWEDENHIELM: He thinks it is, and so it *is* a question of honor. But why take it so tragically? You can certainly wait a few years until the boy has something to offer you.

ASTRID: And in the meantime I must content myself with absolute boredom!

SWEDENHIELM: The only absolute boredom is having nothing to wait for.

ASTRID: And just because Bo doesn't want his wife to provide for him, we have to give up our happiness.

SWEDENHIELM: A man who can give up happiness is a strong man, and a strong man is happy. I am indeed the boy's father, but I know him a little all the same. He isn't a brilliant intellect, he has no great interests, he's just a good-natured young blade, but he has one thing that balances all the rest:

he has a sense of honor. If he were a great musician, and you knew that you could save his musical genius only by leaving him—could you do it?

ASTRID: Of course.

SWEDENHIELM: Well, he's no genius, but he's an honorable man. And you should never tamper with a man's sense of honor.

ASTRID: How you can talk! Fortunately we have arrived at quite a different conclusion.

SWEDENHIELM: He didn't break the engagement?

ASTRID: He never will!

SWEDENHIELM: Then you must, for the sake of your own happiness. Happiness isn't really as necessary as you think. It's not necessary at all. But in any case. And by happiness, I suppose, you mean happiness in love?

ASTRID: How you can guess!

SWEDENHIELM: But love will be gone the day you say: remember, it's *my* money!

ASTRID: That day will never come, never!

SWEDENHIELM: It *may* be that you have such a noble character, that this day will never come. But the matter also has a practical side. Unfortunately, Bo has rather expensive tastes, and a rich wife could never discipline him in the lessons of thrift—

ASTRID: He can have exclusive control of everything I own, every last penny!

SWEDENHIELM: Thank you. And you might have a cottage full of children—

ASTRID: —and I would provide for them, even if I had to go out begging!

SWEDENHIELM: More pathetic than ever—you've already been going down for such a long time!

ASTRID: There's no going down if people can remain true to each other—

SWEDENHIELM: But one fine day he may fall in love with someone else.

ASTRID (*hurt*): That's all right! I can do the same thing!

SWEDENHIELM: Wouldn't improve matters. And what would
you do then?

ASTRID: Get a divorce.

SWEDENHIELM: Why should he divorce you? Unless the new
one is richer, or just as rich as you are. He no longer loves
you, but he has probably learned to value your money.

ASTRID: Well, he must have at least a shred of honor!

SWEDENHIELM: Honor? But you don't put any value on his
honor. Besides, his new flame might be poor. He may feel
obligated to leave her well provided for—

ASTRID (*infuriated, quickly*): Remember, it's *my* money!

SWEDENHIELM (*smiling*): Bang! I knew it would come, but I
didn't think it would come so soon.

ASTRID (*defeated, on the verge of tears*): You are the most
frightening, the most evil old troll there is! Why must you
old people always be so detestable!

SWEDENHIELM: True! We're born human beings, but age into
trolls. We become less attractive as the years accumulate; but
we do become more sensible.

ASTRID: Oh, yes, it's very sensible to have such an exaggerated
idea of honor as you two do!

SWEDENHIELM: Very sensible. One shouldn't sell one's birthright for a mess of pottage. Our honor is our birthright—

ASTRID: And I'm the pottage?

SWEDENHIELM: And very delicious pottage. But not to be com-
pared with the satisfaction of a clear conscience. When a
man has forty years of hard work behind him, and his hands
are as empty as a new-born child's, then he knows the real
value and meaning of honor. My dear, in a few months or

perhaps in a year or two, you'll see a tall old man shuffling along the streets of Stockholm, threadbare, ragged, green from mold and blue with cold, muttering to himself, a bit confused, taunted by children in the streets, cursed by motorists, buffeted by the crowd, pitied by the charitable, moved on by the police—a cartoon character, brother of bums, protected by soft-hearted street vendors. Who is that? Just some poor devil who thinks he was a great inventor. What is he? A crank. What does he have? Who knows? Where does he live? Who knows? What does he live on? Who knows! What's his name? Who knows! (*With rising emotion*) His name is Swedenhielm, gentlemen, and he bears the name with honor. What is he? He is deliriously happy! They took everything from him: credit, fame, fortune, home, happiness—everything but honor. That he cradled in his arms, guarded jealously, never let go of. He was robbed, but he never stole. He was falsely dealt with, but he never betrayed. You made him into an abortive genius, an idiot, a crank. But a happy crank—happy unto death. Because happiness and honor are the very same thing! (*He sinks into a chair, a little ashamed.*) Well, there you have a concise picture of your father-in-law's future. Now I hope you'll give him up of your own free will.

ASTRID: Will things really turn out that badly?

SWEDENHIELM: It looks like it.

ASTRID: Then I'll marry you, instead.

(*She kneels by his chair, her head in his lap.*)

SWEDENHIELM: These small hands want to play with everything. And they are perfectly free to, provided they don't touch a man's honor. It's too substantial for them, and yet too fragile, too strong and too vulnerable, too poor and too rich. It isn't suitable as an ornament or as a toy. It is neither helmet nor sword nor shield. It is the clean white shirt which must be kept spotless, ready for the final sleep.

ASTRID (*rises, weakly resisting Swedenhielm's argument*): That's a damnably outdated notion.

SWEDENHIELM: True! But it saves one from damnation.

(*Julia enters from her room.*)

JULIA: What are you two doing? You look as though you're rehearsing a scene.

SWEDENHIELM: Yes, and you've been standing just off stage, waiting for your entrance. Now wouldn't your stage manager rejoice if this were to become a habit?

ASTRID (*somewhat unwillingly*): We've decided to postpone our engagement.

JULIA: No.

ASTRID: The family honor is worse than Boman's floors. You can't even walk on it in your stocking feet.

SWEDENHIELM: Bah, our honor is nothing but old habit! But Papa Swedenhielm has a mania for providing well for his children: he ruins his oldest son, he leaves his daughter penniless, and from his youngest he steals a rich bride. Yes, you've done your best by them, old fellow, and now—let's get on with it!

(*Rolf comes in through the dining-room doors. He looks worried.*)

ROLF: Father.

SWEDENHIELM: Yes, my boy.

ROLF: I'm afraid I have something unpleasant to tell you.

SWEDENHIELM (*with a bit of comic exaggeration*): Unpleasant! This is the day of big surprises. Let me guess. A judgment against me in one of my thirteen patent suits?

ROLF: No—

SWEDENHIELM: New revelations of Rolf Swedenhielm's scientific incompetence?

ROLF: No, no—

SWEDENHIELM: Bankruptcy petition? Eviction notice? Canceled liquor ration books?

ROLF (*imploring*): For once in your life, will you please stop joking?

SWEDENHIELM: Is that what you want? But that's asking too much. If I stop joking, I stop living.

(*Bo enters from the dining room.*)

BO: There's an important telephone call for you, Father.

ROLF (*nervously*): Tell him to wait.

SWEDENHIELM: I have no account to settle with a single Christian soul. Tell him to go to hell!

BO: Literally?

SWEDENHIELM: Literally.

(*Bo goes out.*)

SWENDENHIELM: Well?

ROLF (*nervously*): I'm afraid I have to talk to you about . . . well, about my personal affairs, and Bo's too. You can't imagine how it hurts me—

SWEDENHIELM: Skip the mental torment.

ROLF: Well, then, to begin with . . . Bo, well he's run into debt. Not very large amounts in themselves, but he's employed a rather risky method.

BO (*re-enters, laughing*): Papa, the fellow says he'll gladly go to hell, if you'll kindly make an appointment to meet him there.

SWEDENHIELM: He sounds like fun! I want to talk to him.

(*He exits at the back, humming the "Toreador Song."*)

ROLF (*anxiously*): That wasn't Eriksson, was it?

BO (*shrugs his shoulders*): I forgot to ask who it was.

JULIA: What's wrong with you two? Is this some sort of conspiracy?

ROLF: No, it's just our debts. Bo's aren't so bad, but mine . . . And I hate to mention them to father today . . . when he was so frank about admitting my real value this morning—I have to come up with something like this!

JULIA: Don't get excited. One debt more or less in the Swedenhielm crash won't make any difference at all. But you were certainly sensible to leave the sinking ship in time, Astrid. Congratulations!

ASTRID: I haven't the least intention of being sensible!

(*She runs to Bo.*)

JULIA: Don't touch him! Bad luck is contagious. Think of your glowing future!

BO: Don't listen to her!

JULIA (*with unbelievable speed*): Imagine Bo Swedenhielm, hollow-eyed and emaciated, traipsing down the streets of Stockholm in his threadbare jacket, meeting the Countess Astrid lolling in her luxurious limousine! Alas, the countess, with a disdainful air, turns from the ragged reminder of her youthful indiscretions to accept with a seductive smile the gallant salutation of Prince Wilhelm—himself out promenading on the other side of the street. Ha! *Now* tell me that I have poor breath control and slow down the dialogue! But from her heart of hearts she sends a thankful prayer to Providence for saving her from little Bo—and now, consumptive little Bo trudges in his ragged little coat to his lonely little stall in a dingy little tenement in the little little town between the bridges. Congratulations!

BO: Spiteful ham!

JULIA (*passionately*): I'm not spiteful, I'm bloodthirsty. I've destroyed Axelin, and I'm looking for a new victim!

ROLF: Can't any of you be serious? God help the unfortunate corpse that has a Swedenhielm speak at his funeral.

(*Boman enters from the dining room.*)

BOMAN: Children! I think Swedenhielm's taken sick.

JULIA: Papa?!

BOMAN: Or lost his mind.

(*Swedenhielm comes slowly through the folding doors. He holds his right hand over his eyes, as if dazed; with his left hand he makes a vague, uncertain gesture. When the children try to approach him, he waves them away. Swedenhielm sinks into a chair and leans his elbow on a table beside it.*)

SWEDENHIELM (*softly*): Fool—numskull—clown—charlatan—dullard—dud—microbe—wretch—tosspot—idiot—(*He takes his hand from his eyes, but keeps it held up as a visor. He looks from one to the other; finally he says in a low, but distinctly audible voice*) Children, I've—won the Nobel Prize.

(*No one can speak. Swedenhielm leans over the table and, supporting his head in his hands, bursts into tears. The children and Astrid come slowly up to him—no one says anything, but they try to comfort him, stroking him over the head and shoulders. Last of all, Boman comes forward, makes a little curtsy, which Swedenhielm doesn't see, and goes quietly out through the dining room. At last, the silence is broken by*)

JULIA (*slowly, imploring*): Papa—don't cry—don't cry—

SWEDENHIELM (*between sobs*): You want that, do you? Well you ask too much.

(*Silence. He pulls himself together. He gives them a reassuring nod and then begins to walk up and down slowly, rubbing his hands together reflectively as he speaks. He is now calm.*)

SWEDENHIELM: It's true, really true. I've won the Nobel Prize.

It was the chairman of the committee himself who called. He didn't want me to know until it was settled. There was probably quite a heated argument over my name. I suppose the majority in my favor wasn't exactly overwhelming, and I can understand that.

ROLF: You have so many enemies in that group.

SWEDENHIELM: That's not what I mean. But there certainly were grounds for legitimate objections. God knows how I would have voted, myself. What have I really accomplished? Taken up other people's ideas, pursued them, completed them, put them into practice. But anything of purely original scientific value? No. He should not have had my vote. At least not Swedenhielm, Sr.—possibly Swedenhielm, Jr.

ROLF: Oh, the way you talk!

SWEDENHIELM: Never mind. I have the prize. All I have to do now is say thank you and hold out my hand.

JULIA (*striking her forehead*): Good heavens, this is a moment of overwhelming joy! Isn't it joy supreme? Why aren't we properly gay?

SWEDENHIELM: We will be, all in good time. Besides—when one is happy, he doesn't need to be gay.

JULIA: This will be good for all of us, won't it?

SWEDENHIELM: An improvement, at least. I think the sun's finally rising over the Swedenhielms. It's always coldest just before dawn, you know—and it certainly has been cold.

(*The doorbell rings. Rolf goes toward the dining-room doors.*)

SWEDENHIELM: Wait a minute! We have to deliberate. Now, children, how do you propose we solemnize the old man's entrance into the ranks of the Princes of Science?

JULIA (*shouts*): Champagne, champagne, champagne!

(*Boman enters.*)

BOMAN: There's a man in the hall who wants to see Dr. Swedenhielm.

SWEDENHIELM: A reporter?

BOMAN: He might be anything.

ROLF (*anxiously*): I'll go—

SWEDENHIELM: No, Swedenhielm himself will receive—today he is polite.

(*He goes out. Silence.*)

ROLF (*suddenly*): This is terrible, terrible! I can't stand it—
(*Rushes out into Julia's room*)

JULIA: What's the matter with him?

BO: Well, he's borrowed some money, and to get it he signed some notes. But I don't understand why he's so worried.

(*There is a silence, broken by Swedenhielm's laugh from off stage. Bo calls out*)

BO: Rolf! (*As Rolf appears in the doorway*) Father's laughing, so it can't be Eriksson.

JULIA: Who is Eriksson?

BO (*curt*): A loan shark.

(*Swedenhielm is heard in the dining room.*)

SWEDENHIELM: Right this way, Eriksson, come right on in. Don't worry yourself about scratching the floors.

(*Those on stage give a start, exchanging looks of astonishment. Swedenhielm enters from the back, followed by Eriksson. As they come on, Swedenhielm puts his arm on the other man's shoulder and introduces him.*)

SWEDENHIELM: My children—my son Rolf—my son Bo—my daughter Julia—my daughter-in-law—oho! now I say daughter-in-law again!—And here, my children, you see: Usurer Eriksson! (*Breaks into resounding laughter, then*) Yes, and for once I can't claim the joke. I went out into the hall— there he was. "How do you do, sir. Do you recognize me?"

"No. Who are you?" "I—am—Usurer Eriksson!" And you see, the amusing thing, children, the really amusing thing is that the man is actually an authentic usurer, by his own immediate confession! Now any other man would have surely said: "Bank Director Eriksson," or "Banker Eriksson," or stockbroker, or house owner, or any of a number of things. But this one bows and says: "Usurer Eriksson"!

ERIKSSON (*quietly*): I know, of course, from way back—that you like a good joke!

SWEDENHIELM: Yes, you see, children, this is the amusing thing, this is the most amusing of all! Do you know who he is? He's my foster brother! My own beloved nurse's son! The old Eriksson lady up in Nora—surely I've told you about her? Oh, a marvelous woman! And he is her son! You understand, I remember him very well—well, what I mean to say is: generally speaking, I remember that he *was*. And that we were very good friends. And do you know what? He has already found out that I have received the Nobel Prize!

ERIKSSON: I have to know what's going on.

SWEDENHIELM: And now he comes to congratulate me. But, my good man, why haven't you come before this? When was it that our paths really separated? Good God, we even went to grade school together! I remember it very well! But then what?

ERIKSSON: You went on to high school, of course, and your father arranged a position for me.

SWEDENHIELM: Where was that?

ERIKSSON: In a cell.

SWEDENHIELM: A—a cell? As?

ERIKSSON: As a prisoner.

SWEDENHIELM: Well, that was, I'm very sorry, a little unpleasant, yes. Good Lord, have you just been released?

ERIKSSON: No, no, of course not, the position was only for two and a half years. Since that time I have had nothing to do with the law. And that's nearly forty years ago, so I thought—

SWEDENHIELM: Yes?

ERIKSSON: —that you wouldn't be ashamed if I paid a visit—

SWEDENHIELM: Are you crazy? How could I be ashamed of my foster brother? No, I don't care how many penitentiaries they've set you up in. And on top of that, I've received the Nobel Prize. I can afford not to be ashamed of anything. No, now we've got to have a good time. What'll we do? Shall we go out somewhere and eat a bit—

ERIKSSON (*astonished*): You can't show yourself out in public with me!

SWEDENHIELM (*slightly annoyed*): No, that's true. Besides we want to enjoy old memories in peace and quiet. First you get the Nobel Prize, and then you get to sit and talk about the home you knew as a boy. Children, we're going to have a good time— (*He looks about the room, his mood begins to spiral.*) A good time, yes, a good time, that's what I said— (*Breathes deeply and shouts with full lung power*) Boman!

BOMAN (*enters at once*): If I were deaf it wouldn't help to shout, but since I can hear—it doesn't help, either.

SWEDENHIELM (*quietly, but with implicit strength*): Boman, I have received the Nobel Prize.

BOMAN: Yes, and I acknowledged with a curtsy, although you didn't see it.

SWEDENHIELM: Boman, does this place look as if I've received the Nobel Prize?

BOMAN: I have no idea how it should look.

SWEDENHIELM: Boman, you are a very, very great unhappiness!

BOMAN: Yes, I've heard that before.

SWEDENHIELM: You are, quite simply, my life's unhappiness! You have driven me with your brooms and soap buckets at a gallop through a whole half century; you've scattered my papers, disturbed me at my work, you have turned my joy sour and torn my sorrow to tatters. If I wanted to have a party, you nagged me; if I wanted to travel, you nagged me; if I wanted to stay at home, you nagged me; if I wanted to rise early, you nagged me; if I wanted to sleep, you nagged me; if I wanted to spend money, you nagged me; and if I wanted to save, you nagged me—

BOMAN: What's that about saving?

SWEDENHIELM: Your purpose in life is threefold: you nag, you clean, and you pinch pennies. You are the personification of everything that is prosaic in this world. You are the silence and the depression of poverty. You are the very wretchedness that destroys souls. But now I have become a rich man, Boman, and now you shall get out of my house!

BOMAN (*calmly*): And what's to become of me then?

SWEDENHIELM: Well! I shall buy you the very finest red cottage that's up for sale in the whole of Askersund. And there you can nag, be as miserly as you wish to, and clean to your heart's content—

BOMAN: That's fine with me; you can thrive anywhere as long as you keep the place clean. But what will become of Swedenhielm then?

SWEDENHIELM: I shall ascend straight up into the seventh sphere of heaven, and there I will fly about in flowing white robes that never need to be washed!

BOMAN: Agreed. We meet in heaven, Swedenhielm. (*Turns to go*)

SWEDENHIELM: Stop! I have an ultimatum. Within the hour, you shall restore perfect order in this house: every last object will be in its place, every curtain in its window, the dampness will evaporate, the rooms will be warm, and the scrubwomen, pails, and brushes will be thrown out the door—

(*From the right come two charwomen with their equipment; they lumber calmly across the stage and exit at the back.*)

SWEDENHIELM (*standing his ground*): I've received the Nobel Prize, and I do not intend to let myself be dominated in my own house any longer!

BOMAN (*upset*): Did you say that all this has to be done in an hour?

SWEDENHIELM: One hour!

BOMAN (*looks with amazement from one to the other*): Listen to me, children. He's been very difficult many times. But now he's really taken leave of his senses!

CURTAIN

ACT III

The scene is the same, but the rooms are now beautifully arranged and tidy. The dining room is strongly lit, but the downstage room is very dim by comparison. Swedenhielm and Eriksson are sitting at the dining-room table—they have just eaten dinner, and on the table remain several dessert dishes and coffee trays. They are pursuing a conversation about the old days which now and then is interrupted by Swedenhielm's bellowing laugh and Eriksson's more subdued tones.

In the downstage area's darkest corner, Bo and Astrid have sought privacy; as the curtain rises all that the audience can see of them is the occasional glow of their cigarettes.

Silence.

BO (*softly*): Give me a kiss.

ASTRID: No.

BO: Why?

ASTRID: No—I said that before!

(*Through the dining room Boman enters, dressed to suit this special occasion; she casts a critical eye around the room and straightens up some small object wherever she goes. Occupied thus she moves into the living room, where she turns on the lights.*)

BO (*softly, impatiently*): Mummy! Turn off the light and go away!

BOMAN (*calmly arranging some small item*): Certainly! I don't believe in making a nuisance of myself. But when there is a stranger in the house, one would think that some people might be able to behave themselves for a couple of hours. Although it doesn't look like it, does it? (*Goes slowly and with dignity into the dining room and finally disappears*)

(*Suppressing an oath, Bo rises and hurries on his toes over to the light switch and turns it off.*)

ASTRID (*stern and serious*): If I allow you to turn off the light, it's only to pursue a higher purpose: I want to see Boman squirm a little herself. (*She smacks her lips in an exaggerated fashion, imitating the sound of kisses. Boman passes through the dining room and coughs loudly in the open doorway.*)

BO (*turning to Astrid, eagerly*): Wait for me!

ASTRID (*coldly*): No. A couple of hours ago you didn't want to
be kissed. Now you do. What's happened in the meantime?
Have I become more attractive, more beautiful, more de-
sirable? No. But a few silly old men in their silly old academy
have given your father some money. And if you think these
gentlemen can decide who *I* get to kiss—

BO (*sardonically*): Darling, the Royal Academy of Science
wouldn't dream of doing anything like that.

ASTRID: I call that sort of thing meaningless.

BO: You should also be able to give me a completely meaningless kiss! Notice: I didn't say innocent!

ASTRID: When you behave like a wary, cold-blooded amphibian?
I wasn't able to kiss you because you were poor. Well, now
you're rich, but who says you're honest?

BO: I do.

ASTRID: I can almost believe you! But even if you should prove
to be, there may be a criminal element in your family. Your
brother may have misappropriated funds.

BO: Unthinkably impossible!

ASTRID: Not at all! He's been acting so strange all day: nervous,
forgetful, impolite. His very behavior is telling evidence of
genuine criminal activity. One fine day he'll be sitting out
in the prison on Långholm—

BO: A little less imagination, please!

ASTRID: And I, poor thing, I'll have to drag through life, my
conscience weighted down by having kissed a man whose
brother sits on Långholm. Thanks!

JULIA (*enters from her room; she holds a script in her hand*):
Who speaks of misfortune will find misfortune at his door!
Who utters an unkind word will find the word return to
haunt him! (*With a tremendous shudder*) Do you feel how
the very vapors chill at the approach of the inevitable?

BO: Please, Julia, couldn't you manage just as well in your own room with that stuff?

JULIA: Impossible. The role is much too large. I demand space! How do you think Axelin would say this: "Do you feel how the very vapors chill at the approach of the inevitable?" Would she shiver and let her voice die away? Or would she swell to a crescendo?

ASTRID: Aha, you're going to mimic Axelin!

JULIA: Nothing of the sort! But I've got to visualize how she would play the part, so I can do just the opposite. (*Hands the script to Bo*) Be a nice boy and listen to me.

BO: I'm busy. Ask Rolf.

JULIA: Well, where is he?

BO: Sitting by the telephone receiving congratulatory calls. Papa wants to be left in peace.

JULIA (*pointing at Eriksson, whispering*): How long is that orangutan going to stay?

BO: Until father's recollected all five hundred and eleven of his schoolboy memories. By that time the other one will finally have realized that he was entirely unnecessary.

(*Swedenhielm laughs heartily.*)

JULIA (*tenderly*): Poor little Papa, he's having such a marvelous time today! (*Goes slowly toward the dining room*) Sir Herbert, try to put yourself in my situation! I am the mother of two radiant, pure-hearted girls; I love them beyond my own happiness, beyond my own life. Shall I then allow a criminal act to wend its way between me and my children? No, rather would I sacrifice love, position, happiness, peace!

SWEDENHIELM (*greets her with applause*): Bravo, my dear, that's what I call high tragedy!

JULIA (*hugs him*): No, darling, it's comedy. Although there are tragic elements.

ERIKSSON: Exactly the same as life, Miss Julia, absolutely the same as life itself.

JULIA (*moves away*): Something like that, yes. (*Disappears, murmuring her lines. In the downstage area a little scuffle has broken out and now terminates in a kiss.*)

BO (*triumphantly*): It is more blessed to give than to receive, but it's best when you can do both!

ASTRID (*infuriated and flaming*): And they told me you were an honorable boy!

SWEDENHIELM (*conversing with Eriksson, stretching himself, greatly satisfied*): Yes, thank God, all of my children are highly talented, although in widely different ways.

ASTRID: A defenseless girl can't always protect herself. And furthermore that kiss was totally lacking in moral value—

BO: You can save your moral kisses for at least a quarter century!

ASTRID: Well there won't be any more today!

(*Suddenly Boman enters from the back—she turns on the lights and begins to pace back and forth in the open doorway, all of the time coughing and clearing her throat.*)

BO (*whispering*): All right! Just to see Boman squirm!

ASTRID: That's the only thing that could entice me—

(*Bo takes her in his arms and they kiss. After a moment's confusion, Boman resolutely closes the dining-room doors and stands on watch with her back turned to the young couple.*)

BO (*sardonically*): How sweet to love, even with a forbidden passion, as the gentle moon watches over our kisses— (*With feigned astonishment, striking his forehead*) My God, they've taken us by surprise!

BOMAN (*turns slowly to them, drily*): Is this being done to give that Eriksson a good impression of the family?

ASTRID: Boman, you ought to have realized that we don't care about Eriksson!

BOMAN: You wouldn't find it so easy to dismiss Eriksson if you were a Swedenhielm.

ASTRID: Why?

BOMAN: Because he holds some notes that the boys have signed.

BO (*quickly*): Did Rolf tell you that?

BOMAN: A moment ago.

ASTRID: So what? It's just a question of paying them.

BOMAN: Yes, but they're going to be expensive.

BO (*with rising anxiety*): Did Rolf tell you anything else? All he said to me was—

BOMAN: You can relax, dear, there's no hugger-mugger with your papers.

ASTRID: But with Rolf's?

BOMAN: It varies.

ASTRID: Varies?

BOMAN: He's pale as death itself. Because it looks like—

BO (*swiftly*): Shut up!

(*Silence.*)

ASTRID (*slowly, offended*): Is it my presence that keeps you from discussing family matters? (*Starts to go*)

BO (*stopping her*): But you understand—

ASTRID: —that I'm a stranger. Yes, I understand. (*She suddenly puts her arms around Bo and draws him to her; she then says with quiet determination*)

ASTRID: Now, Boman, what is it that you know?

BOMAN: This man, Eriksson, has bought up the notes from another dealer. He bought Bo's because he knew that he was engaged to an heiress, Rolf's because he believed that they were signed by Swedenhielm himself.

ASTRID: What made him think that?

BOMAN: The names are identical, and they write in much the same manner. Eriksson knew Swedenhielm's signature, and so he thought the notes were his.

ASTRID: But there must be some difference between their signatures.

BOMAN: Of course there has to be. Rolf usually puts "Jr." after his name.

BO (*tense*): Well?

BOMAN (*reluctantly*): Now Rolf is afraid he may, at one time or other, have forgotten to put the "Jr." there.

(*Bo stands for a moment, staring straight ahead. He then frees himself from Astrid and goes quickly into his room.*)

ASTRID (*whispering*): Bo! (*Takes several steps after him, stops*) Tell me, can't there be some other explanation?

BOMAN (*reflectively*): If the signatures weren't so absolutely identical, someone might suspect another of having forged it.

ASTRID: Are they that much alike?

BOMAN: Yes, or a man like Eriksson wouldn't have been deceived.

ASTRID: So there's no other explanation?

BOMAN: The only explanation is that trouble has come to this house. That's why you ought to mind your manners, that's my opinion, at least. We've got to keep up appearances.

(*Astrid takes several more steps toward Bo's room, and stops again.*)

BOMAN (*after a moment, severely*): Didn't you see that the boy's upset?

ASTRID: Yes.

BOMAN: Then why don't you go to him?

ASTRID (*several more steps, stops*): I can't.

BOMAN (*somewhat kinder*): It's not a question of what you can or can't do . . . not in a case like this.

ASTRID (*by the door*): But he doesn't want—

BOMAN (*mildly but decisively*): Never mind what he wants.

(*Astrid exits to the right. After a moment Boman goes slowly toward the dining-room doors and opens them. Rolf and Eriksson are discovered standing face to face. Rolf appears to be threatening Eriksson, who stands his ground. No words are exchanged, and the tableau breaks up when Rolf sits on the edge of the table and Eriksson moves a short distance away from him. During the next scene we see that brief snatches of conversation are exchanged between them; their mood is now very calm.*)

(*Julia comes in through the dining room reading quietly from her script and complementing her reading with appropriate gestures. She comes into the downstage area, rolls up her script, and strikes herself on the head with it—as if to pound the lines in.*)

JULIA: Mutti, our father is on the telephone talking to the Prime Minister. What do you think of that?

BOMAN (*with a slight curtsy*): The later in the evening, the more respectable the people.

JULIA: Where did the happy couple go?

BOMAN: Into his room.

JULIA (*with a heavy sigh*): A couple of mudlarks! They're happy, though! (*Another heavy sigh accompanied by a sad gaze out into space. Then slowly*) Consider that I never loved my husband. Consider that he neglected me, deceived me! And yet, I have remained faithful to him for ten long years. I swear that I have always been a respectable woman—

BOMAN (*scandalized*): Shh—don't talk about such things at a time like this!

JULIA: Have you lost your senses, Mutti dear—it's only my role!

BOMAN: Yes, well—one never knows what to think with you comediennes.

JULIA: Furthermore, you can just as well help me!

BOMAN: Is this your lesson?

JULIA: Yes, you see, one also has to give a little thought to the text. All right. We'll begin with the third act. Here.

BOMAN (*takes the script and rattles off the words without the faintest expression*): But why let this bitterness poison our cup of joy?

JULIA (*employing all her powers*): Because such is life! A mixture of mild goodness and heartless evil!

BOMAN (*studying the script*): Yes, I guess that's right. At least, that's what it says.

JULIA (*impatiently*): Well, now, what do you find so terribly remarkable about it?

BOMAN: Nothing, I just thought it sounded a little funny. (*Continues*)—your lovely youth.

JULIA: Alas, Sir Herbert, I am already a martyr.

BOMAN: No, no, that's all wrong. It says here: "I am already a mature woman."

JULIA (*impatiently*): Never mind about that! I intend to play the role a little younger.

BOMAN: I see. (*Continues*)—to help you bear this crushing fate?

JULIA: I could say: "God." But the word is much too pious for my mouth. I'll say: "Love"—and then I'll say: "Tenderness!"

BOMAN: —and let me kiss your cheek before we part. Farewell, thou hated one, farewell, oh wretch!

JULIA (*confused*): Does he really say: "oh wretch"? (*Grabs the script*) Where could you possibly be reading from? It says quite clearly: "Farewell, beloved."

BOMAN: I see that, but it must be a misprint, since he just said he hated her. Or else the fellow's taken leave of his senses.

JULIA: It's the insanity of love, you've got to realize that!

BOMAN: Oh, that's what it is.

JULIA: Anyway, you're reading like a block of wood. Haven't you got a drop of feeling left in your body?

BOMAN (*deeply hurt*): Me? Well if this isn't to your satisfaction, you can just go find someone else!

JULIA: No, no, go ahead! Take it again.

BOMAN (*one step forward, she sings out*): Let me kiss your cheek before we part! Farewell, thou hated one! Farewell, beloved!

JULIA (*inspired*): Farewell, Sir Herbert! One thing I shall always remember: you are a man!

(*Pedersen has just entered at the back in the dining room. He bows before both of the gentlemen and cautiously approaches Rolf with a question which clearly receives a short, gruff reply. Pedersen draws back, bowing, and is prepared for a total retreat when he discovers Julia; unobserved by the two women, he sneaks into the downstage area and stops by the doorpost, where he listens: sometimes astonished, sometimes spellbound.*)

BOMAN (*with overblown pathos*): In vain I struggled, in vain I suffered!

JULIA: No, not in vain! He who really struggles, truly suffers— but never in vain! No—

BOMAN (*in her eagerness, she interrupts Julia*): —but when— when did I ask for my reward?

JULIA: No, you are unselfish and many would have wearied—

BOMAN (*as before*): —and do what you will—but do not deny me!

JULIA (*distressed and infuriated*): No, Boman, you're being infernally difficult! I don't even get to say half my lines! I pity the actress who had you for a juvenile lead!

BOMAN (*catching her breath, short and rasping*): I can emote, if I want to! (*Pointing out Pedersen*) Shall I get him a cup of coffee? Because there's still some left.

JULIA (*discovering Pedersen's presence*): Heavens, is the public here? Isn't it—Mr.—Mr.—

PEDERSEN: Pedersen. Valfrid Pedersen.

JULIA: Well what can I do for you?

PEDERSEN (*several steps toward her*): Miss Körner, I have come on business of the utmost weight and importance. That is, for myself. And also for the press in its entirety. But I would like to speak in private to Miss Julia Körner in person.

JULIA: Go right ahead.

(*Pedersen crosses to her, stands one step from her, puts his hands behind his back, and bends forward in order to whisper in Julia's ear.*)

JULIA: I see. (*Whispering*) Oh? (*Whispering*) Yes of course, I understand. (*Whispering*) Yes but, dear Mr. Pedersen— (*Whispering*) Yes but, darling Mr. Pedersen— (*Whispering*) Yes but, adorable Mr. Pedersen— (*Whispering*) Yes but, dear, darling, adorable Pedersen—

(*Rolf enters from the dining room. He meets Boman at the door; she gives him a searching look—and during the following she slowly approaches Eriksson.*)

ROLF (*sternly*): He wishes an interview with Father, but I've already told him it's impossible. Would you be so kind, sir, as to leave us in peace?

JULIA: What's that?

ROLF: It is our father's implicit wish—

JULIA: Our father has become a balloon full of pride! Mr. Pedersen didn't come to see him. Mr. Pedersen has come to look at my famous canary. As soon as a man gets the Nobel Prize, he thinks everyone is running after him. But there are also such things as young, beautiful, talented actresses. This way, Pedersen. (*She takes Pedersen by the hand and leads him to the right.*)

PEDERSEN: I am—I am absolutely overjoyed—

JULIA (*again at her lesson*): But never forget, Sir Herbert, the more attractive Mother Fortune becomes, the more deceptive she also—(*Both exit right.*)

(*During the preceding, Boman has clearly made some kind of request of Eriksson, who has given a negative response. He now makes an energetic deprecatory gesture and comes into the downstage area, leaving Boman alone in the dining room.*)

ERIKSSON (*to Boman*): No, no, no—don't try to. Besides I've never said that I know for certain who the culprit is.

ROLF (*with subdued urgency*): Why won't you show me the notes?

ERIKSSON: I see no use in it.

ROLF: I want to see if there really isn't a "Jr."—

ERIKSSON: Trust me, please trust me.

ROLF: Are you going to show them to Father?

ERIKSSON: It depends. On how things turn out.

(*Boman, who has been standing motionless in the dining room, now begins to cough and move about; soon Swedenhielm comes into the dining room from the back and moves on into the downstage area. He walks powerfully, enjoying a certain peace of mind. Boman gives attention to her work and then disappears.*)

SWEDENHIELM: That was the Prime Minister who just called. Wanted to extend his personal congratulations.

ERIKSSON: Oh really?

SWEDENHIELM: Well, I don't put much value on titles and earthly fame, but it was good to hear a friendly voice—my dear old Hjalmar Branting. Rolf, go out and wait by the telephone. But remember, no more well-wishers today. One can have too much, even of the good things.

(*Against his will, Rolf goes into the dining room. He remains there through the next few speeches; then he exits at the back.*)

ERIKSSON: What should I say—now you can't really climb any higher, can you, Swedenhielm?

SWEDENHIELM (*smiling*): No, this can certainly be regarded as the very top.

ERIKSSON: Well, how does it feel?

SWEDENHIELM: To be frank, it feels good. But good in a very special way. It feels restful and pleasant.

ERIKSSON: Now you can rest on your laurels, so to speak.

SWEDENHIELM: God forbid! But, anyhow—life is nothing more than a struggle to win respect and recognition. To be just as good as the others and even a little better. You have that in you from childhood. Then it's a matter of turning cartwheels, kicking a can, or standing on your head. Later on it's other tricks, but the idea's just the same.

ERIKSSON (*with a thin laugh*): Yes, I remember that you were always very good at standing on your head.

SWEDENHIELM: You know, I think it's simply wonderful that you should come just today and revive old memories!

ERIKSSON: There's an obvious explanation, so to speak.

SWEDENHIELM: The older a man gets, the harder he holds on to his childhood memories. Distances in time seem to shrink, instead of grow. Finally he becomes brother and comrade to both his father and his son.

ERIKSSON (*gently touched*): A beautiful thought, Swedenhielm, a very beautiful thought.

SWEDENHIELM: When something absolutely wonderful happens to me, like today for example, the first thing I do is go to my children and tell *them*. And then there's shouting and rejoicing. But you know what I do next? I go to the old house where I was born, to the mayor's house in Nora. Yes, in memory, of course. And I go straight through the living room until I reach the big, gray door, you remember, the one with the black knob.

ERIKSSON (*involuntarily grimaces*): The door to the mayor's room.

SWEDENHIELM: Yes. I knock. "Come in." I enter and stand upright on the threshold, hands down at my sides like a soldier, the proper way. "Now what's the matter?" says the old man, looking over his spectacles. Then I tell *him*, clearly and precisely. No use coming to him with fancy words. But his hearing is a little poor. So I must step closer to his desk. And then I have the pleasure of telling it once more. And while I'm talking—my mother comes—
  (*Silence*)

ERIKSSON (*gently*): She was very kind, the mayor's wife.
  (*Swedenhielm nods and smiles. Silence*)

ERIKSSON (*slowly*): But the mayor was severe.

SWEDENHIELM: Yes, I can promise you that. No one tried any nonsense with him. I wish I had a dollar for every box on the ears he gave me.

ERIKSSON: Oh, he couldn't have been all that bad with his son.

SWEDENHIELM: Three blows with the cane and one meal a day—that was our punishment. No, as a child I certainly wasn't pampered, thank God.

ERIKSSON: In any case it surely was more of a game—

SWEDENHIELM (*rubbing himself behind*): Thanks a lot! I wish you could have been the son in that house, Eriksson.

ERIKSSON: I've wished that too. Once especially.

SWEDENHIELM: When was that?

ERIKSSON: Once when I stood in front of that big gray door with the black knob.

SWEDENHIELM: When was that?

ERIKSSON: The time I had to tell him that I was short with the company's cash.

(*Short silence*)

SWEDENHIELM (*unpleasantly distressed, he crosses to Eriksson and claps him on the back in a friendly manner*): Such memories ought not to be rekindled.

ERIKSSON: That was a day I regretted I was not his son.

SWEDENHIELM: It really wouldn't have made things any better.

ERIKSSON: I hardly think I should have gone to prison.

SWEDENHIELM (*impatiently*): Let's not talk about it.

ERIKSSON: Because it *could* have been straightened out quietly.

SWEDENHIELM: Do you really think so?

ERIKSSON: Yes, but the mayor didn't want to. I *had* to go to prison.

SWEDENHIELM (*impatiently*): But, my dear old friend, it was your own fault.

ERIKSSON: Of course. Still it could have been hushed up.

SWEDENHIELM: My father got you that job. He placed great trust in you.

ERIKSSON: He placed great temptation in my way also.

SWEDENHIELM: Everyone has his temptations.

ERIKSSON: But everyone doesn't go to prison.

SWEDENHIELM (*genially*): No, thank God! Everyone doesn't yield to temptation.

ERIKSSON (*bitterly*): Most of us do.

SWEDENHIELM (*quickly*): A criminal's delusion!

ERIKSSON (*after a pause*): So, then, you think the mayor was right?

SWEDENHIELM: Listen to me, please. You must remember that my father did more than secure you a position and act as your supervisor in the bank. He was also mayor of the town, arbiter of impartial justice. It was his irrevocable duty to let this justice take its course.

ERIKSSON: I see.

SWEDENHIELM (*wandering back and forth*): I'm not saying this to make it harder for you! I can remember it now, as if it were yesterday, how deeply I was hurt when I heard what had happened. My foster brother, brought up with me! No one could have taken it as hard as I did!

ERIKSSON: Oh yes, there was one.

SWEDENHIELM: Yourself, of course.

ERIKSSON: And one more: my mother.

SWEDENHIELM (*quietly*): Yes, naturally. Of course.

ERIKSSON (*after a moment*): She went to the mayor's wife.

SWEDENHIELM (*stops*): Oh?

ERIKSSON: And begged for help.

SWEDENHIELM: I never knew that.

ERIKSSON: Yes. And your mother promised that the matter would be hushed up, even if she had to plead on her knees.

SWEDENHIELM (*moved*): Of course—two mothers get their heads together—

ERIKSSON: But the mayor wouldn't do it.

SWEDENHIELM (*strongly*): Couldn't do it!

ERIKSSON: But now I want to ask! Not who was right, the mayor or I—naturally the mayor was—but I want to ask: who was right, your father or your mother?

SWEDENHIELM: I won't answer that. The whole affair was over a long time ago, and now is meaningless.

ERIKSSON: You think so? But just a few minutes ago you said that a man clings to his childhood memories. Mine may not be as pleasant as yours, but they have their significance!

SWEDENHIELM: All right, then, all right. My dear little mother, bless her!—but my father was right. You can't compromise on a point of honor.

ERIKSSON (*after a moment*): I see. Well, then, I must give way to you. Although you make it difficult.

SWEDENHIELM (*pleasantly*): Yes, you'll have to give way . . . and go your way. It's getting late, and it's been a rather hard day.

ERIKSSON: Yes. They say that too much happiness is tiring. I'm afraid it's not quite the moment, then, to ask you to look at those notes?

SWEDENHIELM: Damn! I'd forgotten! Certainly. After all, you came especially to show them to me.

ERIKSSON (*strongly, seriously*): No, that wasn't the reason! You mustn't believe that! My first purpose was to congratulate. Secondly I wanted to relive old memories—

SWEDENHIELM (*jokingly*): —and thirdly to present old notes.

ERIKSSON (*taking out his wallet*): Yes, in my business one has to be a little careful. And when I found out that Swedenhielm would soon have so much money—

SWEDENHIELM: You wanted to get here before Swedenhielm celebrated away his fortune! (*Claps him on the back*) Yes, you do know your old foster brother. Do you remember how we nearly killed each other over that rock candy that time in Örebro?

ERIKSSON (*discreetly pulls himself away from Swedenhielm's grasp*): Yes, you've always been a little heavy-handed. (*Files *through the papers in his wallet*) Say, isn't it strange that you, with your keen sense of honor, want to share even a degree of confidence with me? After all, I have been convicted and punished for a rather serious crime.

SWEDENHIELM: Good heavens, I don't view the faults of a friend as contagious. Let other people take care of their own honor. I'll take care of mine.

ERIKSSON (*still filing through his wallet*): Isn't that being a little egotistical? To think of nothing but your own honor?

SWEDENHIELM: It may be. But I don't intend to discard this sort of egotism.

ERIKSSON: Yes, yes—that was exactly what he thought, your father, I mean. When he sent me to prison. One thing, though—shouldn't your sons be here too, so they can answer for—

SWEDENHIELM: Shh! It's going to be a surprise for them.

ERIKSSON: A surprise!

SWEDENHIELM (*a little sheepishly*): I intend to put these notes in their stockings.

ERIKSSON (*not understanding*): In their stockings?

SWEDENHIELM: Boman will put them in.

ERIKSSON: The notes?

SWEDENHIELM (*as before*): It's another childhood memory. On Christmas Eve, when we children were asleep, Mother used to fill our stockings with toys. Didn't your mother do the same?

ERIKSSON: I don't remember. She probably had nothing to fill them with.

SWEDENHIELM: Then you're poorer by a memory. Why that was the most fun of all—

ERIKSSON: And you're going—to put these notes—aren't you letting them off a little easy?

SWEDENHIELM: Of course! Of course I ought to call the fellows in and hold a little conference. My sons, this is the best way to bring your father's old white head with shame into the grave! But you see, I've never had much of a gift for solemnities. And furthermore I myself have had so damned many financial involvements and debts. Many a time I've wished that some benevolent soul would cross out all my bills and take them and stuff them into my stockings. So I don't see why I shouldn't give in to the temptation of being a little frivolous myself.

ERIKSSON: Your father would never have done it!

SWEDENHIELM: I guess he wouldn't have, no.

ERIKSSON: But your mother?

SWEDENHIELM: Perhaps.

ERIKSSON (*suddenly*): Swedenhielm! Shall we do it this way? We'll take all the notes—all together—and tear them up without looking at them and stuff them into their stockings? And then you'll pay me one lump sum for everything.

SWEDENHIELM: Are you crazy?

ERIKSSON (*goes to him, tries to grasp him, nervously*): I'm not going to cheat you in this matter, Swedenhielm. Please believe me! I will not cheat you. You've got to believe me!

SWEDENHIELM: The way you talk! You're a bit of a sentimentalist!

ERIKSSON (*trying to grasp him*): Believe me! If only for old time's sake, believe me!

SWEDENHIELM (*a little annoyed*): Of course I believe you. But there's a proper and orderly way of doing this. When it comes to matters which concern your money, you don't want to jest.

ERIKSSON (*suddenly losing his strength*): Jest?

SWEDENHIELM: Now let me add up the different figures, so that

I'll know how much I have to answer for. (*He searches through his pockets and comes up with a small notebook and a pen.*)

ERIKSSON (*suppressing his feelings and again trying to touch Swedenhielm*): I still think that you should have understood—

SWEDENHIELM: What are you talking about?

ERIKSSON: —should have understood me that time. When I was careless. After all, I was only a boy—

SWEDENHIELM (*indifferently*): *Tout comprendre c'est tout pardonner.*

ERIKSSON: What?

SWEDENHIELM: To understand everything is to forgive everything.

ERIKSSON (*slowly*): That's—beautiful.

SWEDENHIELM: Yes, but I've come to a different conclusion. The more I learn of human nature, the less sympathy I have with forgiveness.

ERIKSSON (*after a moment*): That sounded just like the mayor himself. (*A short pause, during which he arranges his notes with trembling hands; a complete change comes over his voice, he is now dry and cold—very polite, but impersonal.*) If you please—here we have a note signed by Lieutenant Bo Swedenhielm: six hundred and eighty crowns.

SWEDENHIELM (*writing in his book*): Six hundred and eighty. How old is it?

ERIKSSON: Two years, three months.

SWEDENHIELM: Karlberg.

ERIKSSON: Bo Swedenhielm: two thousand, two hundred.

SWEDENHIELM: When?

ERIKSSON: June, a year ago.

SWEDENHIELM: Aha! He was just beginning to fly—

ERIKSSON: Bo Swedenhielm: three thousand, eight hundred, January this year.

SWEDENHIELM: Thanks! Engagement gifts. It's going to be expensive—just for toys in a stocking, hmm? I think I'm beginning to regret—

ERIKSSON: These notes are all signed clearly by the lieutenant.

SWEDENHIELM (*adding up the amounts*): Signed clearly?

ERIKSSON: Merely a figure of speech.

SWEDENHIELM: Making a total of six thousand, six hundred and eighty crowns. Tell me, how much of all this did the boy actually receive?

ERIKSSON: I can't say; I bought the bills from a man named Andersson.

SWEDENHIELM: Rolf's too?

ERIKSSON: No, I bought those from a Mr. Bergström—perhaps you know him?

SWEDENHIELM: No, thank God, I don't know any such people. Tell me, why did you really buy these notes?

ERIKSSON (*evasively*): There was a reason. Suppose we look at Rolf's.

SWEDENHIELM: Phew! I'm starting to sweat—

ERIKSSON: Yes, these are a little worse. Here's one for four thousand, six hundred crowns from March, 1920.

SWEDENHIELM: March, 1920—ai, ai, ai, Rolf, that was a costly experiment—

ERIKSSON: May, the same year, three thousand crowns—

SWEDENHIELM (*writing in his book*): The devil! The dunce! My boy—

ERIKSSON: And June, the same year, five thousand crowns—

SWEDENHIELM: Ye Gods, wait a minute! Twelve thousand, six hundred! I assure you, I wouldn't have been nearly so provoked if he had squandered the whole sum on one big party! But these stupid experiments. And anyway I told him long before that they'd never get us anywhere. I really begin to feel it—let me see now: six thousand, six hundred eighty, plus twelve thousand, six hundred, makes nineteen thousand, two hundred and eighty. No, I'll be damned! (*Restrains his growing bitterness*) No, Swedenhielm: You are now a wealthy old man. *Richesse oblige.* You have the money to put up with sons who fly, go courting, and perform experiments. But when I think how carefully I had to watch myself at their age! Bah, it's only right that they should have it better than I did. Although I've a good mind to borrow Boman's carpet beater! Well. Well. Well. They're a couple of decent boys, in any case. Devilish, but decent! God be praised for the young ones, thank God for them! But a little Nobel Prize every now and then certainly comes in handy!

ERIKSSON (*completely unconcerned with the other's growing anxiety*): And then there are two more.

SWEDENHIELM: Two more! No, the cup must be overflowing—

ERIKSSON (*dry and businesslike*): One for two and the other for four.

SWEDENHIELM: Thousand?

ERIKSSON: No. Hundred.

SWEDENHIELM (*writing*): Thank you, thank you ever so much! Well, that's relatively merciful. Are they Bo's? Most likely tailor bills: those everlasting uniforms—

ERIKSSON: They're signed Rolf Swedenhielm

SWEDENHIELM: Oh, so it's Rolf.

ERIKSSON: Looking at them one might almost think you'd signed them yourself.

SWEDENHIELM: I? Absolutely not! How can you possibly say that?

ERIKSSON: Your son usually signs himself "Rolf Swedenhielm, Jr.," but this time he didn't.

SWEDENHIELM: He probably forgot.

ERIKSSON (*hastily*): He seems to believe that himself, but it isn't so.

SWEDENHIELM (*after a pause*): Do you mean that he intentionally—

ERIKSSON: Your two signatures are so alike that anyone could be fooled.

SWEDENHIELM (*controlling himself*): Are you saying that my son intentionally—

ERIKSSON: I am saying that Rolf Swedenhielm neither wrote nor signed these notes. The handwriting is certainly an imitation of yours, but not done with enough skill to deceive anyone like myself.

SWEDENHIELM (*with quiet despair*): Yes, that's fine. What you mean to say is that someone has forged my name.

ERIKSSON: Precisely.

SWEDENHIELM: Let me see them!

ERIKSSON: Here are Rolf's notes. Here are Bo's that we have passed as genuine. And here are the ones in doubt.

SWEDENHIELM: But this is a most obvious forgery. And you actually went and bought these?

ERIKSSON: From Andersson. The one Bo used to go to.

SWEDENHIELM: And where did Andersson get them?

ERIKSSON: Surely you know that people like Andersson and myself never discuss our clients. As long as we get our commission, we don't ask any questions. Andersson said nothing definite.

SWEDENHIELM: No, but he said something, or an old fox like you wouldn't have snapped them up.

ERIKSSON: Quite right! He said, "Old man Swedenhielm didn't sign these notes, but he'll pay them!"

SWEDENHIELM: Well this time he'll burn his fingers! Tell him that from me.

ERIKSSON: He thinks you'll pay, and so do I.

SWEDENHIELM (*nervously fingering the paper*): Why should I—should I—

ERIKSSON (*watching him carefully*): Are you comparing the papers?

SWEDENHIELM (*still more nervously*): Why should I—I— compare them?

ERIKSSON: The watermark on these is the same as the watermark on these clearly signed notes of Bo's.

SWEDENHIELM (*without raising his voice but with deep anger*): Be quiet with your "clearly signed"!

ERIKSSON: . . . but the top with the monogram has been cut away . . .

(*Swedenhielm draws a deep breath and advances threateningly toward Eriksson. The latter, without undue haste, gives way. Swedenhielm throws the papers on the table and passes his hand over his face.*)

SWEDENHIELM: It's unthinkable—impossible—Bo—Bo—my— little—

ERIKSSON: Don't take it so hard, he's only a boy, and you won't be as harsh as the mayor.

SWEDENHIELM (*in the same tense voice*): It's—it's just impossible!

ERIKSSON: Bergström told me that the lieutenant had been to see him but couldn't get any money. And it seems that the first forgery—oh, excuse me—had been committed the same day. So there was some slight difficulty which needed to be

straightened out. I can only say that a young man has his
temptations—

SWEDENHIELM (*he has regained his composure—but he is now
very tired*): When do you want the money?

ERIKSSON (*quickly*): You'll pay the forged notes, then?

(*Swedenhielm bows his head in assent.*)

ERIKSSON (*decorously triumphant*): I thought you would. But
there's no hurry! Swedenhielm's credit is good—and I'm
accustomed to waiting.

SWEDENHIELM (*with a great effort*): I believe that the money
is distributed with the prizes. If that is so, please come here
in the evening after the ceremony.

ERIKSSON: I couldn't do that! Come here and disturb you in
the middle of the celebration! No, no—I couldn't!

SWEDENHIELM (*sharply*): The same evening! Do you understand?

ERIKSSON: Yes, yes. Mayor—I mean, Swedenhielm.

SWEDENHIELM (*with difficulty*): Have you any objection to my
keeping these papers? Now. This evening?

ERIKSSON: Of course not. Your word is worth more than any
note, genuine or forged.

(*Swedenhielm takes up the papers from the table. Suddenly he crumples the papers up in his hands and tears them
again and again into tiny pieces which fall to the floor.*)

ERIKSSON: Just one more thing. May I request that you make
the percentage on these particular notes a little generous?

SWEDENHIELM: Whatever you want.

ERIKSSON: They're worth it. If someone else had gotten hold
of them—well, you never can tell how it would have worked
out. One can go to prison for things like this—if they aren't
hushed up.

SWEDENHIELM (*tonelessly*): Whatever you want.

ERIKSSON: Shall we say one hundred per cent? But if you think that's unreasonable, I won't take anything! You see, it's the principle of the thing. It's very risky buying up such notes. You never can be sure if the forger's relatives will be willing to hush things up. One of them might insist on justice taking its course.

SWEDENHIELM (*tonelessly*): Whatever you say.

ERIKSSON: Then we'll say one hundred per cent—and—thank you, very much.

(*Himself affected by Swedenhielm's loss, Eriksson moves toward him and gestures with his arm, as if he wanted, but doesn't dare, to take Swedenhielm's hand. Swedenhielm then lifts his own hand and thrusts it toward the other in an indifferent manner. Eriksson grips his hand with both of his own and presses it with a warmth which reveals the shame which he himself feels; he then drops Swedenhielm's hand.*)

ERIKSSON: Whether you believe me or not, Swedenhielm, this is true. I only came here to congratulate you—and to talk over the old times. These notes I had in my back pocket, you might say. If things had turned out differently, I might never have brought them up. But that's not the way it worked out. (*Bows and goes toward the dining room; in the doorway he turns around and says with a tired and subdued voice*) It's not so often that we meet, Swedenhielm, and I would have liked it to have been a happier meeting, I really would have. People aren't any more inhuman than they're forced to be. (*He bows, goes out through the dining room, and exits. As long as he is present, Swedenhielm remains motionless. A door is heard shutting.*)

SWEDENHIELM (*cries out*): Bo! Bo! My . . .

(*Bo comes in quickly from the right, stops, and stands
still, alarmed and bewildered. Swedenhielm turns and advances slowly toward him. He raises his trembling, clenched
fists. After a few steps he stops and presses his hands to his
eyes.*)

BO (*alarmed*): What is it, Father? What is it? Something to
do with Rolf?

SWEDENHIELM: It's nothing. Nothing. Ask Boman to come here.

BO: But something's wrong.

SWEDENHIELM (*stops him with a commanding gesture*): Do
as I tell you.

(*Bo goes out through the dining room. At the same moment Julia enters from her room.*)

JULIA: Did you call, Father?

(*Swedenhielm shakes his head.*)

JULIA (*crosses to him*): I thought I heard you calling. (*Caressingly*) Tell me, Papa dear, are you very tired?

SWEDENHIELM: Yes, a little.

JULIA: You see the fact of the matter is that in my room there's
a young journalist waiting—

(*Swedenhielm makes a deprecatory gesture.*)

JULIA: Well, I suppose it's terrible, but I'll come straight to the
point. He's a young man, just a boy, in fact—and I don't
think he's especially bright—but he's really very sweet. And
he thinks he would make a great splash in the press if he
could only speak to you for five minutes. Just five minutes.

SWEDENHIELM (*wearily*): If I can make a young man's success
so easily, well, I suppose I must.

JULIA: Thank you, darling! Pedersen! Pedersen! (*She goes
toward the door and is met by Pedersen.*) Remember, only
five minutes, and not too many foolish questions! (*She exits.*)

PEDERSEN (*with a respectful bow to Swedenhielm*): My name

is Pedersen, Valfrid Pedersen. I am frightfully, unspeakably grateful! You see, sir, I intend to consecrate myself in earnest to interviewing and to develop it into a fine art. In fact, I've just been thinking a great deal about this subject. First and foremost, it seems to me that, before the interview, one should try and find out what one will get to know. Otherwise one is *so* liable to be taken by surprise and may even entirely lose the thread. Or else one may ask stupid questions and get badly snubbed. And that's the worst of all, because then I completely break down! This is why I've been sitting the whole day in the library, looking at the biographies of the Swedenhielm family. I already have all your inventions, sir, at my fingertips, and all the dates and so on. And I've been rummaging around in the pedigrees and genealogies and what's their names. Bless me! It's an awfully ancient and distinguished family, I've discovered. Though one has a sort of impression that it is slowly but surely on the downward grade, isn't it? Your grandfather, sir, as you know, was a general, your father a mayor, whereas you, sir, are merely an ordinary engineer. But a great luminary, of course. But now I want to know something that isn't in any of the reference books.

SWEDENHIELM (*indifferently*): What is it?

PEDERSEN: Well! How does it feel!

SWEDENHIELM: How does it feel?

PEDERSEN: To get the Nobel Prize! To stand, so to speak, at the top of the heap. For it is, I suppose, the very top?

SWEDENHIELM: For me it is certainly "the very top."

PEDERSEN: And how does it feel? Giddy?

SWEDENHIELM (*quietly*): To be frank, it feels rather good. And restful.

PEDERSEN: Resting on your laurels!

SWEDENHIELM: No, not exactly. If I didn't know that tomorrow would be another day of work, I think I'd go crazy. Life is a struggle to win respect and recognition, at least it has been for me. Now that I've got it, I have nothing left to work for.

PEDERSEN: Can it really be that delightful?

SWEDENHIELM (*calmly*): It's peaceful. It's lovely. You feel that the whole thing may burn up, be flung away like scraps of paper without mattering at all. (*Pause*) It wasn't worth anything. Nothing at all.

PEDERSEN: Not worth anything? I don't quite follow—

SWEDENHIELM: Nothing—worthless. You have a fine, time-honored name, and you do your best to keep it respected. Then, one day a relative, a brother or a son, comes along and dirties it. And then? You don't have to make a fuss about it. Why, what's more natural than being betrayed? We're all tempted, and most of us fall. No, let's say all. It's a criminal's delusion, but it's true.

PEDERSEN: I certainly didn't expect this.

SWEDENHIELM (*gradually losing his composure*): When you're young, you don't see so clearly. But, never mind, the years bring things into focus. Sooner or later, your sight sharpens. Lucky for those who become keen-sighted early. At least they escape the pitifulness and shame of trusting others. They don't work like slaves, like fools, so that they can finally stand, weighted down with people's respect, branded with the mark of honor. Defeated, degraded, disgraced, and indescribably ridiculous! Do you understand how it feels? It feels as if I were standing on the gallows! (*Silence. Quietly again*) I have probably not expressed myself very . . . (*Pause. Laughs softly*) I was going to say, "not very clearly," but the word "clearly" has a rather unpleasant ring, don't you think? (*Laughs*) You shouldn't adulterate the

the truth with unclear words. (*Seriously, wearily*) I have probably expressed myself obscurely. But, when you get to my age, you'll surely have made the same observation: the the whole thing wasn't worth very much. Is there anything else you'd like to know?

PEDERSEN (*quietly*): No. (*He bows and goes silently toward the back, but turns suddenly and grasps Swedenhielm's hand.*)

SWEDENHIELM (*smiling*): My daughter was right. You're not very bright, but you are a good fellow. More feeling than sense. Poor you, poor you! But now let me give you some advice. Condense my remarks. Write: Dr. Swedenhielm feels it delightful and restful to have his life behind him. Or better, his life's work—it doesn't sound so pathetic.

(*Pedersen bows again, goes quietly and silently toward the back; Swedenhielm stands for a while immobile. Boman enters from the back.*)

BOMAN: You sent for me, Swedenhielm?

SWEDENHIELM (*calmly, wearily*): Boman, please gather up all those bits of paper.

BOMAN (*almost to herself, looking at the floor*): Nobody would believe we'd just finished housecleaning.

SWEDENHIELM: Burn them. Be sure that every single scrap is burned.

BOMAN: I'll see to it.

SWEDENHIELM: Thanks.

(*Boman picks up the last bit of paper and goes toward the folding doors.*)

BOMAN: The room has been aired out and warmed, and your bed is ready—if you want to rest, Swedenhielm.

SWEDENHIELM: Thanks. (*He stands a moment immobile; then his erect figure slowly bows with weariness. He walks with tired steps toward the back, as the curtain falls.*)

ACT IV

The scene is the same. Evening. In the dining room the table is piled with chairs; it is not, however, a question of a general housecleaning, only a minor operation which is being taken care of by Boman herself—who has a broom in hand and a kerchief around her head. She sweeps and arranges, is seen bustling back and forth, and finally disappears. At the beginning the dining room is strongly lit.

The illumination in the downstage area is only at half of its strength. Rolf, Julia, and Bo are sitting here waiting. Rolf is in formal attire, with the pin of an order in his buttonhole. Julia is in elegant evening attire, and Bo is in his dress uniform. Now and then Rolf looks at the clock and shows signs of nervousness. Julia seems to be in the depths of meditation. Bo is sitting a little hunched up in his chair and stares straight in front of himself.

Silence.

BOMAN (*in the doorway at the back*): Children, this will never do if Swedenhielm isn't ready soon.

ROLF (*moodily*): There's plenty of time.

BOMAN: Yes, but the taxi's here already, and the meter keeps on ticking and ticking. (*She turns and goes out, but returns again.*) And if Swedenhielm is late, you never know, they might give the prize to somebody else. As a sign of general indignation. (*She turns and goes out, but returns again.*) If people want money they ought to be well in front and early, too. Besides, His Majesty may have something better to do than to sit and wait for Swedenhielm.

ROLF: Well, then, you go right ahead and hurry him up.

BOMAN: Go and face him? No thank you: I'd rather leave him alone. (*Disappears*)

JULIA: It's true: we're acting in a tragedy, a classical tragedy. The curtain will soon be rung down on the house of Swedenhielm for good.

ROLF: Kindly spare us your occupational jargon.

JULIA: Day after day he's just the same, not a word, not a smile —hardly a greeting in the morning, not a caress, not even a kiss. If it lasts much longer, I'll go completely mad. Don't you know what's wrong with him?

ROLF: I know nothing—and don't want to know anything.

(*Bo looks up and regards his brother and then lowers his eyes again.*)

JULIA: Boys, boys, it's all been so very nerve-shattering, these past few weeks! And we Swedenhielms, who always used to be so happy, so very pleasant! Didn't we? Didn't people used to say: Oh, those Swedenhielms; oh, but they're so happy and pleasant, natural and attractive, quick and amusing, elegant and delightful, such an agreeable collection of people! But now? Now! Just look at us, how we sit here! Like the madding crowd in one of those awful films! Puh. (*Throws one leg over the other*) My God, but I'm out of sorts! And furthermore I was such a colossal success! Well, wasn't I? Even last Sunday, thirteen curtain calls after the last act. Well what do *you* two think?

ROLF (*apathetically*): Ham—

JULIA: And our poor father, what in the world could have induced him to meditate so? Or what if it's just an upset stomach? Think we'd better call the doctor?

ROLF: Yes, from an asylum. For you!

JULIA: No, I have a presentiment. I feel it in every limb: in my legs, in my heart, and there's such a terrible lump in my throat—I don't even think I can speak. Puh. Why are you both so bloody silent? When you can neither laugh nor cry, neither dance nor sing, and not even quarrel—then it's the end! An absolute fiasco. Puh! (*Changes leg position and becomes suddenly aggressive*) Bo?

BO (*apathetically*): Hm?

JULIA: Where's my little mirror?

BO: Don't know—

JULIA: You've taken it!

BO: No, I just said—

JULIA: You've taken it!

BO (*as before, apathetic, uninterested*): And what did I do with it?

JULIA: Looked at yourself! Or else you went and gave it to that dreadful little scarecrow!

BO (*sadly*): I haven't seen Astrid in two weeks.

JULIA: Two weeks, such enterprise! Here you have such a charming, lovely fiancée and you don't pay your respects daily. Usch, a regular dullard!

ROLF: Perhaps Bo's expecting a tragedy, too.

BO: Me? (*He looks at Rolf, but lowers his eyes again.*)

BOMAN (*enters from the back*): Children, I'm beginning to worry. Certainly Swedenhielm can't have done himself any harm?

ROLF: Be quiet—that's absurd!

BOMAN: All right! But the last time I saw him he had a razor in his hand. And he's been so strange lately—(*Exits*)

JULIA: What a bore it all is! (*Miserably*) Can you please explain this unmitigated gloom? Today we ought to have been leaping about from morning till night.

ROLF (*bitterly*): Perhaps we've celebrated the occasion in advance.

JULIA (*miserably*): Oh, is that it? Yes, that would be so terribly Swedenhielmish, to dance before the music begins.

ROLF: But if there's going to be any kind of a—confrontation— or, to use another word, "tragedy"—we ought to be able to spare father the shame of seeing our name blasted again by the papers.

BO (*slowly*): I don't understand—what you're driving at.

JULIA: Neither do I, but I do feel terribly out of sorts!

ROLF: I'm only suggesting that one of us might sacrifice himself for the sake of the family's honor and disappear—oh, not by suicide!

BO (*with a spiritless smile*): By plane!

ROLF: By train!

JULIA: Good God, boys, if you would only learn your lines. You've been going around now for weeks mumbling like a couple of Egyptian priests. It's absolutely futile, trying to get you to sing out! If you've robbed or murdered, well then say so, once and for all; but don't spoil the happiness your father is so keenly anticipating.

ROLF: It seems that his happiness was spoiled before tonight.

JULIA: Oh yes, he *has* become so terribly sad! What if he refuses to appear?

ROLF: Appear where?

JULIA: On the stage!

ROLF: Do you think he's about to act?

JULIA: Well, all great people do. This very minute he's sitting in front of his mirror, studying his face and rehearsing what he will do when he takes the prize from the King. My loyal gratitude, Your Majesty, for graciously bestowing upon old Swedenhielm so much honor and gladness in his declining years! You have done well, oh King, for of all the inspiring words in the world, the two dearest to Swedenhielm are "Gladness" and "Honor." (*She breaks off suddenly and bursts into tears.*) Can anyone tell me why I have to be so very nervous?

BOMAN (*quickly enters, frightened, whispering*): Children, listen to me! It's all over with him! He's sitting there in front of his mirror, like a stone image, staring at himself.

JULIA: What did I tell you?

BOMAN: It's the beginning of the end! When an old man sits staring at himself like that, it's the beginning of the end! Who would've thought he'd have taken it so hard!

JULIA: What do you mean?

BOMAN: The papers, of course, that Eriksson gave him—

ROLF: Did he get the forged ones as well? Do you know for certain?

BOMAN: I made sure of those before I burned the torn-up bits.

ROLF (*as if seeking his sister's protection*): No. Julia, I can't take it—

JULIA (*tenderly*): Now my little boy mustn't get excited—

BO (*rises*): Yes, you don't need to get excited—I can promise you that.

BOMAN: He's coming, he's coming! No, I don't dare to stay— (*She hurries out into Julia's room.*)

(*Rolf goes quickly to the window; Julia and Bo remain motionless. Swedenhielm's step is heard—it is a very slow pace—he comes into sight in the dining room. He is in evening dress with the Vasa Order ribbon on his breast. His bearing is erect, except for his head, which is bowed. He looks out as if there were nothing in front of him. He comes into the downstage area and stands in the center of the room. He takes out his watch and looks at it for a long time before he realizes what he is looking at. His voice is hollow, without any feeling.*)

SWEDENHIELM: Is everybody ready?

JULIA (*trying to speak lightly*): As if we weren't ready!

SWEDENHIELM (*taking out his watch again*): All right, then, we'll go. Shall we take the streetcar?

JULIA: Yes, but Papa, there's been a taxi waiting half an hour for us.

SWEDENHIELM (*looking at his watch again*): Really, half an hour? Well, we'd better be going then, hm?

JULIA: Wait a minute—(*She arranges a small detail on his costume.*) Oh, but you look magnificent!

SWEDENHIELM (*smiling weakly*): I must be that—I'm your father. (*He takes out his watch again.*) Yes, we'd best be off, don't you think? (*He turns slowly as if unwilling to leave.*)

JULIA: Oh, but my face is burning so! Does it look like I've been crying?

SWEDENHIELM (*listlessly, without turning his head*): You've been crying? Why?

JULIA: And I don't have my little mirror! (*Stamping on the floor*) What have you done with my mirror?

BO (*impatiently*): No, but Julia, please—

SWEDENHIELM (*still listless*): What is it?

JULIA (*indignantly*): Bo has stolen my mirror!

BO: That's absolutely impossible—

SWEDENHIELM (*turning suddenly, fiercely*): What is it that's absolutely impossible?

BO (*bewildered*): That I should have stolen—

SWEDENHIELM (*rushes toward him, screams*): Is it also absolutely impossible that you are a forger? (*Strikes him on the face*)

BO (*staggers back to the wall; for a moment he is silent, breathing hard. Then he says in a low voice*): You shouldn't have done that, Father. After all, I'm in uniform.

SWEDENHIELM (*beside himself with anger*): Are you a forger? Are you? Answer me, or I'll tear that uniform right off you! Did you forge my name?!

BO (*turns and looks at Rolf, then back to Swedenhielm, quietly but firmly*): Yes, Father.

(*Swedenhielm's tenseness suddenly weakens; his arms fall to his sides; his head sinks. Silence*)

SWEDENHIELM (*exhausted*): Forgive me for striking you. I didn't want it this way. But it's been on my mind for such a long time. It has completely exhausted me.

ROLF (*tormented, hesitantly*): Father—you can never be entirely certain that it was Bo—it could—just as easily have been me—

SWEDENHIELM (*wearily*): Yes, why not? If one could do it, so could another.

(*Silence. Boman enters from the right. She advances slowly, holding her shawl around her tightly as if she were very cold. Swedenhielm makes an effort to pull himself together; he takes several steps back and forth.*)

SWEDENHIELM: No. I can't do it. I can't accept the Nobel Prize. Who am I to wear any decoration at all? If I haven't been able to make honorable men of my own sons, then a decoration can't be worth much.

BOMAN (*with affected serenity*): What is it now?

JULIA (*turning to her and speaking very seriously*): Mutti, something terrible, Bo has forged father's name.

BOMAN: Did Swedenhielm say that? About his own son?

SWEDENHIELM (*again indifferent*): Yes, it's true.

BOMAN (*regards him for a moment with great contempt, then*): Well, you were always a genius at inventing things, but to start inventing about the little one—(*points at Bo with her thumb*) well, that's too much.

SWEDENHIELM (*as before*): What do you mean, Boman?

BOMAN: Those bits of paper are haunting you, are they? Well, I should have thought that when you were so anxious to see them burned, we'd hear no more about them. You see, that would have been considerate and generous.

SWEDENHIELM: We'll say no more about it.

BOMAN: Oh, yes, we will. I know you, Swedenhielm, and you won't rest until you know who signed your name. Well, it was Marta Boman, if you remember who that is.

(*Silence*)

BO: Mummy?!

JULIA: Mutti! I'm going to faint.

BOMAN: Then faint in the dining room, for Swedenhielm and I have got to talk things out.

SWEDENHIELM (*seizes her by the shoulders and shakes her*): If you're lying about this, woman, I'll kill you!

BOMAN (*taking a paper from her bosom*): See for yourself! Here's another of them, written as well as I could. It's only for a hundred, so I was able to pay it back.

SWEDENHIELM (*nervously handling the paper*): But this is Bo's paper, too.

BOMAN: I can't afford any myself.

SWEDENHIELM (*with feverish cadence*): Why in the name of blazes have you done this?

BOMAN: To raise money. If you will dimly perceive.

SWEDENHIELM: But what did you need the money for?

BOMAN (*exasperated*): You ask me that? Have you any idea

how much it costs to run a house for a young officer, a star actress, and two raving geniuses?

SWEDENHIELM: But haven't I given you money?

BOMAN: Yes, when you had any. But when you were broke, you didn't expressly order me to let you starve to death. Besides, people in this house have illusions. Some of them order caviar for breakfast—(*Gives Bo a ferocious look*)

BO (*humbly, pleading*): Mummy—

BOMAN: Oh, don't worry, dear, you're not the only one.

SWEDENHIELM: And because of that you've been to a—

BOMAN (*interrupting*): Put me in prison, Swedenhielm!

SWEDENHIELM: Do you mean to say that I didn't give you enough to—

BOMAN (*interrupting*): Do you know what enough means? In spite of your talent for discovery, you plainly can't keep account of our daily finances. And every now and then we've had to give parties with lanterns and champagne so that some of us could give the impression of East Indian luxury.

JULIA (*as Bo was before*): Mutti—Mutti—

BOMAN: Oh, don't worry, you're not the only one!

SWEDENHIELM: And for the sake of such frivolity—

BOMAN (*stretches out her arms*): Put me in prison!

SWEDENHIELM: What, for example, did you do with the last four hundred?

BOMAN: Paid for the little one's silk shirts

SWEDENHIELM (*exploding*): Silk shirts!

BOMAN (*stretching out her arms again*): Perhaps he was to go without one? Or else he was supposed to go unnoticed among the other fine lieutenants? But since his name is Swedenhielm, this is the way it's got to be.

SWEDENHIELM: You're driving me crazy!

BOMAN: Put me in prison!

SWEDENHIELM (*with a desperate attempt to preserve his authority*): Boman, how long have these—how long has this been going on?

BOMAN: None of your business. Up to now I've paid back every single note the day it was due, but this time because someone—

ROLF: But, dearest Auntie, it is absolutely necessary that we know—

BOMAN (*in a rage*): Well if it's *that* necessary! The first of the notes was written just seven years ago, when someone began to bring home glass tubes, gas ovens, lamps, poisonous powders, and smelly chemicals to demonstrate that he was a genius, too.

ROLF: You don't mean that the little I borrowed tempted you to—

BOMAN: Don't get excited. You're not the only one. There are several geniuses in this house.

SWEDENHIELM: Do you mean to say that you've paid for my experiments? Perhaps you've also been conducting them for me!

BOMAN: If I had I wouldn't have made such a mess of everything as you've always done! But put me in prison, put me in prison.

SWEDENHIELM: Hold your trap with your prison!

BOMAN: Educated, a truly educated man.

SWEDENHIELM: Woman, what am I going to do with you?

BOMAN (*calmly but rather worn out*): Do as I say, Swedenhielm. Put me in prison. That will be an end of all the bother and the noise, an end of all the cleaning and tidying—the darning and mending and sweeping and scheming over accounts and I don't know what else. It will be as good as a vacation for me. Because the way things are—though I haven't made any world-shaking inventions—I can get a little tired, too.

BO (*fondly and anxiously*): Mummy, mummy—

JULIA: Mutti—

SWEDENHIELM (*quietly*): Tell me one more thing—and you will be completely forgiven.

BOMAN: Thank you.

SWEDENHIELM: How could you—could you let me go through all of these days—without saying a word?

BOMAN (*ferociously*): What, for example, should I have said?

SWEDENHIELM: That it was—that it was you—

BOMAN: Could I have any idea that you would be so dense? Didn't you see what terrible scrawling it was? God be thanked, I did have some education, but I never took any prizes for penmanship. And when you asked me to burn those scraps of paper, you gave me a look that made my heart stop. What else could I believe but that you knew everything! And if you didn't understand, you could have come and asked me. But you were too stuck-up for that. And pride has its punishment. So I'm not in the least sorry for you! I'd offer much more sympathy to my poor sister who went and married such a numskull.

SWEDENHIELM (*taking her head in his hands, he looks searchingly into her face*): Boman, sometimes I forget that you're my sister-in-law.

BOMAN: I've noticed.

SWEDENHIELM: Marta, do you remember your sister?

BOMAN: Most likely I do.

SWEDENHIELM: She was a very beautiful woman.

BOMAN: Yes, she was.

SWEDENHIELM: And you are very ugly.

BOMAN: So they say.

SWEDENHIELM (*laying his cheek against hers*): Yet no other

woman has ever made me quite so happy as you've done today—

(*Boman is suddenly shaken by a sniffle.*)

JULIA (*alarmed*): Look there! Now Mutti's beginning to cry. We'll have to go to the ceremony in a rowboat.

SWEDENHIELM (*stretching himself out*): All right, children! Enough of that. But there's still one more thing. (*Takes hold of Bo on either side of his chest and shakes him*) What unhallowed spirit got you to say (*imitating*): Yes, Father!

BO (*embarrassed*): Well, you see—I was afraid that—I thought that maybe Rolf had—

ROLF (*exasperated and bewildered*): What's that, you young fool? I was absolutely convinced that you were the guilty one!

SWEDENHIELM: So—you've been going around suspecting each other! That's a good one! That's a very good one! To suspect your own brother!

JULIA (*innocently*): But Papa darling, is it any better to go around suspecting your own son?

SWEDENHIELM (*impatiently*): Are you implying that I have—

JULIA: Just look at him! He's already forgotten that he wasn't fit to receive the Nobel Prize because of his dishonorable sons! And that's what I thought was so very touching!

(*Swedenhielm and his sons become very grim in appearance; they exchange sly glances and then direct them threateningly toward Julia.*)

JULIA (*joyously and innocently*): Have you also managed to forget that only five minutes ago you knocked poor little Bo on his ear?

BO (*infuriated*): Does that even remotely concern you?

ROLF: Ham!

BO: Ham!!

SWEDENHIELM: Ham!!!

JULIA (*assuming an attitude of tragic despair*): Why do these three men always plot against me, a defenseless woman! Sir Herbert, my life is beyond endurance!

BOMAN (*seriously*): Swedenhielm, you shouldn't insult your children! It's not so easy to live in the same house with you, waiting for an explosion any minute of the day. Sometimes I think you're a genius, but most of the time I pray to heaven you're not a lunatic!

SWEDENHIELM (*putting his hands on her head*): Boman, you are my life's unhappiness. You are the total spectrum of Swedish poverty. Your special genius is that of a Swedish Egeria.

BOMAN: It's quite possible, for I don't have the slightest idea what you're talking about.

SWEDENHIELM: In simple prose, then, for all of your double dealing, you are the perfect pattern of a respectable woman.

BOMAN: I think I'm a little more refined than that!

SWEDENHIELM: And now, children, let's empty a bottle of champagne—in honor of Boman!

ASTRID (*comes hurrying in through the dining room, wearing evening dress and a cloak*): You all must be crazy! Do you know what time it is?

(*Swedenhielm looks at his watch, makes a grimace of alarmed surprise, and rushes out at the back, followed by Rolf and Julia.*)

ASTRID (*to Bo*): Perhaps you cursed Swedenhielms are going to show the King his place, by obliging him to wait for you! What's delayed you so?

BO (*putting his arms around her and kissing her; laconically*): Housecleaning. (*Both exit at the back.*)

BOMAN: Well, just so the King doesn't get angry now. For

with Swedenhielm, you've got to have the patience of Job. If you ever want to get anything done. (*She goes out into the dining room and turns off the light, but comes directly back into the downstage area with a coffee cup surrounded by sweet rolls. She sets this down on a table in the vicinity of the door at the back. Suddenly Swedenhielm returns, wearing his cloak and carrying his hat in his hand.*)

SWEDENHIELM: Boman, in a little while you will be receiving a visit from a gentleman named Eriksson. You know him very well. He's my foster brother. But you shall treat him as if he were a brother of my own flesh. You shall offer him the best chair and give him a flask of the best wine and a cigar from the best case—but above everything else: you shall beam down upon him with your very best humor! For Boman! This man Eriksson is my foster brother. And we will not overestimate ourselves. Have you understood me?

BOMAN: No.

SWEDENHIELM: This is the way I want things, and I hope you can respect my wishes.

BOMAN: Been doing that now for thirty years, so I suppose I can do it tonight.

SWEDENHIELM: A woman of honor! (*Quickly exits at the back*) (*Boman exits into the dining room. The stage is empty for a moment. A car is heard accelerating and driving away. Boman enters from the dining room.*)

BOMAN: Now, they're gone. (*As she comes into the downstage area it is seen that she is armed with a powerful carpet beater, which she sets by the table. She then takes a sip from her coffee cup.*) And Eriksson can come. (*Very much satisfied with herself, Boman dips her sweet rolls into her coffee, as the curtain falls slowly.*)

Introduction to
MR. SLEEMAN IS COMING

DURING 1916–17 Hjalmar Bergman wrote one two-act play, *The Harlequin of Death,* and two one-act plays, *The Shadow* and *Mr. Sleeman Is Coming (Herr Sleeman kommer).* It is this last play that we shall now consider. When the author published all three of them in one volume, he called them *Marionette Plays.* Asked what he meant by this general title, he answered, "I have called my plays *Marionette Plays* since they belong to a group of my plays which embody a common basic idea. In them I look upon my people as marionettes directed by a power behind them of which they themselves are unconscious. In one case it is their own past which decides their fate, in another the force of circumstances, and in still another it is a strong person who has arranged his environment according to his own purposes like a stage director. And finally the greatest power of all, Death, makes his appearance."

The theme that people are really puppets who dance to the will of a higher power runs through all of Hjalmar Bergman's writings. They may be strong and obstinate or weak and irresolute, but finally their wills are paralyzed and they turn into the living dead. Although these Bergman people may seem rather independent in their youth, sooner or later the mysterious power sends a messenger for them; in the end it is always the dread power who summons them, and in the end it is always he who wins.

Marionette plays are among Hjalmar Bergman's most original creations. This form gave him the disguise and the remoteness his sensitiveness demanded. With this symbolic form he could feel himself able to give vent to his own anxiety complex. In the figure of Mr. Sleeman the author created a symbol for the quiet, apparently friendly force which drains the will to live and makes marionettes of people. He wrote: "We are born people, but we become marionettes when we are forced to give up. We struggle and struggle to hold on to our youth, our health, and our vital existence. But Mr. Sleeman comes." This pessimism is based on the author's constantly recurring personal reflections about life in its healthy and in its petrified forms and on his experience with the greatest of tragedies—how living is reduced to mechanism and grimace. In *Mr. Sleeman Is Coming* he handled this subject more thoroughly than ever before and by means of its obviously idyllic setting even more affectingly. This little play is among the author's most frequently performed works, and for the last quarter of a century it has been in the standard repertory of dramatic schools and amateur theaters in most European languages.

The play describes how a poor girl, Anne-Marie, is sold by her guardians to a rich old man. But if a person follows the dialogue closely, he perceives that the play is really about how a young girl reaches maturity and gives up. She is told that the rich but ailing old Mr. Sleeman is coming at exactly eight o'clock the following morning to fetch her as his bride. But Anne-Marie loves the green-clad hunter from the green forest, and he comes and lures her out into the beautiful summer night. Youth yearns to youth but is kept apart through the meddlesomeness of old age. The hunter and his Anne-Marie have their golden moment together. The scene with the two young persons has an ambiguous poetry which floats like a light mist above the witches' brew from the Bergman moors. The girl's anxiety about the minutes which bring her nearer and nearer to the meeting with the terrible Mr. Sleeman, and the hunter's uncomprehending devotion, fresh as the fragrant forest, lend an aura of painful happiness to the scene.

And when Mr. Sleeman arrives at precisely eight o'clock, the scene is repeated, frightful and distorted, as the gruesome Mr. Sleeman declares his love for Anne-Marie in almost exactly the same words the hunter had used. Love and the caricature of love employ the same poor vocabulary—a genuine Bergman touch! Thus, when Mr. Sleeman comes, the drama is concluded and Mr. Sleeman has been betrayed. But the sacrifice takes place, nevertheless; and when Mr. Sleeman, with his hump-back, his stiff legs, and his mechanical squeaky voice repeats exactly the persuasive love talk which came out strong and vi-brant from the hunter's mouth, Anne-Marie weeps her bitterest tears. And Mr. Sleeman tells the old ladies soothingly, "Ah, yes, ladies, joy also has its tears."

When the play was performed in Stockholm in 1919 and the author was asked if he intended Mr. Sleeman to represent Death itself, he answered only: "There is an old gentleman who limps stiffly along the highways and byways. He is not malevolent, but in some strange way he is able to read people's minds. He somehow figures out the thoughts which once were especially precious to us. He knows the words that once were dear to us and very pleasant to hear—our youthful words of love, the unspoiled and beautiful ideas of our youth." A well-intentioned old man—but a melancholy encounter. Because the words he speaks are so horribly toneless. Is he conjuring with them in his toothless jaws? Or is it simply that it was young healthy teeth and warm young lips that once made the words mean something? And that words, words, words, words by themselves have no significance at all?

In this play it is a poor, helpless, little girl who meets Mr. Sleeman. She is still young; but not even youth is any sure protection against Mr. Sleeman. No, as a matter of fact, he most often seeks out the very young, the delicate and defenseless. He loves a glowing heart. A fervent cheek warms his frozen lips so pleasantly.

Mr. Sleeman is coming. He is not attractive to look at. He is almost nothing but a bag of bones. He is not Death—not even related to the Dreadful One. But he resembles him.

STINA BERGMAN

MR. SLEEMAN

IS COMING

A One-Act Play

TRANSLATED BY WALTER JOHNSON

Characters

AUNT BINA
AUNT MINA
ANNE-MARIE, *their niece*
THE HUNTER (WALTER)
MR. SLEEMAN

Setting

A room in an attic apartment.

At the back a rather large window through which the audience can look out over roofs and chimneys; in the distance a darkening forest.

The room is the two old maids' Sunday parlor, and as a result is filled with all sorts of knickknacks, bric-a-brac, whatnots, pedestals, etc., all of them more or less ugly in form and even more so in color combinations. When the curtain is raised, the furniture and the ornaments are concealed by blue-and-white-striped slipcovers. The room thereby gets a simpler, cleaner, and more pleasant effect, particularly the white sloping ceiling and the light blue wallpaper which harmonizes with the slipcovers. The two old maids' tastelessly ornamented dresses are concealed in the first part of the act by blue-and-white-striped housekeeping aprons. Anne-Marie wears the same dress—a blue-and-green-checkered cotton dress of the little-girl type—throughout the play.

It is evening in the late summer. The sunset gives the room which faces the west a beautiful, friendly lighting.

Three doors: two small low white ones, one on either side of the footlights; a large one on the right wall up stage. The large door is the entrance.

The furniture may be arranged as one wishes. On the right wall between the two doors is, however, a Mora clock, also concealed by a slipcover but running. In the middle of the stage quite near the footlights is a group consisting of two large easy chairs and a round table approximately three quarters of a meter in diameter.

When the curtain is raised, the two old maids are sitting in the two easy chairs. Mina is embroidering; Bina has on her lap a stocking she is knitting, but she is busy reading for the third or fourth time a letter, the lines of which she is following with her knitting needle.

MINA (*embroidering*): Imagine!

BINA (*reading*): Yes—imagine!

MINA: What luck!

BINA: Well—you can say that!

MINA: At such an early age!

BINA: A mere child. (*Short pause*)

MINA (*lets what she is embroidering fall slowly*): But—Bina— if we all the same should—

BINA (*stares fixedly at her over her glasses; abruptly*): What?

MINA (*hesitantly*): If we should ask him to wait a year? She *is* pretty young.

BINA (*bitterly*): A girl is never too young to be happy. She can become too old—(*pointedly*) some women have, goodness knows.

MINA (*sighing*): Yes, goodness knows.

BINA: A year is long. You never know what can happen. (*Mina sighs.*) A young girl is exposed to many temptations. How did it go with our sister Mathilda?

MINA (*disturbed*): Please. Please don't talk about that!

BINA (*bitterly*): Quit talking yourself, then.

(*Anne-Marie pokes her head in through the door at the left.*)

ANNE-MARIE: Are you absolutely sure? Shouldn't there be four cups?

BINA (*sternly*): Three cups, child, as I said.

ANNE-MARIE: From the best set?

BINA: The best set. (*Anne-Marie goes out.*)

MINA (*with a quiet giggle*): Now she's terribly curious, isn't she?

BINA (*seriously*): She has good reason to be curious. (*She puts the letter back into the envelope, strikes it solemnly with her knitting needle.*) Here, Mina, we have Anne-Marie's happiness.

MINA: Yes, imagine—in a little envelope. May I see it? (*Takes the letter, examines it, and smells it.*)

ANNE-MARIE (*pokes in her head*): Should there be all kinds of cookies and rolls?

BINA (*solemnly*): All kinds.

MINA (*shocked*): But not too many!

BINA: Three of every kind. (*Anne-Marie goes out.*)

MINA (*points at the letter, dreamily*): What a firm and manly hand.

BINA (*knits; sharply*): He didn't write it himself.

MINA (*disappointed*): Oh—didn't he write it himself?

BINA: No, he has writer's cramp.

MINA: Well, in his position that doesn't matter, of course. I suppose he never needs to write a word himself?

BINA: Only his name. And he does that with a rubber stamp.

MINA (*after a short pause, hesitantly*): And what about the other things?

BINA (*sharply*): What other things?

MINA: In his legs?

BINA (*curtly*): That's another illness.

MINA (*sighs softly*): Well, he doesn't need to walk very much himself, of course.

(*Anne-Marie enters with a little coffee tray, which she puts on the table.*)

ANNE-MARIE (*happily*): Oh my! Are we going to drink coffee in the parlor on an ordinary weekday? And the best dishes and all kinds! No, I think somebody's coming. (*Her two aunts smile secretively at each other. Anne-Marie takes a small chair and then sits down behind the table with her face toward the footlights.*)

BINA (*in the meanwhile*): You're right, Anne-Marie. Someone is coming.

ANNE-MARIE: Tonight?

BINA: That wouldn't be quite proper.

MINA: Oh, no-o—a man at this time of day

ANNE-MARIE (*amazed*): A man?

BINA (*correcting her*): A gentleman. Pour the coffee, Anne-Marie. Two lumps for me.

MINA: And three for me.

ANNE-MARIE (*serving*): Do I know him?

BINA: Perhaps. Well, you have seen him. And you have heard us say very nice things about him. He was your poor mother's guardian and only support.

ANNE-MARIE (*calmly registering the fact*): Oh, it's an old gentleman.

BINA: Middle-aged. If it hadn't been for him, your unfortunate mother would have sunk still—

ANNE-MARIE: What's his name?

BINA (*impressively*): Mr. Sleeman.

MINA (*emotionally*): Now it's said.

ANNE-MARIE (*reflecting*): Oh-h—yes, I remember. I remember him, Aunt!

MINA (*emotionally*): What do you know! She remembers him. That's a happy omen.

ANNE-MARIE (*jumps up, in front of the table*): Isn't he the one who walks like this? (*She imitates a tabetic's stiff, difficult walk, without the characteristic curves.*)

MINA (*giggling softly*): Something like that.

BINA (*sternly*): Anne-Marie! One doesn't imitate a sick person.

ANNE-MARIE (*shocked*): Is he sick?

BINA (*somewhat embarrassed*): Not sick. But sickly.

ANNE-MARIE (*goes back to her place*): Poor man!

BINA: It's because of that that he needs support and care. He wrote to us—

MINA (*anxiously*): The coffee will get cold.

BINA (*stirs her coffee; raises her cup*): Now we'll drink to your good future, Anne-Marie.

MINA: Yes, we will.

ANNE-MARIE (*smiling*): How strange you are tonight. Skoal!

BINA: And now you may hear his letter.

ANNE-MARIE: Is it about me?

BINA: It's about you. (*Reads*) My honored Miss Bina, my respected Miss Mina—

MINA (*beaming*): Yes, he said "respected"—

BINA (*sharply*): "Honored" is just as fine. Don't interrupt me. (*Reads*) As an answer to your appreciated communication of last May 28, I assure you that I have conscientiously and sympathetically taken the complaints stated therein into account. (*By way of explanation*) You see, I complained about our extremely limited circumstances. He answers: Twelve hundred crowns in all truth do not provide luxurious support for three persons, even if these are unmarried women with small and modest pretensions.

ANNE-MARIE: But we get along nicely—

BINA (*sharply*): Oh, you think so? Don't interrupt me. (*Reads*) Although I have examined the matter from every point of view, I see no possibility of increasing your income. (*Mina sighs heavily.*) There is therefore the consideration of the question whether your expenditures in any proper way can be reduced. I believe that I have found that way. It is most likely not unknown to you that my health lately has left a great deal to be desired. Under such circumstances I begin to find the loneliness of bachelor life depressing, and in consequence of that fact I have decided to seek a tender and faithful companion for the remaining days of my life.

(*Mina sighs heavily.*)

BINA (*sharply*): Mina—can't you wait with your sighing?

MINA (*embarrassed*): Yes, yes—I will wait—

BINA (*reads*): First and last I want to give you what I hope will be the happy news that my choice is the unfortunate Mathilda's daughter, your niece, dear Anne-Marie.

ANNE-MARIE (*shocked*): But why? Why, he doesn't know me—

BINA: Wait and you'll hear. (*Reads*) Naturally I have reached my decision after mature consideration, primarily basing it partly on the photograph you enclosed in your letter and still more on the recommendation you give Anne-Marie as being an innocent, by the world yet untouched, young person with a happy, friendly temperament, besides being domestically inclined and not without talent in respect to music —(*Gives Anne-Marie a friendly pat on the cheek*) Yes, Anne-Marie, you got a splendid recommendation from Aunt Bina.

MINA: Yes, thank your kind Aunt Bina!

ANNE-MARIE (*depressed*): Thank you kind—

BINA (*reads*): At the same time I lift a heavy burden from your shoulders, I shall realize my own objective in that as soon as possible I receive dear Anne-Marie in my house.

ANNE-MARIE (*anxiously*): Yes, but everything's fine for me here. Do I have to?

(*Short pause. Mina sighs.*)

BINA (*relentlessly*): I'll read the sentence again. "At the same time I lift a heavy burden from your shoulders . . ." Don't you want to let Mr. Sleeman free us old people of a heavy burden, Anne-Marie?

ANNE-MARIE (*sadly*): Yes, yes. But what am I supposed to do at Mr. Sleeman's?

BINA: I understand your distress, child. You probably think you're to be some higher sort of maid. But listen to what Mr. Sleeman says very clearly. (*Reads*) Even in advance filled with the warmest feelings, I shall hasten tomorrow to meet my young bride. (*Short pause*) Do you understand?

(*Anne-Marie lowers her head.*)

BINA (*reads*): From and including that day I assume all expenditures necessary to her person and hope that I in compensation will receive a friendly and happy reception. I am leaving here on the night train, and, if nothing unforeseen occurs, I shall arrive at your residence at exactly eight o'clock. Trusting that I shall continue in your respected favor, I remain your devoted J. O. Sleeman, Chief of the Secretariat.

(*A short pause. Anne-Marie sits with her head bent low.*)

MINA (*to break the silence*): Has—has he written his name himself?

BINA: No-o—with a stamp.

(*A short pause. The Mora clock strikes eight times.*)

ANNE-MARIE (*jumps up in alarm*): Aunt! It struck eight!

BINA: You crazy little girl! It's early tomorrow he's coming.

It'd be something for a suitor to pay a call at this time of day.

MINA (*giggles softly*): There are suitors like that, too.

BINA: Mina!

MINA (*gets up*): No, now I must look at the sunset. (*Goes to the window*) How beautiful it is over the forest.

ANNE-MARIE (*hesitantly*): Aunt Bina—am I really such a heavy burden?

BINA (*embarrassed, but resolutely*): Yes, my dear child. Ever since your unfortunate mother . . .

ANNE-MARIE (*hastily*): Yes, yes—I know. You don't need to say any more. May—may I go to bed now?

BINA: Go to bed? Are you crazy? Mina, she wants to go to bed! I think we should talk it over—

ANNE-MARIE: Why, there's nothing to talk over. Mr. Sleeman is coming. And so there is nothing more.

BINA: You're crazy! What about receiving him? Do you even know how to greet a man like him?

ANNE-MARIE: I'll shake his hand, I suppose.

BINA (*scornfully*): Yes, of course! You shake his hand—Good day. Good day—just as you do with that—(*sniffs*)—person dressed in green. Oh, I've seen the two of you. But now there'll be an end to things like that. Do you really know what a Chief of the Secretariat is? He is—the highest-ranking person—in—the whole—province—after the governor.

ANNE-MARIE (*weakly*): Is—is he?

BINA: Well, apparently you haven't quite understood how fortunate you are.

ANNE-MARIE: No—perhaps—

BINA: He ranks so infinitely above you. Not so much above me and Mina. Our father was at least a lieutenant when he retired. But your father, dear child—

ANNE-MARIE: Aunt, may I get out of—

BINA: No, you may not. Since you don't seem to appreciate your good fortune. Your father was an ordinary simple laborer in the forest. Yes, he was.

ANNE-MARIE (*looks toward the window; softly*): That's probably why I like the forest so much.

BINA: Good heavens! You like the forest because it's full of young hunters. But if you don't watch out, it will go for you as it did for—

MINA (*claps her hands lightly*): Bina dear—Bina dear—but this is a day for rejoicing.

BINA: Yes, it ought to be. Well, well. First and foremost you're to take off all the slipcovers and dust very carefully.

ANNE-MARIE: Yes, Aunt Bina.

BINA: But you mustn't stay up too long or you'll be pale. Mr. Sleeman expects to see a radiant young girl. Now we'll imagine receiving him. Come here, Mina. Don't stand there gaping at the sun. I almost believe we should let them be alone to begin with. What do you think, Mina? A tête-à-tête—

ANNE-MARIE (*pleadingly*): Oh no—Aunt—

BINA: Yes, that's what we'll do. We can't begrudge him that little bit of freedom since he's a mature man. And then Mina and I have a little surprise ready. You didn't forget to order the bouquets, I hope?

MINA: Not a chance! The engagement bouquets!

BINA: You can, for example, stand by this chair. Mina can keep a lookout in her window and let us know when he comes. Yes, you'll get plenty of time. You'll hear his steps on the stairs—he—walks a little slowly, of course—Anne-Marie— are you listening to what I'm saying?

ANNE-MARIE (*coming to*): Yes—yes—I hear his steps on the stairs—he walks a little slowly, of course—

BINA (*impatiently*): Well, I mean that you're to stand here in a perfectly natural way. Then he'll knock. Mina, pretend you're Sleeman and go out and knock.

MINA (*trips, giggling, toward the door*): What that Bina can't think of! (*Goes out*)

BINA: Don't stand there listless. Be cheerful and friendly. Knock, Mina! (*Mina knocks.*) Well, what do you say now?

ANNE-MARIE (*with a slight shudder*): Come in.

BINA (*scornfully*): Yes, of course! Come in. No. Please come in! (*Mina enters, giggling.*)

BINA: At first you can look a little surprised. Like this. But then you change that look at once to a smile of recognition. And what do you do then, Anne-Marie? (*Anne-Marie curtsies.*)

BINA: No, dear child! Like this! (*A deep curtsy*) You're exceedingly welcome, Mr. Sleeman. (*Anne-Marie curtsies deeply.*)

BINA: Wait a little. We'll put his letter in your bosom—like this—then he'll understand that you know its contents— that will make it easier for him to propose. Then I imagine he'll take a couple of steps. Say something, Mina; think up something—

MINA (*disguised voice, giggling*): My lovely girl—

BINA: Then you walk up to him and take his hand. Mina, what do you think? Should she kiss his hand? No—no, I don't think so. It would emphasize his age too much. It's better if he kisses your hand. Oh, you have to be so careful—so careful —you'll raise your hand—like this—

MINA: But Bina dear—what if he should kiss her cheek—or— or perhaps her mouth?

BINA: You ought to be ashamed—an old woman having such thoughts. Do you understand, Anne-Marie? It takes so much to catch a man. Especially a man with a good position and sure income. Well, we'll have to do it over again early tomorrow. Just see to it the slipcovers are taken off. Mina —it's almost nine o'clock. We mustn't be too sleepy-eyed, either. Good night, my child. Think of this: your happiness is coming closer every minute that passes. Mr. Sleeman is already on the train. Good night, Mina. You did put the bouquets in water, didn't you? Yes. Well then. Sleep well. (*Goes out through the little door to the right. Mina locks the entrance door and takes the key. Anne-Marie goes quickly up to her.*)

ANNE-MARIE: Aunt Mina, may I go out into the forest tonight?

MINA: No, no, no, dear child. You mayn't do that any more.

ANNE-MARIE: Just tonight. Mr. Sleeman is coming tomorrow.

MINA: Yes, thank goodness—after that I won't have any responsibility. And once you're really married, dear child, you may go out into the forest as much—as much as you want to—

ANNE-MARIE (*goes over to the window*): But then—but then I probably won't want to—

MINA (*goes giggling softly toward the door at the left*): I wonder, Anne-Marie! (*Giggles*) Sleep well. And dream about the forest. (*Goes out*)

ANNE-MARIE (*at the window; clasps her hands back of her neck, slowly*): Dream—about—the forest. (*Forces herself out of that mood*) No. I have to take off the slipcovers. (*Goes over to the clock and begins to loosen a cover; suddenly covers her eyes with her arm.*) No . . . I can't look at the clock—(*The clock strikes nine. Anne-Marie lets her arm fall.*) Poor me—it keeps going, going—anyway. And Mr. Sleeman is coming. (*Goes to "the" chair*) So—I'm to stand here. And then I hear his footsteps on the stairs. I have plenty of time—for he walks—a little slowly. But he knocks at last. (*Knocks on the arm of the chair; bows invitingly*) Please come in!

(*There is a loud knock on the entrance door. Anne-Marie jumps. There is a still louder knock. Anne-Marie steals toward the door on her toes.*)

HUNTER'S VOICE (*muffled, but rather strong*): Anne-Marie! Anne-Marie!

ANNE-MARIE (*very softly*): Walter!

HUNTER: Open, Anne-Marie!

ANNE-MARIE: I can't.

HUNTER: Come out. Come with me into the forest. It's very beautiful out there tonight.

ANNE-MARIE (*looks toward the window; repeats*): It's very beautiful out there tonight. (*Changes her tone*) I can't, Walter. Aunt Mina has locked the door. It's all over now. (*Pause*) It's all over, Walter. You have to go. (*Pause*) You have to go.

HUNTER: I'll go, but I'm coming back.

BINA (*enters from the right*): Anne-Marie—were you talking with someone?

MINA (*enters from the left*): Anne-Marie?

BINA: She was talking with someone.

MINA: She was talking with herself, the crazy girl.

ANNE-MARIE (*calmly*): I was talking with Walter. He knocked on the door just now and asked me to come out.

BINA: Mina, you have the key, I hope?

MINA: The door's locked and barred.

BINA: Mina, I'm afraid you haven't kept an eye on Anne-Marie.

MINA: I've done as well as I could, Bina. But I will say— thank goodness Mr. Sleeman is coming.

BINA: Yes, thank goodness he's coming. (*Goes out*)

MINA (*shakes her finger reprovingly*): You—yes, you—

ANNE-MARIE: Oh, you don't need to shake your finger, Aunt Mina. He's gone.

MINA: Just see to it he doesn't come back.

ANNE-MARIE (*indifferently*): How should he get in?

MINA (*soft giggle*): Oh, one never knows—(*Hums with a cracked voice*)

> When the linden turns green
> The hunter gets his queen
> In the forest.

(*Goes out. Anne-Marie stands by the chair again, begins slowly to loosen the slipcover but stops, stares straight ahead, hypnotized.*)

ANNE-MARIE (*half chanting*): Then-n—I hear his footsteps. He walks a little slowly—of course. Then he knocks. Then he comes in. Then I do like this. (*Curtsies deeply*) You're exceedingly welcome, Mr. Sleeman. Then I go up to him and raise my hand like this. Then he kisses my hand. (*Looks at her hand*) Exactly at—eight o'clock—tomorrow.

HUNTER'S VOICE (*whispering, but strong enough to be heard*): Anne-Marie! Anne-Marie! (*She is startled, then steals over to the door and listens.*)

HUNTER: Anne-Marie! Open the window!

(*Anne-Marie goes up to the window. The Hunter, a young man dressed in green [there is a feather in his cap] swings himself up on the sill and takes Anne-Marie in his arms while he continues to sit on the sill. The sun has set, but the light is still red and rather strong. After a moment Anne-Marie frees herself and hurries over to her aunts' doors to listen. The Hunter comes in. His clothes are somewhat in disarray, and when he throws his cap on a chair, the feather is loosened and falls to the floor. Anne-Marie goes toward him happily.*)

ANNE-MARIE (*laughs softly*): How you look, you poor thing! How did you get up on the roof?

HUNTER: Climbed like a cat. Ah, it wasn't anything. The fire escape goes all the way up to the edge of the roof. Then all I had to do was to climb over the ridge. It went like a dance. Do you know what? You could do it, too. (*Enthusiastically*) Dear Anne-Marie—I'll help you. Come on! It's not right to have to sit here locked up. Come on, Anne-Marie!

ANNE-MARIE: That's what you say! And my wide skirts?

HUNTER: I know. Take off your skirts and make a small bundle. We'll throw it down first.

ANNE-MARIE: I can't—can't—because my old stockings have been darned.

HUNTER: No one will see them.

ANNE-MARIE: I can't—can't—I'm absolutely too heavy.

HUNTER: So heavy I'll carry you!

ANNE-MARIE (*covers her eyes with her arm; says slowly*): I can't—can't. For tomorrow—(*suddenly points at the clock*) at exactly eight o'clock Mr. Sleeman is coming.

HUNTER: Who's he?

ANNE-MARIE (*indifferently*): You don't know him. (*Changed tone*) Sit in the chair—no, there—so I can look at you. (*They sit down on the easy chairs.*) So—it's very beautiful in the forest?

HUNTER: If you could only imagine! And there are a lot of people out there tonight. Why, it's a holiday. They have an orchestra at the dancing pavilion, and a lot of people are dancing.

ANNE-MARIE (*childishly*): I'd rather walk in the real forest. Way, way into it. Where only you and I would be.

HUNTER (*softly, pleadingly*): If you want to, Anne-Marie—why don't you?

ANNE-MARIE (*hesitantly*): Because—because—(*whispers, pointing at the clock*) tick-tock—tick-tock—tick-tock—(*Changed tone*) Tell me more. Is there anything else that's fun?

HUNTER: Shooting galleries, of course. And an old woman who has talking parrots. Yes, and what's most fun of all! A trained monkey!

ANNE-MARIE (*interested*): Really? What tricks can it do?

HUNTER: A little of everything. It's dressed like a gentleman and walks very slowly and with much dignity on its back paws—

ANNE-MARIE (*suddenly*): I know. Do I know how it walks? (*Jumps up*) It walks like this. (*Walks as when she was imitating Mr. Sleeman, suddenly screams and strikes out with her arms*) Walter!

HUNTER (*jumps up*): Anne-Marie!

ANNE-MARIE (*anxiously*): No, sh-h, sh-h! Imagine if we wake them up. (*Listens*) Sit down. Like that. And I'll sit here. And you'll tell me something. (*Childishly, pleadingly*) No, no, not tell—you're going to say something—Walter —say something—

HUNTER: What do you want me to say?

ANNE-MARIE: You see—I'm going away. Soon.

HUNTER: Where are you going?

ANNE-MARIE (*"sensibly"*): Far away. I'm going into a better family, you see—I'm very hard to have about—I eat a lot— and I wear out clothes—I'm a heavy burden for my aunts—

HUNTER: I'd like to carry you!

ANNE-MARIE (*smiling*): Imagine if you could? I'm very heavy. (*Seriously*) But Mr. Sleeman can. You see—he's the highest ranking person in the whole province—after the governor.

HUNTER: Then he's old, I suppose?

ANNE-MARIE: Oh yes. Pretty old. Middle-aged. He was—was very kind to my mother. Mother was very unfortunate. You see my father was only an ordinary laborer in the forest. Merely that. And Sleeman—well—I don't really know anything about him. I know only—that—that he is coming. (*Glides down out of the chair and leans against Walter's knee; looks toward the footlights; more enthusiastically*) You'll have to hurry, Walter. It's going, going—the nasty thing—tick-tock. Say something. You must understand that when I'm far away in that fine family, I must have something to think about. (*Suddenly puts her hands to his head*) Walter! Look me in the eyes. Really. Don't you see what you're to say?

HUNTER (*half-embarrassed*): That you have beautiful, beautiful eyes.

ANNE-MARIE (*disappointed*): Oh well, that was pretty good. Though it wasn't . . . *that.* (*Gets up, listens involuntarily, hypnotized*) Then I hear his footsteps. He walks—a little slowly—of course—

HUNTER (*jumps up*): No—now you have to tell me what's wrong! Has something happened?

ANNE-MARIE (*indifferently*): Happened—happened—yes, something's always happening—during every minute that passes —(*Suddenly, anxiously, whispering*) Listen—listen—if we could—could stop that thing? (*Points at the clock*)

HUNTER: Would it be such a trick to stop an old Mora clock? (*Undoes the cover, opens the clock's door*)

ANNE-MARIE: How mean it looks! Has it stopped?

HUNTER: Until judgment day. Unless someone sets it going again.

ANNE-MARIE (*goes up to him with open arms; caressingly*): You could do it. You could! (*Puts her arms about his neck*) But you can't carry—such a heavy, heavy burden. No, no! Don't try! Say something instead—(*half singing, caressingly enticing*)—something—something—something—(*Suddenly becomes silent, embraces him violently, and stares into his eyes*)

HUNTER (*after a moment, shyly, childishly*): I love you, Anne-Marie.

(*Anne-Marie bends her head forward against his and kisses him. Then frees herself slowly, but puts her arm about his neck, he puts his arm about her waist. They go up to the chairs.*)

ANNE-MARIE: Sit here for a little while longer. No—I won't sit on your lap. That's not nice. I'll sit as I did before—(*in her earlier position*) And then you're to say something else. I need it so. I want a lot, a lot. Say something—(*roguishly*)—almost—almost as beautiful as what you just said.

HUNTER: Won't you say something?

ANNE-MARIE: No, I can't say anything—anything beautiful.

HUNTER (*bends over her*): Then I'll say that you are my dearest friend, the only one I have.

ANNE-MARIE (*smiling*): Yes, that too was beautiful.

HUNTER: And then I'll say that you're in my thoughts wherever I go and in my dreams when I am asleep.

ANNE-MARIE (*sadly*): Imagine! I could never have thought of all that! Did you read it in a book?

HUNTER: I read in my heart.

ANNE-MARIE: More.

HUNTER: Only this: I want to die the same day and the same hour and the same second as you, Anne-Marie.

ANNE-MARIE (*slowly, gravely*): That sounded sad—but very, very beautiful. (*Suddenly bursts into tears*) I'm so unhappy, Walter. I'm afraid if I start weeping, I'll never stop.

HUNTER (*caresses her hair, gently, naïvely*): Sorrow has many tears.

ANNE-MARIE (*with rising intensity*): No—no—I won't weep—not tonight—not now. I *can* put off sighing. I *am* going to be happy now—(*Gets up, extends her arms*) Yes, darn it—happy, Walter dear! We will dance now. Wait—no wait—I want to dance alone. (*Takes a few dance steps, caressingly*) You have given me so much that's beautiful. I have nothing to say to you, the man I love. I'm poor and have nothing to give you. I want to dance before the man I love. (*Dances*) Like this? I have never learned to dance—but I think I can anyway—now I curtsy to you—and take a step and rise on my toes—it is the way to your heart—now I'll swing around —around—(*lightly dizzy*) It's like flying—I get far, far away—into the forest—though I am heavy—I can still fly— look at me—look at me—(*panting breathlessly*) Walter! Walter! (*Her dance becomes stiff; with uncertainty*) No— no—I become older—now I'm a respectable wife—trip along so neatly—one step forward—one step to the side—then I move very lightly—very lightly—in a pirouette—and then a step—a step—(*the dance becoming ever heavier, with a changed tone*)—footsteps—I hear—his footsteps—footsteps— (*stops dancing, stares straight ahead*)—he walks—a little slowly—(*supports herself on the chair*)

HUNTER (*takes her hand, softly, insistently*): Anne-Marie— come—come with—come with me out there. Can you see the red glow still on the forest? Doesn't it draw you? Do you hear the music? There's no one at the pavilion who can dance like you. You can get in without paying because you're so beautiful. But I'll treat you . . . to all the tent shows . . . so you can see everything. And buy what you want. And I'll do it at the shooting gallery. There are so many fine prizes. I'll shoot them down for you. For I can shoot—do come.

ANNE-MARIE (*smiling*): But you're so poor, Walter—

HUNTER: Nonsense! I certainly have money tonight. I have two dollars and sixty cents. That'll go a long way—

ANNE-MARIE (*gently, childishly*): Deep in the forest one doesn't need money. I've always wanted to be there.

HUNTER: You may be there all night. There'll be many hours, Anne-Marie, many minutes, many seconds. What does it matter to us who's coming at eight o'clock tomorrow—

(*Anne-Marie starts, straightens up, and immediately curtsies deeply, takes a few formal steps toward the door while she slowly raises her hand, stops, jerks it suddenly back, breaks into a ringing laugh, swirls about on her toe tips, jumps up on a chair*)

ANNE-MARIE (*calls out*): Come, Walter, come! Take me! I am so heavy, heavy, heavy! (*The Hunter carries her to the window.*)

ANNE-MARIE (*while he is doing so, jubilantly*): Carry me far, though I am heavy—far, far. Into the forest. My poor boy, my friend, the heart of my heart, the man I love.

(*He puts her down on the windowsill and swings himself over it. Anne-Marie puts her arms about him and looks into his eyes.*)

ANNE-MARIE (*passionately and childishly*): You're to tell me once more—far, far in the forest. And you're to say it a hundred times and a thousand. That beautiful thing. It shall sigh in my ears as the forest sighs. It shall sigh in my ears all through my life. And I will want to hear nothing else.

(*The Hunter glides down out of the window. The audience can see his hands stretched out to help Anne-Marie.*)

ANNE-MARIE (*to the room, shrilly, defiantly*): You're exceedingly welcome, Mr. Sleeman—(*Slides hastily down out of the window*)

(*A short pause. It is becoming somewhat darker. Bina comes in from the right, dressed in a long nightrobe, carrying a candle.*)

BINA: Anne-Marie? Anne-Marie? (*Looks about, stops, cries out angrily*) Mina!

(*Mina enters, dressed as before. During the whole scene she has a hard time concealing inward giggling.*)

MINA: Bina dear?

BINA: Where is Anne-Marie?

MINA: How do I know? She's not in her bed.

BINA: I heard her a few minutes ago.

MINA: Then she can't be far away. (*Patters about. Bina finds and picks up the feather from the Hunter's hat.*)

BINA (*sharply*): Mina, what's this?

MINA: Well, what a big feather! Can a bird have got into the room? The window's open.

BINA: Mina—you're in on the plot. You have helped them.

MINA (*puts her hands on her breasts as if to protest on her honor*): No, dear—if I've lived for sixty years without an adventure, I certainly won't help others to have any—in my old age.

BINA (*furiously*): Leech!

MINA (*righteously, as if she did not quite hear*): Yes, this'll teach us.

BINA: And if Mr. Sleeman finds out?

MINA (*uneasily*): Dear, surely he won't find out?

BINA: Aren't we going to tell—?

MINA: We haven't the right, Bina—

BINA (*scornfully*): I thought it was our duty.

MINA: To destroy the girl's future?

BINA: You old witch!

MINA (*gently*): Each one to her own taste.

BINA (*goes toward her door, turns*): What if she isn't home when he comes?

MINA: She knows better, I hope. She'll be back at seven.

BINA (*at the door*): You old reprobate!

MINA: Yes, at the latest by eight!

(*Bina goes out. Mina shakes with silent giggling. Goes slowly toward the door, turns about and throws a kiss toward the feather and the window. Hums with her cracked voice*)

> When the linden turns green
> The hunter gets his queen
> In the forest.

(*Goes out*)

The curtain is lowered but is raised again immediately. The scene is unchanged, but the light is that of a gray, gloomy dawn.

Anne-Marie is standing a short distance from the window with her face turned toward the footlights. She is pale, lacks expression, is stiff—otherwise unchanged. Her eyelids are kept somewhat lowered during the whole scene until toward her very last speeches. At first she stands immovable and seems unaware of sounds and touch.

When the curtain goes up Mina, without her apron, in all her finery, is standing in front of the clock which she has just set going. She closes its door and hurriedly begins to remove the slipcovers from the furniture. After a moment Bina comes in to help; the two sisters flutter from piece to piece of furniture like ugly gray butterflies; they do not say a word but give each other directions and tasks by means of gestures. They pay no attention to Anne-Marie, except that Mina at one point stations herself in front of Anne-Marie and pinches her cheeks to give them color.

Anne-Marie is completely unconcerned.

First when the Mora clock begins to strike she is startled— quite mildly—and walks with slow, measured steps up to the chair, where she assumes the position she has memorized. All this is done absolutely calmly.

The sisters have now finished their preparations—dusting, straightening up, etc. Mina notices Anne-Marie has moved and points at her.

The clock strikes eight.

The sisters listen intently. Bina hurries over to the entrance door, opens it a little, signals that she hears someone coming. After a last hurried survey of the room, the sisters disappear into their respective rooms.

Anne-Marie stands absolutely still.

The audience hears more clearly slow, hard footsteps on stone stairs. Silence. Someone knocks.

ANNE-MARIE (*softly with an empty but not unpleasant voice*): Please come in.

(*Mr. Sleeman enters. He walks as Anne-Marie has described, bent backward, slowly and mechanically raising his legs. Even the movement of his arms seems automatic— approximately the movements of a tabetic, although with-*

out being genuinely characteristic. His voice is flat and petulant. He is bald. His eyes seem dead but light up occasionally when he observes Anne-Marie. He stops right in front of the door and takes off his hat. For her part, Anne-Marie carries out her movements as instructed. Slightly surprised she raises her head—but not her eyes—and thereupon presents "a smile of recognition," takes one step forward, and curtsies deeply.

ANNE-MARIE: You're exceedingly welcome, Mr. Sleeman.

SLEEMAN (*bows slightly*): Miss Anne-Marie?

(Instead of answering she does what she has been told to do, walks with measured steps toward him, and while doing so raises her right hand slowly. This gesture must be neither a strange act nor a parody, an effect that is prevented by Mr. Sleeman's coming forward somewhat to meet her in order to kiss her hand. Her hand then sinks down heavily. They stand silent for a moment.)

SLEEMAN: You have probably read my letter, dear Anne-Marie?

ANNE-MARIE: Yes.

SLEEMAN (*with a stiff roguishness*): You probably have it on you?

ANNE-MARIE: No. I've lost the letter.

SLEEMAN: Lost the letter?

ANNE-MARIE: I've lost the letter in the forest.

(Short pause)

SLEEMAN: But at any event it has been read and considered? What do you say about my proposal?

ANNE-MARIE (*quickly, but not defiantly*): Nothing.

SLEEMAN: Do you mean by that that you agree to fulfill my and your aunts' wishes?

ANNE-MARIE: Yes. (*Sleeman kisses her on the cheek.*)

SLEEMAN: Come, dear child. I'm somewhat tired after the trip.

(*Supports himself against her shoulder and walks up to the chairs, places her directly in front of him, and observes her with a glowing look. Walks in a half circle around her*)

SLEEMAN: You surpass all my expectations. (*Whispering a little slyly*) Can anyone hear us?

ANNE-MARIE: No one.

SLEEMAN (*as before*): Then it's proper that I make my proposal. I love you, Anne-Marie. (*She starts, looks up.*) It may seem strange that I tell you this when we meet for the first time. But you have been in my thoughts for a long time during the day when I have been working and at night in my dreams.

ANNE-MARIE (*moves away a little, very slowly*): Oh-h—

SLEEMAN (*smiling*): I want you, Anne-Marie, to be my dearest friend, the only one I have. (*Short pause. Anne-Marie takes a couple of steps toward him and stares at him in horror.*)

ANNE-MARIE (*her voice about to choke*): How beautiful. Did you read that in a book?

SLEEMAN: I read in my heart. (*Short pause*)

ANNE-MARIE (*with anguish*): Can you—can you say anything more?

SLEEMAN: What else is there to say? I want you by my side all the way through my life, Anne-Marie. I want to die the same day, the same hour, the same second as you, Anne-Marie. (*Short pause*)

ANNE-MARIE (*tonelessly, but without anguish*): That sounds very beautiful. But very, very sad.

(*Sleeman puts his arm about her and draws her to him. Anne-Marie puts her hand over her eyes.*)

SLEEMAN: And what do you say, Anne-Marie?

ANNE-MARIE (*as before but without tears*): I am so happy. But if I begin to weep, I'll never stop.

(*Both the side doors are opened; the two sisters sweep out in all their finery, each with a large bouquet, both "smile" sweetly, both curtsy deeply, both say*) Congratulations! (*Mr. Sleeman nods condescendingly.*)

BINA (*suddenly*): Anne-Marie—are you crying?

SLEEMAN: Be calm, ladies. Happiness, too, has its tears.

CURTAIN